P R O L O G,
Children
and
Students

Fifth Generation Computing in Education Series

PROLOG,
Children
and
Students

Edited by Jon Nichol (Series Editor),
Jonathan Briggs and Jackie Dean

**Kogan Page, London/Nichols Publishing
Company, New York**

First published in Great Britain 1988 by
Kogan Page Limited
120 Pentonville Road, London N1 9JN

First published in the USA in 1988
by Nichols Publishing Company,
PO Box 96, New York, NY 10024

British Library Cataloguing in Publication Data
PROLOG, children and students.—(Fifth
   generation computing in education; 1).
   1. Computer-assisted instruction 2. Prolog
11(Computer program language)
   I. Nichol, Jon II. Briggs, Jonathan
   Harland III. Dean, Jacqueline IV. Series
371.3'9445   LB1028.5

   ISBN 1-85091-341-2

Library of Congress Cataloguing-in-Publication Data
PROLOG, children and students/edited by Jon Nichol, Jackie Dean, and
   Jonathan Briggs.
      p. cm. — — (Fifth generation computing in education : 1)
      ISBN 0-89397-290-8
   1. Computer-assisted instruction 2. Logic programming.
   3. Prolog (Computer program language) I. Nichol, Jon. II. Dean,
   Jackie. III. Briggs, Jonathan. IV. Series.
   LB1028.5P734 1988
   371.3'9445——dc19   87-22451 CIP

Typeset by Texet, Leighton Buzzard, Bedfordshire.
Printed and bound in Great Britain by
Billing & Sons Ltd, Worcester

Contents

Introduction
Learning opportunities through computer systems

Professor R Lewis
Economic and Social Research Council
Information Technology and Education Programme
University of Lancaster
Lancaster LA1 4YF
UK

Like most people concerned with or even devoted to children's opportunities for learning, I scan, at least, many research publications. I must admit that it really is hard to do more than 'scan'. The sheer volume of publications is insurmountable if one aspires to reading in depth.

As a result we read rather more carefully those papers which look as if they may support our own intuition. This is a natural part of the selection process: we need to have our prejudices reinforced in order that we can sleep more easily.

This, of course, can be very dangerous. In such a rapidly evolving field we need to be prompted to look sideways, as the contributions from a number of specialisms and disciplines may spark off new lines of thinking.

There is also a tendency to seek universal solutions to learning difficulties. This must be avoided as one basic tenet of educational theory indicates the values of diversity in learners' activities. Learners become jaded quite quickly when confronted with similar tasks: 'Oh no, not another PROLOG problem!'.

The interest in PROLOG has grown very rapidly after ten years of relative inaccessibility. This interest, and the diversity of PROLOG-based experiments, is clearly illustrated in this book. But let us be sure that we do use the correct tools for the learning we have in mind.

Learning opportunities are influenced by the environment in which learning takes place. Software environments have recently been added to the range of possibilities for pupils and students. Software systems differ in the ways in which they allow humans to express their thoughts and it is the variety of these differences that provides richness to the possibilities of learning with microcomputers.

High-level computer languages have all been devised with particular human activities in mind. There are two features in particular which reflect this: the data structures corresponding more or less to the ways in which knowledge is represented by humans, and the strategy chosen to perform processing of the data. LOGO programs consist of sets of procedures, each performing defined actions. PROLOG programs, in contrast, are constructed from facts and rules (of the form A if B and C) and a problem is solved by logical inference based on the principles of formal logic.

How can these languages be used to provide learning opportunities?

At the basic level, both languages may be used directly by students to solve problems of different types. These are exemplified by problem-solving in various mathematical domains through turtle geometry and by problems related to the expression of pupils' knowledge (for example, biological taxonomy) in PROLOG. With LOGO, pupils most commonly work directly with LOGO procedures, either of their own compilation or prepared by their teachers. PROLOG toolkits have been prepared too and, in contrast to LOGO, these take a variety of forms. LOGO, with whatever procedures are to be used, offers a common front-end syntax to the pupil. This is an enormous benefit as no new syntax has to be mastered when working with different procedures and so the extensibility of LOGO (into so-called micro-worlds) becomes a natural continuation without syntactic barriers. This easy extensibility is less apparent in PROLOG.

Much effort has been directed to the development of logic programming shells or front-ends. These become the tools for academic researchers and educational developers of expert systems. To some extent many in the community have been distracted by the promised land of artificial intelligence. This has deflected much work away from a curriculum emphasis towards the goals of intelligent tutoring systems. In such systems the feedback given to students depends upon a student model in order that a relevant 'intelligent' reaction is provided by the software. This contrasts strongly with the micro-world work in LOGO and PROLOG where the teacher makes the decisions as to what kind of environment and problem is appropriate to the students' current stage of development. The teacher forms the student model and modifies it in the light of a student's actions which identify changes in knowledge.

Both languages can be used to provide unintelligent CAL software. The choice of either language, or of some other algebraically based language, will depend upon the domain for the CAL which it is intended to develop. No one language can be said to be universally the best. One would expect that some powerful graphical tools would always be important, even if only for displaying text. The choice beyond this does not have any impact on the learner if the programmer has done the job properly. However, the programmer/developer's task is made much easier if the features of the language allow an efficient representation of the domain being considered.

The main point of these reflections is to emphasize the need to consider any learning objectives carefully and to have sufficient knowledge of a range of tools in order to select the most appropriate. Opportunities to delve into the work of those working from different perspectives from one's own must always be taken.

Part I: PROLOG Across the Curriculum

Preface

Jon Nichol

By the late 1970s PROLOG was a bright idea twinkling in the firmament of computer science and linguistic research. It was as far removed from schools and children as theoretical atomic physics is from the contemporary classroom. However, PROLOG as an educational idea was launched upon an unsuspecting and unprepared world in 1980, when Professor Kowalski headed a small school-based curriculum development project, 'Logic as a computer language for children'. The project's aims were clear: to teach pupils logic programming, and through that process to transfer the logical patterns of thinking they developed to their other curricular activities. The project was based on a single Wimbledon Middle School, and it was conducted under the enthusiastic and expert guidance of Richard Ennals.

Richard subsequently went on a series of national and international tours, disseminating the ideas which he had developed to a varied audience. The dissemination process was similar to the progress of early rock bands who subsequently soar to super-star status, even down to the loading of the equipment in the back of transit vans. The result of Richard sowing the seeds of logic programming as an element in the every-day education of normal children was that a series of projects and activities have sprouted up world-wide. These have seen PROLOG applications according to the expertise and knowledge of the particular enthusiast.

The process has involved two main communities which have become increasingly interlocked: academic psychologists and educational researchers/teachers. The academic psychologists have been interested in children's cognitive development, both in terms of cognitive processes and peer interaction. This work has involved pupils both learning logic programming and interacting with CAL written in PROLOG. Some of the results of this research are presented in Part 4.

Educational researchers and teachers have been more concerned with experimenting with different ways in which the pupils can use PROLOG to develop their understanding of subjects, or to foster their general educational progress. Educationalists' activities have involved three separate elements:

1. The writing of programs on topics within a subject domain, once a certain mastery of elements of PROLOG programming has been achieved.
2. The use of shells — structured authoring environments — with which to represent an understanding of a topic within a structure based on predicate logic. Such shells enable pupils to represent their understanding of a topic in their *mother tongue*.
3. The use of expert systems — both programs which contain expert knowledge with

which the user can interact, and expert systems shells with which the pupils can write their own programs.

This section examines the use of the first two elements, logic programming and shells, within a variety of subject disciplines, spanning the humanities and sciences, and the education of pupils with special educational needs. A striking feature of the chapters is the varied approaches to teaching which they detail, and the wide range of ages and abilities which have experienced PROLOG-based teaching. The use and writing of expert systems has a section devoted to itself.

1. Using PROLOG in the teaching of Classics

Kevin O'Connell
Head of Classical and Religious Studies
Queen Elizabeth's School
Crediton
Devon
UK

The last seven years have seen a spectacular growth in the use of microcomputers in schools. Teachers have in a professional way responded as best they could to the realities of Britain in the 1980s and have rightly taken advantage of government and LEA schemes in order to get computers into their schools. Yet the proper applications of these machines to attain educational objectives have not been fully identified, particularly by those teachers who have not had any previous contact with computers. While scientists have readily exploited them and while the study of computing has developed rapidly as a subject in its own right, the response of the humanities has been uneven and lacking in confidence. Yet the humanities can help satisfy a general social need *vis-a-vis* computers: that of the population at large to be able to see computers as machines that they can control, by virtue of understanding through direct experience the functions they can perform.

Teachers of the humanities have a critical role in helping pupils to gain this understanding. The moral and social implications of computers are of direct concern to them. Indeed, it is the teachers' subject matter that will exemplify how computers may be used by the non-specialist. Classicists share in this responsibility.

I would advise that we need to become acquainted with three broad categories of use of computers in education, in ascending order of importance. First, we must know about the computer programs that require a limited response from the user. These will include learning programs such as Jeremy Fenton, described in the Autumn issue of the *JACT Review* (1984), adventure programs like *Jericho Road* (1983), in which the user travels from Jerusalem to Jericho in the 1st Century AD, and simulations like Ginn's *Expedition to Saqqara* (1983) and *Mary Rose* (1982), in which the user conducts archaeological excavations. Secondly, we need to know about programs that allow us to use a computer for our own specific purposes. eg word-processing (of great value to children of low ability), the creation and manipulation of databases, and programs such as *Telebook* (1984) (which allow us to create our own versions of teletext). Thirdly, we must be prepared to investigate to what extent we and our pupils can hope to be able to program computers. This brings me to the main thrust of my argument.

To program a computer one uses a language that the computer understands. Most computer languages are imperative — that is, they consist of a series of interrelated instructions to the computer in order to achieve an end result on the screen. The popular BASIC is of this kind. The results that can be achieved without a great deal of time and skill are usually of little value. In any case, the programmer is working for the benefit of other people who will use the completed program. It does not help the programmer to solve any of his or her own problems (in contrast to problems caused by the actual programming). Is there not, we might ask, a language that allows us to communicate with a computer in something approaching English in order to help us with our own problems, is accessible to everybody at some level, and has intrinsic educational value? The answer is ..... yes: PROLOG (PROgramming in LOGic).

PROLOG has now been adapted for use in education on microcomputers in the form of micro-PROLOG. The use of micro-PROLOG in secondary schools has been the subject of intense development over the last five years, but is still not widespread. Some of that research has been conducted at my school by Dr Jon Nichol of Exeter University (Nichol, 1985). When I first encountered micro-PROLOG I could scarcely believe what I had found — the perfect point of contact between the humanities and computing. Micro-PROLOG is a descriptive language. It enables us to record in the computer a description of any situation we may choose. This is done by typing in statements, which are immediately held in the computer's memory and are ready for retrieval at any time. Using the simple front-end program supplied with the language statements can take either of two forms:

1. Two words, eg 'Earth round', where the second word is recorded as a property of the first — this is equivalent to the English sentence 'the Earth is round'.
2. Three words, eg 'Earth satellite Sun', where the second word is recorded as a relationship between the first and third — this is equivalent to the English sentence 'the Earth is a satellite of the Sun'.

It is important that we type in two or three units. These will usually be single words but could be composite, hyphenated or abbreviated according to taste. Hence the second statement above could have been 'the-Earth is-a-sat-of the-Sun'.

Once information of this kind has gone in, we can immediately ask the computer questions about it. We can ask whether it is true that 'Earth satellite Sun', to which it would answer 'yes'. Alternatively we can ask whether it is true that 'x satellite Sun', to which it would also answer 'yes'. If we asked it to tell us what x is, it would answer 'Earth'. Treating x as a variable, the computer looks for any sentence pattern which matches the query sentence. Using variables (x,y,z,X,Y,Z, etc.), micro-PROLOG also enables us to put in rules which define properties or relationships. For example, putting in the two statements:

> **x satellite y if**
> > **x revolves-around y**

and

> **Mars revolves-around Sun**

and then asking for x in the sentence:

> **x satellite Sun**

will produce the answers:

> **Earth**
> **Mars**

Let us apply all of this now to an example from Classical Studies. Herodotus tells us how Phoenician sailors were sent by Necos, King of Egypt, to sail around Libya, and how they did this, returning after two years via the Pillars of Hercules. Herodotus also records the story that the Phoenicians saw the sun on their right as they sailed westwards round the south of Libya. Herodotus says that he does not believe the story. Using micro-PROLOG and what we now know about the shape of the earth, we can work out whether he was right or wrong. Together with our pupils we can decide on statements to put into the computer, as accepted by Herodotus, for example:

Phoenicians sailed-around Africa

and some rules:

**X rounded Cape-of-Good-Hope if
    X sailed-around Africa**

and:

X sailed west if X rounded Cape-of-Good-Hope

We can then look at what we know about the Tropics (your Geography department may prefer these to be referred to as 23 L/2N and 23 L/2S) and put in:

**X south-of Tropic-of-Capricorn if
    X rounded Cape-of-Good Hope**

**X saw sun-in-north if
    X south-of Tropic-of-Capricorn**

**X saw sun-on-right if
    X sailed west and
    X saw sun-in-north**

If we then say:

**Herodotus wrong if
    Phoenicians saw sun-on-right**

We can finally ask whether

Herodotus wrong

is a correct statement.

The line of thinking here may seem obvious to us, but many children even at the age of fourteen have not grasped the significance of the Tropics. Using the computer we can trace the argument with the children, recall any part of it at will, and get satisfaction from knowing that we have successfully taught the computer to manipulate logically information about the problem.

The regularity of Latin inflexions and syntax lends itself to micro-PROLOG but the programming of rules can become very complex. Nevertheless programming in the classroom can be rewarding as long as we have prepared thoroughly and thought out the implications of what we are doing. In Stage 2, Unit I, of the Cambridge Latin Course (1982), we would be alerting our pupils to the phenomenon that most nouns in Latin change their terminations according to the role they play in a statement, initially the existence of nominative and accusative forms. With the pupils' help we could construct a series of rules:

x FormA if x has-ending a   etc
x FormB if x has-ending am   etc
x Verb if x has-ending t

When we have defined 'has-ending' this will test any word that we put in.
  If we simply put in a vocabulary:

ancilla FormA
    etc
Metellam FormB
    etc
salutat Verb
    etc

we can ask the computer to give all the possible sentences that could be generated from this vocabulary by presenting it with the sentence:

x FormA and y FormB and z Verb

and asking for x, y and z.

  Whilst PROLOG can be used with pupils in the construction of rules and databases, research is currently underway on the use of PROLOG to construct 'intelligent' computer-assisted learning programs which will, for example, have the built-in ability to examine termination matches.

  So far we have been exploring how micro-PROLOG might be used, with our pupils, in order to record and manipulate information. The use of variables clearly puts a limit on how far one can go (to the relief of teachers?!) but I believe there are benefits at whatever level one uses the language. With the less able one could avoid variables altogether and use the language to develop the skill of note-taking. Micro-PROLOG can assist our teaching, is intrinsically worthwhile because of its use of logic, and allows both teacher and pupils to be in control of the computer and to apply it to their purpose.

  This chapter is intended only as a brief introduction to micro-PROLOG but it would be wrong to conclude without showing how it might be used by a teacher to create a sophisticated database. In Classical Studies, prime candidates for database construction are gravestones and other inscriptions and we have ready-made material in the cards contained in the *Roman World* pack published by Cambridge UP (1978,1979). For an example see Figs.1.1.

  If we look at the gravestone inscriptions on the cards in Figs 1.1, we see that information on them can be categorized with some profit, eg class (deduced from number of names), occupation, age at death, etc. The examples on the cards have no statistical value but they will allow us to indulge in useful speculation, eg about the significance of ages when they are given. Let us look at a fairly straightforward way of recording information from two of the cards:

(Tiberius Claudius Maturinus) has-info (money-changer parents 28 manes-ascia)

(Aper Illiomarus) has-info (linen-weaver son 85 manes-ascia)

To the Manes

and the everlasting memory of

TIBERIUS CLAUDIUS MATURINUS ORONTIUS

a money changer

and a most sober young man.

He died when he had almost completed the xxviiith

year of his life.

He worshipped all the gods,

but what was the good of it when he died so young?

Cl. Regulus and Severia Severa his parents

are most wretched at the loss of their only son.

Now they are completely childless –

for he had no children.

They had this stone set up and dedicated it

under the Ascia.

Figure 1.1a

To the Manes
and to the eternal memory of
APER ILLIOMARUS
A LINEN-WEAVER.

HE WAS ELECTED FROM THE TRIBE OF THE VELIOCASSES
INTO THE RANKS OF THE TOWNSPEOPLE OF LUGDUNUM.
HE WAS A MEMBER OF THE SOCIETY OF BLADDERMEN
WHO HAVE THEIR PREMISES AT LUGDUNUM.
HE LIVED LXXXV YEARS WITHOUT CAUSING ANY ILL-FEELING.

APRIUS ILLIOMARUS

HIS SON HAD THIS SET UP TO HIS DEAREST FATHER
AND DEDICATED IT UNDER THE ASCIA.

Figure 1.1b

The units on either side of the relationship **has-info** are in fact lists bound together by brackets. We can tell the computer whereabouts on a list to look for a particular type of information with rules. For example:

> **x occupation y if x has-info (y z x Y)**
> **x buried-by z if x has-info (y z X Y)**

Having created a program in this way we can, for example, type in:

> **x occupation y**

and ask for **y**. The question takes the form:

> **which (y : x occupation y)**

The result will be a list of all the occupations recorded. With increased sophistication of rules this can be made a very powerful database indeed, yet the rules are within the grasp of most teachers after a few hours' study.

There is far more to be said about the potential of micro-PROLOG. I hope that I have given some indication of the role it might play in giving both teachers and pupils a sense of control over computers. Classicists must achieve 'computer-awareness'. For those who have shunned computers so far micro-PROLOG may prove to be the most exciting way in.

REFERENCES AND FURTHER READING

Cambridge Latin Course (1982), Unit I (2nd edition), SCDC Publications.

Expedition to Saqqara (1983), Ginn & Company Ltd.

Fenton, J (1984), 'Latin and Computers' *JACT Review* (Journal of Joint Association of Classical Teachers), pp 18-20.

Hughes, M and Forrest, M (1978, 1979), *The Roman World* Cambridge University Press, for the Schools Council, Unit I & Unit II.

Jericho Road (1983), Shards Software, Ilford, Essex.

Mary Rose (1982), Ginn & Company Ltd.

Nichol, J (1985), 'Classroom-based development, artificial intelligence and history teaching' *Journal of Curriculum Studies*, Vol 17, No 2, pp 211-214.

Telebook (1984), 4MAT Educational Software, Barnstaple, Devon.

2. Using PROLOG in the teaching of History

Martyn Wild
The Advisory Unit
Microtechnology in Education
Hatfield
Herts AL10 8AU
UK

INTRODUCTION

Recent trends in the teaching of History emphasize the need for the creation of classroom environments which both help develop children's understanding of History and allow expression of that understanding. The computer has been the focus of many claims to date suggesting that the micro can be instrumental in the development of such classroom environments.

This chapter reflects work in progress where a number of schools are using software 'toolkits' or 'shells' that allow children and teachers to represent and explore knowledge of various sorts on the computer. It is suggested that the use of this type of software may provide a powerful means by which children can develop their learning in History.

Although this chapter is overtly concerned with History, the principles here underlying the use of the micro are applicable in other curriculum areas.

CHILDREN, THINKING AND HISTORY

From January 1986, the *Computers in History Project* based at The Advisory Unit, Hatfield, has been investigating the role the computer may play in the teaching and learning of History. The project is focused upon the use of authoring environments, including software tools for information handling activities as well as software 'shells' which offer the possibility for students to model and generally represent knowledge in the computer.

The points of reference for the project include:

1. Consideration of the nature of children's thinking in History.
2. The philosophy of the New History that is currently so much in vogue.
3. The various claims made for the computer as a tool to facilitate unique learning environments.

THE NEW HISTORY

There are a number of elements which make up the nature of the New History. At its centre it may be said to be concerned with developing an understanding of the methods or process of historical inquiry. Accordingly, the focus of study in schools should not be on the past as a static body of received fact but rather on how we come to acquire our knowledge of that past, as well as developing a dynamic understanding of the past. At best this is to be achieved by the pupils making a demanding use of the sources of History as evidence.

The New History initially gained currency in the 1970s and has now come to be regarded by some as the new orthodoxy. The general acceptability of the philosophy of the New History is most clearly demonstrated by the success of the Schools History Project (SHP), especially in the large-scale take-up of the SHP's 'What is History?' units and, to a lesser extent, the growing number of schools following the AEB's 673 syllabus for A-level History. Some further measure of the influence that the New History has is to be seen in the various GCSE syllabi which clearly carry its mark.

A reaction

Of late there has been a reaction to certain aspects of the New History. The essence of this reaction is that the New History should be broadened out from a narrow concentration on skills related to the handling of evidence (Lang, 1986).

The challenge of History teaching is to stimulate children to identify with people of the past, to recreate past situations. From this, many important aspects of cognitive and affective development can occur, including the important areas of historical imagination and empathy.

The critical factor is how the teacher can encourage the child to have a positive and genuine learning experience within the historical domain. The teacher may use pupil-centred problem-solving methods, provide source materials for group and individual work, create a classroom environment which nurtures the child's understanding of History, and allow opportunities for the expression of understanding. It is in this context that the application of software 'shells' can be considered. The use of such shells offers semi-structured environments within which historical knowledge may be represented and developed.

In part, the software that is currently being used by project schools has been taken from the developments of the PROLOG Education Group (PEG) (Nichol, Dean and Briggs, 1986). This software includes LINX, used to create simulation programs and embryo expert systems (Dean and Nichol, 1987); DETECT, a toolkit which supports the development of problem-solving approaches to learning; PLACES, a shell which enables information to be entered into the computer and then explored according to a logic rule-based framework; and THE PLAN, which may be used to provide and explore computer 'micro-worlds'.

These toolkits or shells are written in PROLOG, and as such reflect the semantic and logical structures of this language (Briggs, 1984a; Conlon, 1985). From the evidence of initial trials it has been suggested that in this software lies the power, flexibility and potential of the use of the computer for teacher and child alike.

POSSIBILITIES

At an early stage the project identified certain key areas, expressed in the form of questions, to be used as initial yardsticks for monitoring the use of these software shells in teaching and learning History:

1. The pioneering work done by Piaget in researching the cognitive development of children has led many educationalists to concern themselves with how children may be encouraged to reach formal levels of thinking at a relatively early stage in their learning. Knowing what and how a child is thinking is perhaps necessary before the educationalist can proceed further.

   Could the use of these software shells facilitate the move into and through formal levels of thinking by allowing children to represent their knowledge within the computer and thereby reveal their thought processes to teachers?.

2. Without denying children's experiences as the basis of learning, some empirical research has suggested that many children examine historical material and demonstrate an understanding based on conventional and stereotyped views. Could the use of certain facilities offered by these software shells enable children to review their misconceptions and false assumptions, without fear of adverse reaction from teachers or peers? Would children using the shells be able to transcend what appears as natural inhibition in the testing and representation of views and ideas against information/evidence?

3. Could the use of these software shells enable new forms of historical activity to take place? The shells offer a flexible if structured environment to work in; and importantly, the shells offer a natural language medium in which to represent and develop knowledge.

   The notion of children being able to represent a problem as a set of statements within the computer, and at the same time use their description of the problem as a procedure for solving it logically, potentially provides a new departure for learning in History.

4. Could the use of the shells provide the classroom focus for structural, logical, or even historical thinking? The New History is concerned with knowledge representation, the modelling of information and the development of conceptual understanding through the use of information as evidence. The shells offer facilities for representing, modelling and developing knowledge in these ways.

5. Could the shells provide the focus for the development of skills such as communication, co-operation, deliberation and reasoning when used in a planned social context?

6. Could the shells provide the context to explore and monitor specific areas of historical activity, such as simulation, recreation, research, use of evidence?

7. Could the shells provide children with power to represent and develop their own learning?

Does the use of knowledge-based systems, as in the application of these software shells, in fact contribute to a special learning environment, where the child may control the rate of and approach to, his/her own learning?

WHY USE PROLOG?

The claims made for the use of PROLOG in education are well documented (Ennals, 1981). These claims range from the consideration of PROLOG as a means of improving logical thinking, to PROLOG being seen as a panacea for all education ills. Certainly it is clear from many studies that PROLOG as a language has inherent features that might justifiably commend its use in the field of teaching and learning (Dean, Briggs and Nichol, 1987). Such features include:

1. the support it lends to both declarative and procedural thinking,
2. its logic basis,
3. the fact that it is easily extensible (so that new predicates can be created by the user to enhance an application of the language), and
4. the fact that its close proximity to natural language and its pattern-matching facility make the language applicable to problem-solving activities in the humanities.

Recognition of the advantages of using PROLOG in education is merely the first step; one must subsequently consider how these advantages can be applied to learning situations. Apart from using PROLOG in its raw state (that is, purely in terms of its internal syntax), it would seem that current possibilities range from the implementation of software interfaces to PROLOG, such as SIMPLE or MITSI (Briggs, 1984a), to the use of toolkit programs written in PROLOG and which include certain characteristics of the language. These toolkits or shells may, perhaps, be used in specific applications and to cater for the varying needs of different disciplines. Other possibilities for PROLOG have still to see the light of day and are not yet within the grasp of the teacher or student (these might include PROLOG as a tool used to produce natural language interfaces to powerful pieces of software already in existence).

Using PROLOG toolkits is perhaps an efficient way of applying the advantages of the language to teach and learn about a subject, rather than about PROLOG itself or even formal logic. For example, the toolkits that have been developed by the PEG team such as LINX, DETECT, PLACES and THE PLAN, allow both History teachers and students to represent their historical understanding in logical frameworks. Not only do these frameworks actually mirror certain aspects of the discipline of History, but the facilities offered by these toolkits allow children to interact with the software at high conceptual levels. This may at first occur by a child using a particular program written within a toolkit and then subsequently employing the same toolkit to adapt the existing program or to create another. That is, both the teacher and student are able to use and write computer programs in a language and structure already intelligible to them.

HOW ARE THE SHELLS BEING USED?

Project schools have largely concentrated upon a sub-set of the available toolkits developed by the PEG team. These have been used in various ways and contexts. For example, with LINX, children have simulated past and present events and explored the reasons why things happened as they did; they have also used the LINX framework to construct historical models to represent their knowledge of a topic or theme. In another instance using DETECT, children have developed a series of imaginative detective cases based upon historical events or incidents. With each of these cases a central problem is presented in the program. In addition to the problem each program also incorporates the possibilities for exploring and solving it.

In all examples of children working in the toolkit software shell environments, the computer provides the means by which historical problems can be represented, explored, re-designed and possibly solved. That is, children are confronted with tasks specific to a particular subject which encourage them both to represent their understanding of a problem (pupil programming) and to seek to solve and/or modify a problem by using a program.

SOME RESULTS

The project has been in operation for two school terms now and in all cases the use of the toolkits has been within History and/or Humanities as part of the mainstream curriculum. In the majority of instances the children are of early secondary school age (11-14 years). It is also important to recognize that teachers are using the toolkits in a variety of ways, addressing their own classroom needs and problems and covering topics that range from ancient Greek mythology to the battles of medieval England to the politics of modern China. Similarly, children have also undertaken to use the toolkits in varying fashions, responding to and directing their own approaches to a subject.

Some early results suggest that the concepts of evidence and method are central to the computer-related tasks being undertaken by the children. In many examples of children working within the environment provided by the shells the ideas of (a) what a Historian does, and (b) the role that evidence plays in historical methodology, feature strongly. That is to say, the use of the shells allows children to address and develop their understanding of what constitutes historical evidence and methodology. Appropriately enough it is these concepts that underpin History as a subject.

The research so far has been largely dependent upon video and audio recordings of what children say and do in relation to both on- and off-computer tasks. Initial observations are revealing. Children seem to develop their understanding of a theme or topic by building upon and re-building knowledge structures. This is particularly evident when children are constructing a program using, for example, the LINX toolkit. Here a child's conceptual understanding (of, perhaps, causation, change, evidence) is initially subjected to representation within the computer. Upon reflection, and perhaps after testing that representation within the LINX framework, a child will often seek to change and develop his/her understanding, perhaps with the help of extraneous information or as a result of peer-group interaction.

Attention has been drawn in the past to the part PROLOG might play in developing the formal reasoning abilities of children. PROLOG arguably 'mirrors the patterns of thought involved in formal thinking' (Nichol, Dean and Briggs, 1986b). The use of PROLOG may indeed be said to promote reflective thinking and enable hypothetico-deductive reasoning to take place. Certainly, the use of LINX, DETECT and PLACES in the domain of History provides problem-solving tools which allow children to involve themselves in the process of making and testing hypotheses (reflecting an important part of the historian's method). This process is facilitated by and depends upon a background of knowledge structures. These structures themselves grow with the assimilation of process knowledge (the process of doing) and objective knowledge (the result of doing) gained by testing hypotheses.

Results achieved so far suggest that children are able to progress through relatively high levels of conceptual understanding by undertaking historical activities that would not be readily possible without the application of the software shells. In many ways the children are working within an environment where the software used encourages them to test ideas and understanding against available data. Using the shells to handle ideas and information in this way is essentially different to handling data with other computer software tools or languages. Problem-solving in the PROLOG toolkit environment is based upon the exploitation of an inference mechanism where logical rules determine the way in which the data may be manipulated. Importantly, these rules can be changed and/or added to by the student. Other data handling programs written in other languages or code are perhaps more sympathetic to the needs of the computer as a machine than they are to the needs of the user. Such programs impose a structure in which the student must work and think, which is often compromised, not complemented, by the software.

CONCLUSIONS

The use of toolkits or software shells in the manner described puts the computer and the child at the centre of the learning experience in the History classroom. The use of the shells provides children and teachers with new ways of thinking about knowledge and with new ways of learning.

Alongside new learning experiences other developments may be seen to occur when the shells are applied in the classroom. They appear to be both machine- and time-intensive which, in turn, has wider curriculum implications. The software makes specific and new demands upon the teacher and also raises questions concerning the classroom relationship between teacher, child and computer. For these reasons the computer becomes a powerful agent of educational change. It is the nature of this change that should, perhaps, be the focus of further studies.

REFERENCES AND FURTHER READING

Briggs, J (1984a), *Micro-PROLOG Rules!* LPA.

Briggs, J (1984b), The Plan, PEG-Exeter, School of Education, EX1 2LU.

Briggs, J (1986), 'Why teach PROLOG? The uses of PROLOG in education'. (See Chapter 11.)

Conlon, T (1985), *Start Problem-Solving with PROLOG*, Addison-Wesley.

Dean, J, Briggs, J, and Nichol, J (1987), 'Why Prolog', in *Educational Computing*, Scanlon, E, and O'Shea, T (Eds), John Wiley/Open University.

Dickinson, A K, and Lee, P J (1978), *History Teaching and Historical Understanding*, Heinemann.

Ennals, R (1981), 'Logic as a computer language for children,' in *Educational Computing*, June 1981.

Lang, S (1986), 'The sacred cow History project,' in *The Times Educational Supplement*, 4.4.1986.

Nichol, J, Dean J, and Briggs J (1984a), DETECT/PLACES/LINX, (PEG).

Nichol, J, Dean, J, and Briggs, J (1984b), 'Pupils, computers and History teaching,' in *New Horizons in Educational Computing*, Yazdani, M (Ed), Ellis Horwood.

Nichol, J, Dean J, and Briggs J (1986a), *Authoring Programs and Toolkits, Logic Programming and Curriculum Development*, (unpublished).

Nichol, J, Dean, J, and Briggs, J (1986b) *Computers and Cognition in the Classroom*, (unpublished).

Nichol, J, Dean, J, and Spedding, R (1986), *The Computer in the Teaching of History* (INSET pack), CET.

O'Shea, T, and Self, J (1983), *Learning and Teaching with Computers*. Harvester Press. PEG Conference 1986.

Schemilt, D (1980), *Evaluation Study: Schools Council History 13-16 Project*, Holmes McDougall.

Schemilt, D, *The Caliph's Coin: Grade Criteria and Adolescent ideas about Evidence in History* (unpublished).

Wild, M (1985), *Children, History and the Computer*, Advisory Unit.

Wild, M (1987) 'Information handling and History in the classroom: the role of the computer in the historical process', in *Conference Proceedings: International Association for History and Computing*, Hopkins, D and Denley, P (Eds), Manchester University Press.

3. Using PROLOG in the teaching of Geography

Terry Goble
Essex Institute of Higher Education
School of Computing
Victoria Road South
Chelmsford
Essex
CM1 1LL
UK

THE USE OF COMPUTERS IN GEOGRAPHY TEACHING

Over recent years computers have been used in teaching Geography in the secondary school in four main ways (Kent, 1985). They are:

1. Statistical analysis
2. Drill and practice
3. Simulation
4. Information retrieval.

Computers are used in many subject areas for statistical analysis. For several geographical activities, especially at A-level requiring quantitative methods, the computer has been a most suitable tool. The software has usually been general-purpose, small-scale statistical package. The drill and practice software, that sometimes has helpful comments and alternative pathways, typifies many geographical software packages. They are normally directed at a small sub-set of the subject and are specially designed for specific age groups (eg. Climate program).

Content-free software such as databases is growing in popularity. At present there appears to be no widespread use of databases for information retrieval in the subject; however, some interesting uses have been developed — for example, *Geobase* (Richards and Hones, 1986). As the use of information retrieval grows it is reasonable to expect PROLOG to be used in this respect.

Perhaps the most successful use of software to date has been in simulation packages. A simulation is the representation on the computer of a geographical process in the real world. The pupils have the opportunity to manipulate the inputs and then to observe the results. A typical and widely used simulation program is *Water on the Land Puddle* (Riley, 1983).

Several simulations have been given a competitive edge and have developed as games, eg *Mine, A Prospecting Game* (Glover and Riley); there is a clear analogy with non-computer games such as those pioneered in the early 1970s.

In the research environment of artificial intelligence there have been two major

Geography-based developments — tutorial interaction and student modelling. Neither has yet had any significant impact on the classroom, but this could be explained by the lack of suitable hardware. Both developments have laid some interesting foundations for future work in the area of computers in Geography.

'Scholar' (Carbonnell, 1970) was designed primarily but not exclusively to investigate tutorial dialogue. The subject matter was the Geography of South America. The database not only contained facts but also had the ability to infer new conclusions. The 'Why' program (Stevens and Collins, 1978) investigates, in the broad theme of Intelligent Computer-Aided Learning, student modelling. The computer analyses the student's responses to questions and attempts to diagnose conceptual errors. The 'Why' program deals with misconceptions in the causes of rainfall.

A recurrent theme in the use of computers in Geography is being able to build in the computer a logical representation of the physical world, and then have the ability to manipulate that representation. The manipulation can serve two principal purposes: firstly to test hypotheses, and secondly to attempt to identify the principal components that control and influence the situations of the real world. Thus the computer in Geography can become a very powerful tool, supplementing the traditional theoretical and quantitative value approaches to the subject which were previously used to make sense of the real world. The teaching of Geography encourages pupils to develop an understanding of the complex processes in the real world. Simplified models of a restricted area of reality can be easily constructed by school pupils. However, the strength of such a tool is that it can produce simple representations which can then be extended to represent more complex situations. The population model and the shop location problem described below show some simple implementations in PROLOG.

PROLOG can be used by pupils to represent simple models but can also be used at the other end of the spectrum to represent 'expert' knowledge. Much work needs to be done in these areas. Towards the 'expert' end there is also a need for suitable design tools so that the complex interrelationships can clearly be studied. Much work has been done in the structural analysis of complex business systems and some of these techniques can be used to advantage in the development of knowledge bases for the teaching of Geography. The knowledge base for industrial location illustrates one use of such a method (see later in this chapter).

MODEL BUILDING IN GEOGRAPHY

There has been much justifiable criticism of subject specialists being encouraged to learn programming so that they can represent subject ideas on the computer. It is not the teaching of a computer language itself that creates problems, for several aspects of programming, such as problem analysis, are useful techniques in many subjects. The principal difficulty comes with the need to concentrate on the programming aspects when the time and thought should be directed at the subject-specific problem. The programming aspects that need to be focused on are the preciseness of the language, ie the syntax, and the methods by which languages solve problems. The more common procedural languages, such as BASIC, require both a description of the problem and a description of a method by which the language is to solve the problem. PROLOG suffers from some of the syntactical problems, which can be distracting, but its declarative nature, carefully used, can ensure that a description of the problem will give the required answer, the PROLOG system itself working out how to obtain the solution.

In the analysis of problems, one method that can help to clarify ideas is to set out the main factors in tabular form. The declarative nature of PROLOG allows for easy translation of the tabular description into the language.

The modelling of reality, ie the world around us, is a cross-disciplinary area of investigation that could give some valuable insights into the use of computers in Geography. Modelling is subsumed under the broad area of cognitive science in which the disciplines of psychology, linguistics, philosophy and computer science are strongly represented. The area is relatively new and is expanding rapidly and so more questions are posed than answers given (Sowa, 1984). It is argued that the manipulation of mental models constitutes reasoning (Johnson-Laird, 1983). There is, however, a certain difficulty with the term 'modelling' in that it has been used in several different ways. Three basic distinctions can be made within the computers-in-Geography-teaching domain:

1. The Geography models typified by Chorley and Haggett (1967) were essentially theoretical models and were developed to move away from the purely descriptive work of previous generations of Geographers (Gould, 1985).
2. Cognitive modelling represents the symbolic relationships developed in the mind to conceptualize the world. The realm of models includes the areas of experimental epistemology (Sloman, 1978), ie the construction of models to give an improved understanding of the world. Using the computer as a tool for pupils to represent their model can not only give feedback to the students, but also help the teacher to identify areas of misconception.
3. In the area of artificial intelligence a component of Intelligent Tutoring Systems is the student model. The model relates the student's learning pattern to the area of knowledge within the system. Many treat the student model as an 'overlay' of the main knowledge base, eg 'Guidon' (Clancey, 1982).

The use of modelling in the context of learning should help to relate the pupil's mental model to the reality of the Geographical world. The link will often be through either a theoretical (analytical) or descriptive (simulation) model on the computer. The pupil can then hypothesize and test out ideas. If the tools permit, it should then be possible for the pupil to build his/her own model which can be tested in the same way. Two of the most difficult aspects that any model building must address are the concepts of change and causation (Roberts, 1983). These can be seen to underpin many points in Geography, whether interpreted in a spatial or a temporal manner.

A SIMPLE POPULATION GROWTH MODEL

The model that follows shows simple population for a specified number of years. It is divided into a number of sections that are explained below. In this PROLOG model recursion is used to step through the years. Recursion can be a difficult topic but the basic principle of it can easily be shown.

Each step of the model is a repetition of the same basic process. The basic process can be illustrated for one year. The inputs are:

the year
population at the beginning of the year
the year in which the calculations are to end

These can be called parameters. Each time the process takes place it will need these parameters but the value of the parameters will change from year to year.

After the inputs comes the section that requires various references, such as the birth rate and death rate. In this case the birth rate and death rate will be looked up from facts already stored in the system. These could equally well be introduced and passed through the system as parameters but as their value does not change they need only be entered once.

After obtaining the reference details the calculations can be performed. The number of births and deaths are calculated to give the natural increase and total population at the end of the year.

The final task is to increment the year in readiness for the transfer of parameters to the next year. The year count in fact controls the recursion.

The output of the population figures is required so the values required to be printed can be passed as parameters to a printing routine.

The final operation is to output the information that is needed by the next step. The structure of this output must correspond exactly to the input structure so that recursion can take place.

In addition to the process indicated, the following are also required to make it a clearly working model:

1. A section to input the initial data.
2. A section to print the headings for the output.
3. A stop point to the recursion.
4. A section to perform the printout.

Tabular Representation of Population Model

Division	Model of Process	Yearly Steps			
Inputs	Year	1970	1971	1972	1973
	Pop	1000	1018	1036	1055
	End Year	1974	1974	1974	1974
References	Birth Rate	0.038	0.038	0.038	0.038
	Death Rate	0.020	0.020	0.020	0.020
Calculations	Births	38	39	39	40
	Deaths	20	20	21	21
	Nat Increase	18	18	19	19
	New Pop	1018	1036	1055	1074
Increment	Next	1971	1972	1973	1974
Outputs	Next Year	1971	1972	1973	1974
	New Pop	1018	1036	1055	1074
	End Year	1974	1974	1974	1974

The Population Growth Model in PROLOG

The model has the process section called 'growth'. The layout is very similar to the tabular method.

```
growth(Year,Pop,End__year):-
    birth__rate(Birth__rate),
    death__rate(Death__rate),
    births is Pop * Birth__rate,
    deaths is Pop * Death__rate,
    natural__increase is Births—Deaths,
    new__pop is Pop + Natural__increase,
    next__year is Year + 1,
    printout(Year,Pop,Births,Deaths,Natural__increase,New__pop),
    growth(Next__year,New__pop,End__year).
```

The references for the birth rate and death rate are:

```
birth__rate(0.038).
death__rate (0.020).
```

The clause to end the recursion, which stops the calling of the process section, occurs when the first and third parameters match.

```
growth(End__year,Pop,End__year).
```

This section prints out the values for each year. The **r(7,0)** part of the instructions results in a tabular output seven characters wide, with whole numbers only.

```
printout(Year,Pop,Births,Deaths,Natural__increase,New__pop):-
    write(Year),
    write(Pop,__,r(7.0)),
    write(Births,__,r(7,0)),
    write(Deaths,__,r(7,0)),
    write(Natural__increase,__,r(7,0)),
    write(New__pop,__,r(7,0)),
    nl.
```

This section prompts for input and then passes the initial parameters to the process model called growth.

```
begin:—
    write('Enter start year.................... ')'
    read(Year),
    write('Enter start population............... '),
    read(Pop),
    write('Enter end year..................... '),
    read(End__year),
    print__headings,
    growth(Year,Pop,End__ year).
```

The 'begin' section, before calling 'growth', displays the headings for the tabular output of the results:

```
print__headings:—
    write('Year...'),
    write('Pop....'),
    write('Births'),
    write('Deaths'),
    write('Incr...'),
    write('New Pop'),
    nl.
```

The model can be called with **'begin'**. The output below shows the input prompts and then the response from the PROLOG model.

Enter start year. . . . . 1970.
Enter start population. . . . . 1000.
Enter end year. . . . . 1980.

Year...	Pop....	Births	Deaths	Incr...	New Pop
1970	1000	38	20	18	1018
1971	1018	39	20	18	1036
1972	1036	39	21	19	1055
1973	1055	40	21	19	1074
1974	1074	41	21	19	1093
1975	1093	42	22	20	1113
1976	1113	42	22	20	1133
1977	1133	43	23	20	1153
1978	1153	44	23	21	1174
1979	1174	45	23	21	1195

THE LOCATION OF A SHOP

Geography by its very nature deals with spatial analysis, and therefore modelling that can be map referenced can be of great use. A typical application is indicated below. A map with 25 grid squares and X and Y coordinates has the population of each grid square indicated. It can be assumed that to move to an adjacent grid square takes one unit of time, and that the optimum location for the shop is where the average travelling time for the total population of the map is at a minimum.

The main part of the representation is in the same form as before, the processing being done in the section labelled:

shop__location(Count,X__coord,Y__coord,Total__Pop,Total__time)

The sub-section **time__to__shop(X__coord,Y__coord, Time)** passes the value of the current X and Y coordinates and works out the time, which is then duly passed back to the main process. The procedure is slightly longer than necessary because of the absence of the arithmetic functions *absolute* and *square root* in some versions of PROLOG.

The count of the squares is used, rather than just coordinates, firstly so that it easily conforms to first style of modelling and secondly so that the recursion does not become unnecessarily complicated.

The arguments for the map__of__population references are:

map__of:population(Count of grid square, X coord, Y coord, Pop)

The stopping point for the recursion is when the count has reached 26 and then the summative information is printed.

The Location of a Shop in PROLOG

```
shop__location(26,Total__pop,Total__time):—
    write('Total population on map . . . . . . . . . . . . . . . . . . . . . . . . . . . . . . '),
    write(Total__pop),nl,
    write('Total time taken for all population . . . . . . . . . . . . . . . . . . . . . . . . '),
    write(Total__time),nl,
    Average is Total__time/Total__pop,
    write('Average time per person . . . . . . . . . . . . . . . . . . . . . . . . . . . . '),
    write(Average),nl.

shop__location(Count,Total__pop,Total__time):—
    map__of__population(Count,X__coord,Y__coord,Pop),
    time__to__shop(X__coord,Y__coord,Time),
    New__total__pop is Total__pop + Pop,
    New__total__time is Total__time + (Pop*Time),
    printout(X__coord,Y__coord,Pop,Time),
    New__count is Count + 1,
    shop__location(New__count,New__total__pop,New__total__time).

time__to__shop(X__coord,Y__coord,Time):—
    shop__coords(Shop__x,Shop__y),
    Diff__x is X__coord — Shop__x,
    Diff__y is Y__coord — Shop__y,
    Positive__x is Diff__x * Diff__x,
    Positive__y is Diff__y * Diff__y,
    ((Positive__x > = Positive__y,
    Time__diff is Diff__x);
    (Time__diff is Diff__y)),
    ((Time__diff < 0,
    Time is Time__diff * —1);
    (Time is Time__diff)).

begin:—
    headings,
    shop__location(1,0,0).

headings:—
    write('X Coord....'),
    write('Y Coord....'),
    write('Population....'),
    write('Time to shop'),nl.

printout(X__coord,Y__coord,Pop,Time):—
    write(X__coord,__,i(11)),
    write(Y__coord,__,i(11)),
    write(Pop,__,i(14)),
    write(Time,__,i(14)),
    nl.
```

shop__coords(2,2).
map__of__population(1,1,1,10).
map__of__population(2,1,2,10).
map__of__population(3,1,3,10).
map__of__population(4,1,4,10).
map__of__population(5,1,5,10).
map__of__population(6,2,1,10).
map__of__population(7,2,2,10).
map__of__population(8,2,3,10).
map__of__population(9,2,4,10).
map__of__population(10,2,5,10).
map__of__population(11,3,1,10).
map__of__population(12,3,2,10).
map__of__population(13,3,3,10).
map__of__population(14,3,4,10).
map__of__population(15,3,5,10).
map__of__population(16,4,1,10).
map__of__population(17,4,2,10).
map__of__population(18,4,3,10).
map__of__population(19,4,4,10).
map__of__population(20,4,5,10).
map__of__population(21,5,1,10).
map__of__population(22,5,2,10).
map__of__population(23,5,3,10).
map__of__population(24,5,4,10).
map__of__population(25,5,5,10).

The output produced by the shop location program is detailed below. For simplicity each grid square is assumed to have a population of 10.

X Coord	Y Coord	Population	Time to shop
1	1	10	1
1	2	10	1
1	3	10	1
1	4	10	2
1	5	10	3
2	1	10	1
2	2	10	0
2	3	10	1
2	4	10	2
2	5	10	3
3	1	10	1
3	2	10	1
3	3	10	1
3	4	10	2
3	5	10	3
4	1	10	2
4	2	10	2
4	3	10	2
4	4	10	2

X Coord....Y Coord....Population...Time to shop			
4	5	10	3
5	1	10	3
5	2	10	3
5	3	10	2

Total population on map..240
Total time taken for all population..............................460
Average time per person..1.9167

A KNOWLEDGE BASE FOR INDUSTRIAL LOCATION

The illustration of the use of PROLOG as a modelling language for pupils is one end of a spectrum that uses PROLOG in Geography teaching. The other end is the representation of expert system knowledge. Industrial location represents a suitable subject area for the development of an expert system in Geography. It is broadly a rule based domain but does have sufficient heuristics to warrant encoding as part of an expert system, and therefore the use of PROLOG is appropriate. Two of the most significant points of industrial location to the geographer are:

1. The relationship between the theoretical and the actual. These aspects are frequently dealt with in isolation. Current theory in industrial location is purely algorithmic, with many basic assumptions and premises. A knowledge base that united both theory and the actual location of industry would use heuristic rules. Heuristic rules are 'rules of thumb' often used by experts to determine conclusions.
2. The weighting of the many inputs to industrial location is of prime importance. This is particularly important in the balance between optimum and satisfier decisions.

The example of the knowledge base given below is in the developmental stage and therefore some aspects, such as a more sophisticated user interface, have not yet been developed.

One major difficulty that arises in developing a knowledge base is the design methodology. The attempt to use PROLOG directly with a significant number of rules causes confusion in two ways. First, in the mixing of the procedural and declarative aspects of the language, and secondly in the ability to predict and thus test the knowledge base at different stages of its development. The more usual design mechanisms, such as JSP, Jackson structured methodology (Jackson, 1975), are not suitable for PROLOG as they were devised for procedural languages. A method that is suitable can be adapted from a structured systems design methodology. The method is used to produce a functional specification for the introduction of computers into a business system. The central core of the design method is a data flow diagram. Each data flow diagram has four possible components, as illustrated in Fig. 3.1.

1. External sources and sinks of information.
2. Data flows.
3. Process boxes.
4. Data stores.

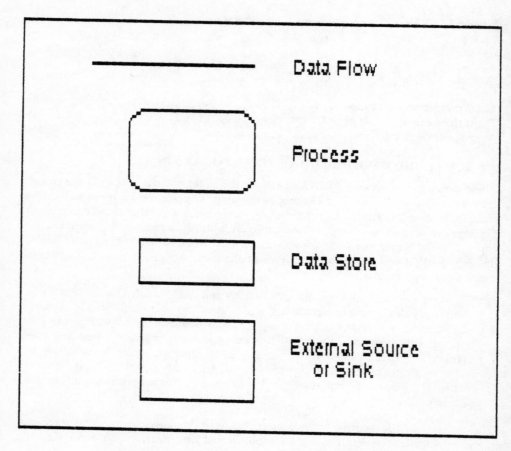

Figure 3.1 *The four components of a data flow diagram.*

The data flow diagram (Fig. 3.2) shows part of the industrial location knowledge base. The details of the method of implementation will not be entered into here. However, the flows are representative of the clauses in PROLOG. The inputs to the process boxes represent the tail of a rule, the head of the rule being the output. Each process box has a very close relationship to the tabular method of constructing models as mentioned earlier. The external sources and sinks of information represent the normal input and output sections. The data stores are comprised of facts. They can be asserted and retracted as the process box dictates. Some of the data stores are 'read only' and therefore can be set for reference before the program is run, in a similar manner to the 'reference' sections in the earlier models. It is possible to use the data flow diagram to identify modules and therefore be able to work on independent sections, for testing purposes. The structured systems analysis methodology is capable of producing 'layered' data flow diagrams so that both generalized and more detailed implementations are possible including, at detailed levels, validation and error checking procedures. This corresponds to the PROLOG method illustrated in the shop location model whereby a more detailed analysis is developed as a 'sub-unit' of the main process.

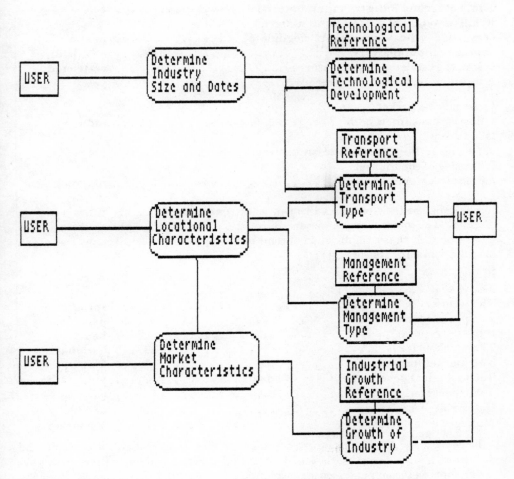

Figure 3.2 *Data flow diagram. (From Gane and Sarson, 1979, Structured Systems Analysis.)*

The trial outputs of the system are represented below. The input details are for the steel industry in 1970. The prompts for information are illustrated below.

Enter name of industry .... **steel.**
Enter year... **1970.**

Name of first industry input material .... **iron__ore**
Weight of first input material
very__heavy heavy moderate negligible .... **very__heavy**
Source of input material one .... **port.**
Is source restricted or everywhere....................... **restricted.**
Is input material natural__resource .... **yes.**

Name of second industry input material . . . . coal.
Relative weight of second input material
very__heavy heavy moderate negligible . . . . heavy.
Source of input material two . . . . coalfield.
Is source restricted or everywhere. . . . . restricted.
Is input material natural__resource . . . . yes.

Is the target market
industry consumer both . . . . industry.
Is industry__size
very__large large moderate small workshop . . . . large.
Is the size of the market
national regional local . . . . national.

The program then processes them in accordance with the details in the data flow diagram. The output screen produced by the computer then shows the required information which is a combination of some of the inputs and the deductions made from the rules within the system.

Industry name is. . . . . steel
The year is 1970
The industry is in a. . . . . specific__location
The precise location being . . . . port
Industry type is. . . . . heavy
The market size is. . . . . national
The market target is. . . . . industry
Technological development is typified by . . . . automation
Transport is . . . . rail
Industrial trend is. . . . . decline
Management style is. . . . . corporate

In any expert system the program should be able to explain by what route and deductions it arrived at its conclusion. This particular stage is still under development but the prompts on the output screen are as follows:

For an explanation of any of the factors

location(1) industry__type(2) transport(3)
industry__trend(4) technology(5) management(6) stop(7)

Please input choice.......?.

So as not to crowd the explanations with long indications of pathways through a complex network that the user does not need to directly understand, the explanation takes the area requested and shows how the answer was devised. The inputs from which the conclusions of that particular section are drawn can come from one of three sources. First, the user may have supplied them, — for example, the industry size. Second, the input may have been deduced from a previous rule within the system, for example, dealing with the type of industry. Finally, the input may have derived from the reference material associated with a particular aspect. In the example below, the management style would be identified as corporate, given the other inputs and the years between 1960 and 1986. Thus the explanation screen would be as follows:

The name of the industry is .... steel
the year is 1970

the following factors influence the management
the industrial growth trend is .... decline
the industrial size obtained from the user is .... large
the industry type is deduced and is .... heavy
for the period beginning in............................ 1960
and ending in 1986
the management style is................................ corporate

CONCLUSION

PROLOG offers a wide potential for the teaching of Geography, stretching from simple student modelling through to the use of expert systems. However, it is not a panacea for all and every problem in the use of computers in Geography. It has difficulties that must be overcome if it is to be used widely. Firstly, some of the less friendly aspects of the many implementations need to be removed so that the Geographer or potential Geographer may concentrate on Geographical issues and not have to worry about syntactical and other idiosyncrasies. Good progress is being made here with 'front-ends' such as MITSI (Briggs). Secondly, many teachers who have stepped out of using pre-written CAL packages have found themselves learning BASIC, and have become disillusioned. This could present a barrier to learning 'another' language, albeit a very different one. A third problem that must be overcome is that those teachers who are introduced to PROLOG are frequently only shown the elementary data retrieval facilities, and no systematic way of introducing further steps or illustrating the potential of the language is adopted.

PROLOG has the potential to play a significant role in the future use of computers in Geography, if it is properly introduced and developed.

REFERENCES AND FURTHER READING

Briggs, J, *MITSI* (1984), Peg-Exeter, England, EX1 2LU.
Carbonell, J R (1970), *Mixed Initiative Man-Computer Instructional Dialogues*, Bolt Beranek and Newman.
Chorley, R J and Haggett, P (1967), *Models in Geography*, Methuen.
Clancey, W J (1982), 'Guidon', in Barr, A and Feigenbaum, E A (eds), *The Handbook of Artificial Intelligence, Volume 2*, William Kaufmann.
Climate, Software, Heinemann Computers in Education Ltd.
Gane, C and Sarson, T (1979), *Structured Systems Analysis*, Prentice-Hall.
Glover, S and Riley, D *Mine, Prospecting Game*, Computers in the Curriculum, Longman.
Gould, P (1985), *The Geographer at Work*, Routledge & Kegan Paul.
Jackson, M (1975), *Principles of Program Design*, Academic Press.
Johnson-Laird, P N (1983), *Mental Models*, Cambridge UP.
Kent, A (1985), 'The Humanities', *Children, Computers and the Curriculum*, Wellington, J J (Editor), Harper and Row.
Richards, P N and Hones, G H (1986), *Geobase*, Longmans Micro Software.

Riley, D *et al* (1983), *Water on the Land, Puddle,* Computers in the Curriculum, Longman.

Roberts, N *et al* (1983), *Introduction to Computer Simulation,* Addison-Wesley.

Sloman, A (1978), *The Computer Revolution in Philosophy,* Harvester Press.

Sowa, J F (1984), *Conceptual Structures,* Addison-Wesley.

Stevens, A L, and Collins, A (1978), *The Goal Structure of a Socratic Tutor,* Bolt Beranek and Newman.

4. Using PROLOG in the teaching of Ecology

Jens Rasmussen
The Royal Danish School of Educational Studies
Institute of Pedagogics and Psychology
Emdrupvej 101
DK-2400 Copenhagen
Denmark

When new information technology has been applied to teaching, interest has mostly been directed towards the technology *per se:* what can the new technology do, or what is it supposed to do, and what consequences will its application have? Such a stimulus/response view and evaluation of IT makes it look as if new technology is dependent on purely quantitative considerations for its impact, such as for which type of pupils, in which context and for how long IT can be applied.

To evaluate technology in a way that *qualitatively* distinguishes between different applications (promoted, interactive, etc) it is necessary not only to observe how IT integrates into the educational process but also how the educational experience forms part of information technology. It means that you have to consider educational intentions which are more or less consciously embedded within the technology as well as the specific pedagogic aims and objectives towards which the technology is being directed. Criteria for the evaluation of the technology derive from its nature, its specific pedagogic application and how it relates to a general theory of IT in education. It is not sufficient in a positivistic way to concentrate on the effects the introduction of technologies will have. You also have to take an interest in the immanent meaning of technology and its relation to the educational milieu in which it has to be used.

THEORETICAL BACKGROUND

This chapter concerns an environmental project about the river as an ecological system, in which PROLOG was used as a general datalogical tool. We chose PROLOG in order to surmount one of the basic problems of education, that of parallelism.

The fundamental role of education is to create a connection across the historically developed separation between knowledge and man. The basic elements of education are knowledge and pupils. Apart from this there are at least two forms of knowledge and two forms of pupils' backgrounds.

Knowledge can be direct or indirect (Vygotsky, 1962; Negt, 1976). Direct knowledge or everyday knowledge is the form of knowledge which answers factual questions of the who or what type, and represents the form in which reality appears. In other words it is the kind of knowledge which can directly be registered and learned, or which can be looked up in a dictionary. Indirect knowledge or positivistic knowledge is the kind of knowledge which gives answers to reasoning questions of the how or why type, and which represents positivistic insight into and understanding of underlying meaning. It is knowledge which cannot be directly experienced.

The aims of pedagogical theory are to establish a connection between knowledge and man and to establish a coherent understanding of links between direct and indirect knowledge in the experiences of the pupils (Fig. 4.1).

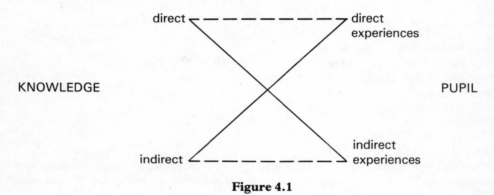

Figure 4.1

Pedagogical theory has tried to solve this problem in two ways (Rasmussen, 1985). Starting with indirect knowledge (Kant, 1964), an effort has been made to promote it in pupils, an effort that has mostly failed. If the pupil has no direct knowledge in advance to which indirect knowledge can be connected, it will remain external to him/her. The goal is to develop pupil understanding but if purely abstract knowledge is supplied it cannot be connected with the concrete reality.

An alternative approach is to start in the basic direct experiences of the pupil and from here aim at indirect knowledge (Rousseau, 1983). However, this has mainly failed as it has only been possible to give the pupils direct experience of direct knowledge. The pupils learn about the appearance of reality, but do not grasp its essence. In a slight paraphrase of an old Danish pedagogical theorist, you could say that the memory is overloaded without the brain being developed.

The axiom for our developmental work is: it is possible to create a connection between direct and indirect knowledge in a teaching project by using PROLOG as a tool for expert systems. In other words, pupils achieve a qualitatively greater and deeper understanding of the learning process. In order for us to say that the use of PROLOG has been a success, the pupils need to understand *how* there has been a qualitative development of their conceptual knowledge.

THE EDUCATIONAL PROJECT

The subject matter of the project was an environmental study of the river as an ecological system. The PROLOG version used is written in Danish and called pico-PROLOG (Bogh, 1986; Briggs, 1984). It is the MITSI front-end translated into Danish and expanded by incorporating some facilities from APES (1984).

The project was carried out with a class of 12 pupils in an ordinary public school. The pupils were about 14 years old. The teaching was done by the class teacher: Hans Jantzen, Biology master. The Royal Danish School of Educational Studies has placed four IBM PCs (MS-DOS, 256k), at our disposal.

The project spread over 35 lessons, split up into the following phases:

I	II	III	IV
pico PROLOG	PREPARATION	EXCURSION	WORKING UP
10 lessons	7 lessons	6 lessons	12 lessons

Each lesson lasted for 45 minutes, but often lessons were combined into double lessons. The excursion and the working up occurred on fieldwork days comprising 5-6 lessons each.

Learning Pico-PROLOG

In the first phase of the project pico-PROLOG was introduced to the pupils. They learned about the syntax, the editor, lists and how PROLOG works: evaluating goals with facts, evaluating goals with rules and tracing evaluation.

The teaching was based on material I had written. This material was written so that the pupils individually, or in small groups, could work with the subjects and try the examples on the computer on their own. This material has now been prepared for a book that can back up pico-PROLOG (Rasmussen, 1986).

After this phase all pupils were interviewed for the first time. From those interviews it appears that none of the pupils found it difficult to learn pico-PROLOG. Statements such as the following are characteristic of the pupils' views on the version:

'Just in the beginning when we didn't know it very well I thought it sounded enormously difficult, but as I learned it I think it has been easier.' (Boy)

'No, I don't think it was difficult. When there was such a small problem I thought the way we could solve it was rather funny. I liked that when we had written something it just told us that it didn't understand one word of it. Then we had to try again. I really thought that was funny.' (Girl)

The river

The phase of preparation began with an initial trip to the river that the pupils later on had to study closely. The purpose of this tour was to teach the pupils how to use the landing net to catch animals. After trying for some time, the pupils worked out how to move the landing net to catch something. All of them caught animals which were put into an aquarium on their return to school.

When the pupils met again they discovered that all the animals were dead except the sticklebacks. They were very indignant, and it was excellent motivation for a discussion about which conditions had to be fulfilled for animals to live in a freshwater system. The following aspects were considered important:

1. There have to be plants and light so that the plants can produce oxygen.
2. The water must be fairly pure.
3. There has to be food and there have to be hiding places for the small animals if they are not going to be eaten by the sticklebacks.

The teacher for this lesson had the foresight to bring in a fresh collection of animals, which the pupils had to identify. In this way they learned the names of most of the macro-animals to be found in a river: tubifix, snails, mussels, crayfish, may flies, spring flies, mosquito grubs, water beetles, bugs and mites — to name just a few of the most common.

Finally there was in the preparation phase an experiment about putrefaction. Three glasses were put aside for a couple of weeks. In the first there was pure water, to the second 0.1 g of fishfodder was added and to the third 1 g of fishfodder was added. As fishfodder is an organic substance it will putrefy. To show what happens during putrefaction the content of oxygen in the three glasses was measured. The results showed that oxygen is absorbed during putrefaction. The amount of oxygen was greatest in the glass of pure water (about 30%), and smallest in the glass with 1 g of fishfodder (about 5%). Apart from that there was a discussion about the gases emitted from the glasses, which smelled unpleasant. The conclusion was that putrefaction reduces the amount of oxygen in the water, while the gases hydrogen sulphide and ammonia are produced.

This experiment brought the pupils to reflect further about which type of animals would be able to live in water with different amounts of oxygen. The result of the discussion which followed was the drawing up of the taxonomy shown in Fig. 4.2.

	RESPIRATION SYSTEM	ANIMAL EXAMPLES
LOTS OF OXYGEN	gills	fish, crayfish
|	tracheae	may fly, spring fly
|	respiration through the surface	tubifix, chironomid larvae
LITTLE OXYGEN	airbreathing	water bugs, water beetles
	snorkel	fly larvae

Figure 4.2

Using this taxonomy the respiration systems of the animals can be regarded as indicators of the quality of the water.

The learning in this phase involved the pupils gaining knowledge that the river can be seen as an ecological system. It is a well-defined principle of nature that there is a cycle of mutual interdependence between living organisms and decaying substances. To support this concept we used Fig. 4.3 (Abrahamsen, 1981).

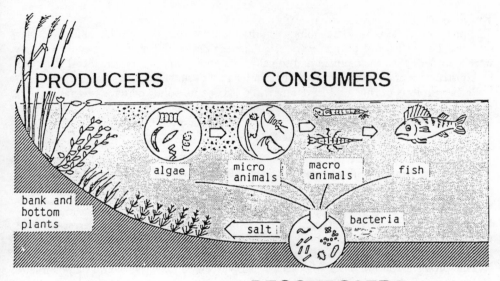

Figure 4.3

The figure shows that the producers are the microscopic plankton algae and bank and bottom plants. The animals are consumers. Plants and animals help each other in such a way that the cycle in the ecological system is kept going. The figure also shows two food chains. The grass food chain is the one where algae are eaten by micro animals, which are eaten by macro animals, which are eaten by fish. The detritus food chain is here just shown by bacteria. The next link is between bacteria and detritus eaters.

The river trip

After our preparations the main excursion to the river finally took place. The pupils were separated into four groups of three. They stayed in these groups for the rest of the project.

Two groups went north and two went south. At each 400-metre point they had to take water and oxygen samples and the test point had to be categorized in terms of breadth, depth, stream, weeds, smell and conditions of the bottom. Animals were caught in a landing net and the oxygen content of the water was measured by the Winkler method. Each group had to make six tests. On return to school all the collected samples, which were in marked glasses, were put into the fridge to keep until the next day. About this excursion one of the girls said quite precisely:

'Actually in the beginning I was very negative about standing outside in the cold and running 3-4 km to find a fish but actually when you are there it is much better than you really believe. Actually in the beginning it was rather cold to stand out there. We would simply not do anything but then when we went further into the wood we actually had to make tests and so on. We did play a little and we got warm and it was more fun to make tests. Without the tour we wouldn't have learned as much.'

Resolution

The phase of working up the results was initiated by going through the collected water samples. Percentages of oxygen were calculated precisely and all the collected animals were identfied. Now the moment had come for the pupils to try to use the pico-PROLOG for construction of an 'expert system' containing all the knowledge they had gained.

Earlier projects of this kind have often stopped at this point; perhaps the pupils were given a lecture or produced some wall displays to show what they had learned. However, it is a common opinion of teachers that pupil interest is often lacking during this phase. The teacher of the class, Hans, expressed his view:

'When we discussed the excursion afterwards nobody really felt like going on working with the problems and the results. The results were a part of the instruction and had no meaning apart from this.'

Earlier there had been pupil interest and engagement when acquiring 'direct knowledge' drawn from everyday concepts and concrete, direct experiences. The interest stops or declines, however, when an attempt is made to link this knowledge with indirect knowledge, scientific concepts, the general or the abstract.

This project had to find out whether by using pico-PROLOG, it would be possible to go beyond this distinction between forms of knowledge. Our aim was for the pupils to obtain an insight into and an understanding of the ordering principles that characterize the river as an ecological system. Secondly our aim was to develop a real understanding of the ecological quality of the river.

The end of the collection of direct knowledge meant we could see if it would be possible to create a connection between this knowledge and the regularities which concern the river as an ecological system. The idea was mainly to represent direct knowledge by facts and indirect knowledge by rules. The pupils had inductively obtained direct knowledge about the river but were not able, in a continued inductive process, to find the principles that ordered its ecological system. So it was decided that the teacher should continually refer to Fig. 4.3 deductively, and should try in class to formulate single regularities in normal language without considering the syntax of pico-PROLOG.

The following facts were listed:

1. Plants produce organic substances.
2. Plants produce oxygen.
3. Plants live by nutrient salts.

The pupils had no problem in understanding these expressions: the first they knew from the science teaching about photosynthesis, the second they knew from the aquarium they had in class, and the third they knew from giving the plants fertilizer. The next step was to formulate rules for these statements in a way that could match pico-PROLOG's syntax.

object — relation — object

Connecting statements 1. and 2. gives the following rule:

+ + +>SOMETHING supplies oxygen if
+ + +>SOMETHING produces organic-substance

Connecting statements 1. and 3. gives:

+ + +>SOMETHING consumes nutrient-salt if
SOMETHING produces organic-substance

In this way we had examples of rules for both producers and consumers.

Now the pupils were asked to formulate more rules on their own. They had gained the knowledge to be able to do so from what they had learnt during the preparatory phase (as far as they were able to remember). They had Fig. 4.3, and we made this frame which they could use as a guide, or disposition, for the formulation of rules:

	produces	consumes
organic substance		
oxygen		
nutrient salt		

Each group ended up by formulating between 8 and 10 rules for supply and an equivalent number of rules for consumption:

supplies:
1. **SOMETHING supplies organic-substance if**
   SOMETHING produces organic-substance
2. **SOMETHING supplies organic-substance if**
   SOMETHING putrefies plants
3. **SOMETHING supplies organic-substance if**
   SOMETHING putrefies animals
4. **SOMETHING supplies organic-substance if**
   SOMETHING is a source-of-pollution
5. **SOMETHING supplies organic-substance if**
   SOMETHING falls into the water
6. **SOMETHING supplies oxygen if**
   SOMETHING produces organic-substance
7. **SOMETHING supplies nutrient-salt if**
   SOMETHING putrefies plants
8. **SOMETHING supplies nutrient-salt if**
   SOMETHING putrefies animals
9. **SOMETHING supplies nutrient-salt if**
   SOMETHING is a source-of-pollution
10. **SOMETHING supplies nutrient-salt if**
    SOMETHING falls into the water

consumes:
1. **SOMETHING consumes organic-substance if
   SOMETHING eats plants**
2. **SOMETHING consumes organic-substance if
   SOMETHING eats animals**
3. **SOMETHING consumes organic-substance if
   SOMETHING putrefies plants**
4. **SOMETHING consumes organic-substance if
   SOMETHING putrefies animals**
5. **SOMETHING consumes oxygen if
   SOMETHING eats plants**
6. **SOMETHING consumes oxygen if
   SOMETHING eats animals**
7. **SOMETHING consumes oxygen if
   SOMETHING putrefies plants**
8. **SOMETHING consumes oxygen if
   SOMETHING putrefies animals**
9. **SOMETHING consumes nutrient-salt if
   SOMETHING produces organic-substance**
10. **SOMETHING consumes oxygen if
    SOMETHING is a living-organism**

We now had a micro-world that consisted of the PROLOG system and the pupils. The PROLOG system contains indirect knowledge which the pupils are able to confront with their own direct knowledge in a knowledge-based micro-world. This confrontation characteristically occurred in two quite different ways.

Most of the groups tried to extend their databases with direct knowledge so that it was possible to get an answer to any questions asked. This meant that they began to add facts with concrete objects which the variables of the rules could match during the goal evaluation. On the basis of the following two rules:

consumes:
1. **SOMETHING consumes organic-substance if
   SOMETHING eats plants**
1. **SOMETHING consumes organic-substance if
   SOMETHING eats animals**

the pupils added facts which enabled the system to declare what respectively eats plants and animals:

eats:
1. **crayfish eats plants**
2. **snails eats plants**
3. **micro-animals eats plants**
4. **fish eats animals**
5. **crayfish eats animals**
6. **micro-animals eats animals**

This approach demanded that the pupils used all their existing knowledge and additional information from reference books. In many ways this could be described as a traditional enquiry pattern for building a domain-specific expert system.

Another, far more interesting, approach was used by a group of boys (perhaps because they were a little lazy). This approach profited by the query-the-user module. Instead of adding facts to the system these pupils only used rules to query and extend the database, for example: [NB In Danish we do not use do/does to indicate a question. (Bogh 1986).)

+ + +>supplies water-thyme oxygen?

[NB In Danish we do not use do/does to indicate a question. (Bogh 1986).]

Pico will then ask:

—————————————— **Is it true that** ————————————

water-thyme produces organic-substances
———————————————————————————— **(yes/no)?**

If the pupils answer yes to this question the answer will be added as a fact to the dialogue part of the database and as long as it is allowed to remain there, the query-the-user module will be activated every time questions are asked by rules where no facts are connected to the condition part.

Pupil interest in this phase of the project was considerable, as they discovered that it was possible to connect the concrete knowledge from their fieldwork with the abstract knowledge from the instruction during the preparatory phase. I had been very sceptical as to whether it would be possible to use PROLOG in this way, as it demanded a great deal from the pupils; but my scepticism was put to shame. In the PROLOG system the pupils had a tool which enabled them to connect their total knowledge in the field, and which worked as an incitement to ask questions of a coherent body of knowledge about the river as an ecological system.

The project ended with an expansion of the database for use in measuring the ecological quality of water in rivers. (The ecological quality is high if there is a varied life of plants and animals.) The basis for this was the above mentioned taxonomy for the respiration systems of animals, connected to a theory about competition among the animals when the quality of the water declines. As this part of the project was not our main concern I will just give an example of the types of rules and facts which were formulated by the pupils in this connection:

+ + +> SPECIES goes down for SOMETHING if
SPECIES respires with RESPIRATION-SYSTEM and
RESPIRATION-SYSTEM is more primitive than OTHER-
RESPIRATION-SYSTEM.

+ + +> snorkel is more primitive than airbreathing.
+ + +> airbreathing is more primitive than respiration-through-the-surface.
+ + +> respiration-through-the-surface is more primitive than trachaea.
+ + +> tracheae is more primitive than gills.

+ + +> sticklebacks respire with gills.
+ + +> spring-flies respire with tracheae.
+ + +> tubifix respire with respiration-through-the-surface.
+ + +> water-bugs respire with airbreathing.
+ + +> crane-flies respire with snorkel.

The underlying logic is:

The ecological quality of the water will be better if there is a great number of species at a testing point *and if* **these species have a highly developed respiration system.**

The method is called The Macro Index System and it is elaborated on the basis of the Biotic Index (Chandler, 1970). It is also called the Trent Index because the idea comes from the Biologists of the Trent Board.

CONCLUSION

The enquiry process was central to the construction of an 'expert system' using the general datalogical tool. It is my impression that the use of pico-PROLOG has contributed to a reduction in the problem of parallelism in education mentioned at the beginning of this chapter. This cannot yet be fully proved, as my evaluation only builds on interviews with the pupils before the preparation phase and after the project ended and on my subjective opinion of the databases that the pupils built. At the moment other observations and evaluations have not yet been analysed. There are tapes of all lectures and videos of the pupils working at the computers. Furthermore, there are classroom observations of pupils' on-task behaviour which show an inclination to ask questions, work independently, pay attention, co-operate, and concentrate. To help us obtain an indication of the pupils' view of the course they were asked to produce a self-evaluation after each lesson. Until this material has been analysed we will be unable to draw any final conclusions.

However, my subjective impressions are that the pupils have developed a much deeper understanding of the ecological system than they would otherwise have acquired. Confirmation of this came from the fact that all pupils, a week after the project ended, were able to answer the following test questions:

1. Can you explain how oxygen is produced and consumed?
2. Can you explain the production and consumption of organic substance?
3. Can you explain the production and consumption of nutrient salt?

Additionally the pupils in my post-project interview expressed the opinion that PROLOG might be linked to that result. A girl said:

'We had to think more about the things: actually you must understand it very thoroughly to write it into the computer. Because if you just understand it superficially then there will be a lot of things you will miss and then the answers will only be the half truth when you ask questions of the system.'

You could say that it is a good indication of pupil understanding that they were able to create rules — because without understanding the principles of order in the ecological system, it will hardly be possible to formulate one's knowledge in such an abstract and formalized way.

Furthermore, my impression of PROLOG's use in this ecological project is that it will be equally educationally valid in other logically-structured subject domains and knowledge bases. However, this project has shown that for success, a high degree of professional competence in the subject domain, and familiarity with different teaching methods, are required.

[*The project was accomplished in co-operation with cand. paed. Hans Janzen in phase I-IV and cand. polyt and phil. Bent B. Andresen in phase IV.*]

REFERENCES AND FURTHER READING

Abrahamsen, S E (1981), *Forurening i ferskvand* (Pollution in Fresh Water), Copenhagen, p.14.

APES (1984), *Augmented PROLOG for Expert Systems*, Logic Based Systems Ltd.

Bogh, K (1986), *On pico-PROLOG*, paper presented at PEG First Annual Conference, University of Exeter.

Briggs, J (1984), *Micro-PROLOG Rules!*, LPA, London.

Chandler, J R (1970), 'A Biological Approach to Water Quality Management,' *Water Poll. Control* **69**, 415-422.

Kant, I (1964), 'Uber Padagogik' in Immanuel Kant *Weke XII*, Frankfurt am Main.

Negt, O (1976), 'Schule als Erfarungsprocess', *Aesthetik and Kommunikation*, Berlin, no. 22/23.

Rasmussen, J (1985), *Informationsteknologi og den didaktisk dannelsesteoretiske tradition*, (Information Technolgy and the Didactic-formation of Theoretical Tradition) The Royal Danish School of Educational Studies, Copenhagen.

Rasmussen, J (1986), 'PROLOG i skolen', (PROLOG in the School), *PROLOG-DATA*, Alborg.

Rousseau, A J (1983), *Emile*, London.

Vygotsky, L S (1962), *Thought and Language*, New York.

5. Using PROLOG in the teaching of Electronics

Giovana Sissa
IPSIAA Meucci
Via dei Platani,
16139 Genova
Italy

INTRODUCTION

This chapter describes the use of micro-PROLOG in the training of students studying Electronics. The case study was carried out within the framework of the project 'Experiencing micro-PROLOG' which involves teaching and using PROLOG in secondary schools[1].

The objectives of the case study were to teach PROLOG programming via micro-PROLOG, and to develop applications relating to professional practice in an electronics laboratory. The project produced learning situations aimed at promoting deductive reasoning, and a learning environment which involved the use of databases by technicians in the electronics laboratory. The final element of the project was the implementation of a rule-based system, aimed at supporting the technician in his selection of electronic components.

The experimental use of PROLOG was conducted in a school for electronic technicians. The students involved in the case study were 16 to 17-year-olds, with no training in information technology — they had never used a computer before. The course was developed from their existing technical Electronics curriculum. The examples developed concerned subject matter which the students had already encountered. The project's goals were that by the end of the course:

1. The students should be able to describe non-trivial, although simplified, problems encountered in electronic engineering and to write PROLOG programs based upon actual situations.
2. The students should be able to discuss their choices and actions, on the basis of the accuracy, completeness and consistency of the criteria of the knowledge base and their mastery of the basic elements of micro-PROLOG.

[1]'Experiencing micro-PROLOG' is a two-year funded EEC project involving PROLOG for teaching, coordinated by CREFI, Marseille, France.

STUDENT EXPERIENCE

Language teaching

The main aim was to teach the computer language PROLOG, emphasizing its declarative aspect and focusing student attention on the problems of knowledge representation in a given field. Our methodology was initially to introduce the main language mechanisms rather than focusing on the logical aspect. It was only during the second stage that we dealt with the control component. The use of extra-logical features was reduced to a minimum, and discussed case by case. The built-in predicates were introduced when specific problems had to be solved.

Examples developed

We use micro-PROLOG for:

1. Object classification.
2. Object description.
3. Implementation of criteria for choosing the best object for any given application.

The first example concerns object classification in a laboratory. Students, after making an inventory of items in an Electronics laboratory, wrote down a classification of the objects. The aim was to produce an intelligent classification of the laboratory's equipment. Students already possessed the necessary knowledge, and worked out a classification of the objects according to their competence. Their classification was expressed in a tree, as in Fig. 5.1.

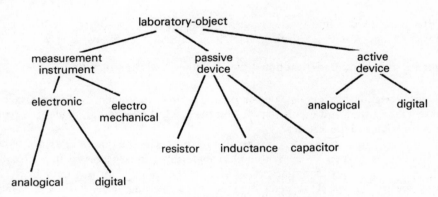

Figure 5.1

In particular, the active devices were described as in Fig. 5.2.

We indicated the hierarchical links through **is-a** relationships, obtaining a simple semantic network that gave an immediate entreé to writing programs in PROLOG.

Students then tried to write a synthetic but complete description of these objects. The problem was to draw information from different sources (data sheet, manuals, brochures, etc) that were either redundant or confused, and to try to put them together in a structured, coherent way.

We would like to draw attention to the digital integrated circuits (DIC) in Fig. 5.2. These circuits are components whereby, in a single chip, a complex circuit is obtained that performs a logic or memory function.

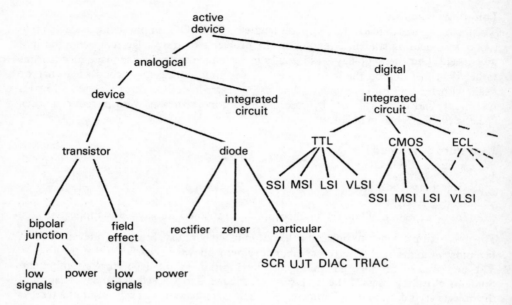

Figure 5.2

DICs were divided into two main groups: gates and logical functions. Each DIC is represented in the database by a fact, which is structured in the following way:

(letters & numbers) has (function-type (features-list) pins-number)

The binary relationship 'has' is based on the use of lists as arguments. The first argument represents the letters and numbers typed on the DIC, the second argument the type of gate or function and the features.

As far as function is concerned, it is not enough to specify the type of function; ie that it is a flip-flop, a counter or an arithmetical logic unit. It is necessary to indicate the function's features. For each function we indicate the features; for example, for the flip-flop we specify the type (D RS, etc), the mode of functioning of the clock, and, if found, with asynchronous inputs. For example, the flip-flop 74L74 was represented as the fact:

(74 L 74) has (FF (D ET-P Y) 2 14)

From the letters and numbers typed on the DIC one can find out which logical family it belongs to. Each family (or sub-family) is characterized by the following features:

logic properties, concerning voltage levels corresponding to logic level 0 and 1 (input higt level, input low level, output high level, etc);

electrical properties, concerning currents either absorbed or provided by the circuit (I/O currents);

performances, concerning delay times, maximum clock frequency, etc.

Each single DIC inherits the features of the family it belongs to.

After building the database containing the description of existing DICs, some rules are written down that allow us to obtain significant information to perform a fast and intelligent interrogation of the database, such as finding out which family a DIC belongs to, or how many elementary circuits a DIC has implementing a logical function. For example, we defined a three-argument predicate:

features-function (__I __T __F)

which connects the DIC -I that performs a logical function of a -T type that has -F features.

We now come to the main and most interesting part of the experiment — the choice of DICs. In real professional life we have different digital integrated circuits at our disposal, built-up with different technologies yet all implementing the same logical function. From a logical viewpoint they are identical, but in fact they have different properties — for example, in relation to their electrical characteristics, power dissipation and speed (and cost!). How can we choose the most suitable component for a specific situation?

A technician makes a choice on the basis of his expertise, and these choices are expressed through a number of *rules*. The main idea of our experiment was to try to reproduce this professional expertise in a PROLOG program, with the twofold aim of:

1. Making the student reflect on real professional use, getting him/her used to formalizing and expressing his/her reasoning in a clear and precise way.
2. Building a useful professional tool to help the technician make a choice of DIC; the tool can be used for training in this field.

Because of its declarative and rule-based nature, PROLOG is particularly suitable for this application. Besides this, PROLOG is particularly suitable for the representation of hierarchical links with inherited properties, such as each DIC inheriting the features of the particular logical family it belongs to.

Our procedure is to define the same relationships among objects. This allows us to decide which components are to be used. For example, we define compatibility among DICs when two circuits can be used together. Two DICs are compatible if they are compatible from the logical viewpoint (which means if voltage levels corresponding to logical 0 and 1 are correctly detected) and if they are electrically compatible (that is, if one circuit does not overcharge the other). Using PROLOG this is expressed in the following way:

__CI compatible __C2 if __C1 logic-compatible __C2 and
__C1 electric-compatible __C2

__C1 logic-comp __C2 if
__C1 has logical-properties (__VOHmin1 __VIHmin1 VOLmax1 __VILmax1)
and
__C2 has-logical-properties (__VOHmin2 __VOLmax2 __VILmax2)
and __VOHmin1 GE __VIHmin2
and __VILmax2 GE __VOLmax1

__C1 electric-comp __C2 if
__C1 has electric-properties (__IOH1 __IOL1 __IIH1 __IIL1) and
__C2 has-electric-properties (__IOH2 __IOL2 __IIH2 __IIL2) and
__IIH1 GE __IOH2 and
__IIL1 GE __IOL2

In the same way we defined the possibility of replacing the DICs. This possibility for replacement can be positive, or have functional limitations. As an example, if we replace one DIC with another, using a certain component of the TTLH family or the TTLS, some performances can be impaired, like power dissipation. This change in performance may not be important in some cases but can be important in others. This means that, for certain applications, we must take this into consideration.

METHODOLOGY

Students study micro-PROLOG and then use it as a logic-based language for problem-solving. First, they develop logic programming expertise, then declarative semantics and finally procedural semantics. In addition, the students are shown solutions related to a variety of circumstances (execution speed, core memory optimization, instruction number, etc).

At the same time the students learn how to describe the environment in which their daily school activity takes place: the electronics laboratory. Under the teacher's guidance, they can try different approaches and structures to describe the same problem. Problems related to the program implementations are not over-stressed. The focus is put upon: adequacy of the knowledge base, representation of the problem, accuracy and correctness, non-redundancy and completeness of the solution (examples are made, bearing in mind their mistakes).

The system has been validated through use in practical cases.

ORGANIZATION

The experiment was carried out in the 1986/87 academic year, in a classroom of 16- 17-year-olds, for 6 hours each week, using LPA micro-PROLOG on Apple IIe computers. In the laboratory the students' activities included classifying, listing and describing the components. It was conducted in conjunction with activities on the computers.

FUTURE PERSPECTIVES

Ideas about the system's future development concern the enhancement and management of the database. At present the system is implemented using a sample database, representing all kinds of existing possibilities, but limited in number. In actual professional activity the number of DICs used is very high. One of our ideas is to build up a database representing the real professional situation. For this purpose another version of the language, more suitable for database management, will be used.

At present the system provides information about which performances deteriorate when one DIC is replaced by another. The aim is to build an interface to query the user about the specific situation, so that EDY can suggest a component in a particular case. It is also interesting to know to what extent performance deteriorates when one circuit is replaced by another.

CONCLUSIONS

The basic idea is that the problems handled must be examples of a broader range of problems concerning classification, description and choice of the criteria of objects and consideration of specific situations. The number and kind of problems from the educational and training viewpoint are infinite — just think of the amount of classification in Biology and the natural sciences. And think of how often in real life we have to choose between different objects to see which one suits us best, or which one is most suitable for a specific situation; for example, the selection of car tyres on the basis of the kind of road one has to drive on.

The main idea is to consider a technician's expertise within a specific limited field, to try to formalize it and express it within a set of rules. In addition, the attempt to represent professional expertise is very important in order to understand the nature of such expertise.

REFERENCES AND FURTHER READING

Bergmann, M (1983), *PROLOG — Programming in Logic*, Paper given at The First European Seminar on Education, Marseille.

Clarke, K L, and McCabe, F G (1984), *Micro-PROLOG: Programming in Logic*, Prentice-Hall

Clocksin, W and Mellish, C (1979), *Programming in PROLOG*, Springer Verlag.

Conlon, T (1985), *Start Problem-Solving with PROLOG*, Addison Wesley.

de Saram, H O (1985), *Programming in micro-PROLOG*, Ellis Horwood.

Ennals, J R (1984), *Beginning micro-PROLOG*, 2nd edition, Ellis Horwood.

Giannesini, F, Kanoui, H, Pasero, R and Van Caneghen, M (1985), *PROLOG*, InterEditions.

The World TTL, IC, DATA and Cross Reference Guide, 1982.

6. Using PROLOG in classroom scientific research

Carole Cole
19 Vanessa Crescent
Glendowie
Auckland 5
New Zealand

For the purposes of this research the children studied used a microcomputer to process data and micro-PROLOG as a programming language. The teacher was employed as a resource for pupil self-learning about a science topic. The children wrote simple descriptive sentences in English — like SIMPLE syntax to create a database which they queried using **is** and **which**. The pupils also produced atomic sentences, some containing variables, and semantic networks.

A science topic was chosen because research reported so far by Ennals (1983, 1985) and by writers in *The Computer Teacher* such as Pon (1984) and Hunter (1985) has been in the use of History or Geography databases.

Within the area of self-instruction, programmed learning and educational technology have played an important part. The early approaches to programmed learning by Pressey (1926), and others foreshadowed the approach of Mager (1961). 'Learner-controlled instruction' within the context of industrial training was Mager's novel thesis. Students were able to ask questions about the topic under study. The teacher was a resource person. The instructional programmes were based on student, rather than teacher, constructed sequences. Hartley pointed out in 1977 that this approach had 'blossomed forth'. However, it is necessary to look further back, to at least 1879, to trace the history of logic programming in order to understand the basis of my research. For centuries humans have had an academic tradition that has used formal logic in describing and representing reasoning. People have hoped for a long time that such deduction could be automated.

In 1879, a mathematician, G. Frege invented predicate calculus to further his goal of a complete analysis of the structure of pure thought so that each piece of deductive thinking could be represented mathematically. The special aspect of Frege's work, 'computational predicate calculus', is the foundation of logic programming. That aspect seeks agorithms to represent the process of deduction systematically. It was the first step towards automating deduction.

It was about 1929-30 that three independent mathematical researchers, Herbrand, Skolem, and Godel, discovered the proof of Frege's invention. The objective of the procedure was that it would present 'formal proof of every sentence in the language which is logically valid — and that this proof would be systematically constructible, given the sentence'. No computers were available to try the procedure.

When the procedure was trialled, using 1950s computers, the results were disappointing. By the year 1961, concurrently with Mager's research, J A Robinson began to study the problem and improved the computational behaviour of the algorithm.

Another important development not directly related to the study of logic, but still a part of logic programming history, was pioneered by two other overlooked researchers of the mid-60s: M Foster and T Elcock. Their computer language allowed the programmer to make assertions that he believed to be true and store them for querying in the computer memory. The assertions were 'read' automatically by the computer to deduce the answer. It was the first example of logic programming. But it was not carried out in the context of formal predicate calculus.

Meanwhile, using Robinson's work on resolution, C Green in the late 1960s considered resolution logic programming as a question-answering system. It was still not successful although the concept of the system was correct.

Many researchers worked on improving the language, including Robinson (1983) and Kowalski (1979). The latter's contribution was to interpret 'statements of declarative logic as procedural instructions to the computer'.

The parts were ready for the synthesis. In 1972 A. Colmerauer designed PROLOG, a linear resolution system, where clauses within the problem were restricted to Horn-clauses (conclusion-if-conditions rule, eg A if B and C). Together with Kowalski's procedural interpretation the concept of logic programming was born. PROLOG was looked at by Kowalski as logic first and programming second.

The use of PROLOG has grown steadily since 1972. The Japanese, planning for the fifth generation computers, have adopted logic programming as the core language instead of the ubiquitous BASIC. As far as the educational use of PROLOG is concerned it is being trialled on microcomputers using a Z80 microprocessor and the CP/M operating system. Micro-PROLOG is the adaptation of PROLOG from larger computers for personal use on microcomputers.

PROLOG is part of the artificial intelligence tradition which includes LOGO. The roots of artificial intelligence are within the theory of computing, psychology and natural language research. As shown above, PROLOG is a declarative language. The view of knowledge adopted by the educator may be procedural or declarative depending upon the questions posed in the computer program (O'Shea and Self, 1983). 'How' questions require a procedural program, such as provided by LOGO or Pascal. 'What' questions, which need facts for answers, require a database of facts, as found in a declarative program.

The project 'Logic as a Computer Language for Children', sponsored by the Science and Engineering Research Council and the Nuffield Foundation, was begun in England in September 1980 by Kowalski. Ennals (1983) has reported on the progress of the English project. He visited New Zealand two years ago when he conducted seminars and was a keynote speaker at the New Zealand Educational Computing Conference in August 1985.

According to O'Shea and Self (1983) the questions for research in PROLOG are:

1. To what degree do pupils have questions they want answered?
2. To what degree are pupils able to express their questions in micro-PROLOG?

My project was formulated to investigate these questions as well as to allow children to study data processing, and for them to use a logic programming language which will assume increasing importance within their future. A comparison of the learning experienced by Forms S2 and F2, the former with a computer-experienced teacher as well as experienced monitors, the latter with a computer-experienced pupil, was part of the research.

METHOD

Having in mind the Socratic dialogue idea, Mager's thesis of learner-controlled learning and Kowalski's project of 'Logic as a Computer Language for Children', I have implemented a research programme using micro-PROLOG with Forms F2 and S2 children studying a science topic in the following manner. Children at F2 and S2 levels, according to Piagetian cognitive learning theory, build their individual schemata of their environment using concrete, symbolic and abstract thinking. Each child develops these thinking attributes at an individual rate (Papert, 1980).

Pupils collected data in a concrete way from environmental observations, film, pictures and diagrams. In the experimental groups (F2 and S2) the collected information was organized symbolically as a database or added to an already prepared one; in other forms pupil findings were recorded traditionally. The database was constructed by the teacher for S2 and a computer monitor (a person) for F2. Those pupils at the formal operational stage of abstract thought, by using further analysis, synthesized new information by combining the data in different ways. The synthesized product was tested and more abstractions were derived from the generalizations. These increased their knowledge and improved their thinking at the same time.

The Form F1 computer monitor was given instruction outside the school timetable by myself. He had proceeded through the five activities mentioned by Hunter (1985) and was ready for a project. The monitor had a working acquaintance with Ennals' book before the experiment began. His teacher gave him some school time to prepare the data and construct the program.

The computer acted as an unobtrusive assistant during the traditional learning activities organized by the teacher. However, the 'assistant' needed the data input to its memory to be organized for speedy retrieval. In order to enlist the 'assistant's' help, beginner users needed the teacher to translate the users' requests into a form of pidgin English acceptable to the 'assistant'. Unfortunately there are no systems available yet that allow requests to be expressed in English. When this is so, and the 'assistant' is able to 'talk back' to the user, the teacher will have an assistant capable of working with pupils in a tutorial mode.

As St Heliers School owns only one Apple 11e 128K system it is placed permanently in the main office block in an interview room. Each class in the school has access to it one morning or afternoon a week, with a limit of four children, which includes two monitors, at any one time. Users' time at the keyboard is therefore limited. Preparation before computer access is desirable once initial exploratory experience of any operating system has been given.

As part of the topic 'Energy', an S2 class at St Heliers Primary School participated in a unit 'Measuring the Wind'. This unit was voluntary and additional to a weather unit taken last term. The mandatory parts were testing of the reading of a Wind Scale and the writing of questions for further research. All activities to accompany it were encouraged but not compulsory, so that attitudes could be observed. The learning outcomes anticipated were:

1. *Knowledge*
   Children describe: directions from which wind blows, and wind speed, using appropriate words.
2. *Process skills*
   Observation: Children use senses to determine wind direction and velocity.
   Measurement: Children estimate wind speed; measure deflection of the anemometer vanes; count revolutions of anemometers.
   Experimentation: Children test model wind vanes and anemometers; alter models if necessary.
3. *Communication skills*
   Children describe: the direction and speed of the wind; the effects of wind on objects in the environment.
   Children discuss: construction of vanes and anemometers.-
   Children complete: tables of data and discuss possible ways wind data could be used.
4. *Attitudes*
   Interest: Children are keen to make and test their models.

SUBJECTS — FORM S2

The S2 class involved had an ability range in PAT (Progress and Achievement Tests, New Zealand Council for Educational Research, for use in New Zealand schools) percentiles for reading vocabulary from 91 to 8 and for reading comprehension from 98 to 10. Listening comprehension range was from 95 to 8 and mathematics from 99 to 0. Children selected for the experimental group were of heterogeneous abilities:

The reading vocabulary range was from 85 to 32 and reading comprehension from 98 to 33. Based on reading comprehension percentiles, three groups in the class were:

1. 75 to 98 percentile range: 7 children (5 boys, 2 girls), aged 7y 8m to 8y 4m on 1/1/85.
2. 40 to 74 percentile range: 3 children (1 boy, 2 girls), all aged 8y 4m on 1/1/85.
3. 33 to 39 percentile range: 2 children (2 boys), aged 7y 9m and 8y 2m on 1/1/85.

PROCEDURE — FORM S2

The research described involved the reading and use of the Beaufort Wind Scale. This scale was represented as a PROLOG database for one group of mixed ability pupils while the rest of the class used a printed Beaufort Wind Scale with no assistance from the teacher in the way it was to be read or used. All groups queried the Beaufort Wind Scale, but the experimental group queried the database Wind Scale as well by using atomic questions and variables, beginning with **is** and **which**, respectively. These were written out for them in micro-PROLOG from their original English questions. These pupils then typed the questions into a 128K Apple 11e loaded with Simple, a beginners' version of micro-PROLOG, and wrote down the answers received.

The PROLOG representation of the Wind Scale was teacher organized: the teacher entered a sentence about each wind. Much research has been undertaken to ascertain the usefulness of semantic networks as a way of representing information. In order to clarify how the sentences represent and create new information a graphic representation of some of the sentences follows.

English: When smoke rises vertically the wind is 0.
PROLOG: (smoke-rises-vertically force 0)
Semantic network. smoke-rises-vertically force 0
Smoke-rises-vertically   **force**   **0**

•————————————————————————————·————————————>•

The names of individual items, hyphenated if more than one word, are the labels for each dot or node on the network. The relationship name is written above the link between the nodes.

The mode of querying can use the atomic sentence exactly, or variables $x, y, z \ldots$ can be substituted.

English: is the wind force 0 when smoke rises vertically?

PROLOG: Is (smoke-rises-vertically force 0)

Response YES if the exact information named in the questions appears in the database, also NO if the computer has failed to find the information requested; but the answer is limited.
Semantic network:

Using a variable for the unknown the question could be:

English: What is the force of the wind when smoke rises vertically?
PROLOG: which (x smoke-rises-vertically force x)
    Answer is 0
    No (more) answers
English: What is a sign that the wind force is 0?
PROLOG: which (x x force 0)
    Answer is smoke-rises-vertically
    No (more) answers

Molecular sentences:

Translated as: Smoke-rises-vertically wind-description calm if smoke-rises-vertically force 0 and 0 wind calm. This long sentence does not appear in the database, however. Instead it is expressed as a rule. Rule-based programming has increased recently, especially in the growing field of expert systems in artificial intelligence. A sentence written using variables arranged A if B and C (the Horn-clause sub-set of the clausal form of logic) expresses all information within the database that conforms to: x wind-description y if x force z and z wind y. Such a sentence is a rule of inference. It is also a description of what the wind is like.

To query a molecular sentence:

does (smoke-rises-vertically wind-description calm)
which (x smoke-rises-vertically wind-description x)

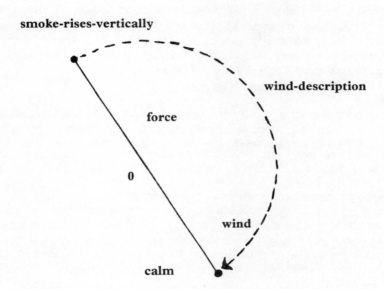

The next stage involved the questioning of the database to discover relevant information for calibrating an anemometer. Again, the experimental group used the computer while the rest used the printed scale.

Extra data collected by the experimental group was added to the database, whether it was from measuring the wind outdoors or reading reference sources.

SUBJECTS — FORM F2

PAT reading and listening comprehension and reading vocabulary range in the Form F2 group was from 99 to 61 for the four girl participants. Their age ranges were from 11y 8m to 12y 6m at 1/1/85.

PROCEDURE — FORM F2

The Form F2 competent micro-PROLOG programmer collected data for a food-chain relating to the topic *oceans*, which his class was studying. He constructed rules for querying the data within his program, FOODCHN. A group of pupils was selected to learn about food-chains by questioning the computer, while the control group was the rest of the class. They researched food-chains in the traditional manner from print sources.

Evaluation depended on the 'illuminative' learning systems model advocated by Nolan (1984) as representative of Papert's (1980), Parlett and Hamilton's (1975) and Codd's (1983) thinking on educational evaluation that has grown out of Piagetian developmental learning theory. Anthropological and educational evaluation in the illuminative sense implies an understanding of the cultural materials that are appropriate to human cognitive development. The computer is an artefact that is used as a learning tool to assist in cognitive development. Evaluation was done on this premise. The complex learning process was described and interpreted. The complex environment was left free of manipulation and control. Significant aspects were noted, relationships between beliefs and practices examined and patterns of responses, both organizational and individual, were pursued, as stated by Parlett and Hamilton. Existing needs were observed within the cultural environment. The way the computer was contributing to these needs was observed by the teacher directly or by video film of the F2 group.

Materials

The test of the experiment will be qualitative statements made by the teachers and diaries kept by the F2 monitor. The criteria for science learning are knowledge, process skills, communication skills and attitudes, which were enumerated in detail under 'Method'.

RESULTS

The results of the S2 class of non-computer users are given first.

Non-computer users' knowledge of wind speed using appropriate words improved in 13/14 cases after the first attempt to read the Beaufort Wind Scale. A small informal test of 10 items was given, with questions of the same type as the original test but with different factual answers. Their communication skills of describing the wind speed and effects improved. But only those who constructed vanes and anemometers improved their communicative skills when discussing the construction because they had the model to display to assist their talk.

The process skills of observation to determine wind direction and velocity were linked to the children's extra-curricular experiences. The girls who first constructed a wind vane were not the ones who necessarily knew how to read a wind vane. When they demonstrated their vane in operation to the class some boys were able to supply practical advice to enable a correct reading. The same girls needed help with observations and places to take wind readings. Subsequently others who constructed vanes were able to operate them correctly.

Estimation of wind speed using an anemometer was attempted. The same two girls read their Wind Scale, decided on the type of wind they were going to measure, and set about looking for the signs that they had decided they should see! The more practical types again corrected them. Both girls had PAT comprehension scores in the 80s. However, their enthusiasm was not dampened by assistance from the boys of lower PAT assessment for they were more ready to set us further experiments than the boy advisers! They were now joined by other girls who tested and modified their vanes and anemometers. The original two girls took regular readings of the wind and recorded their findings in sentences.

Attitudes were significant, as the girls were eager to make and test their models, whereas boys either forgot to bring the materials needed or lacked sufficient initiative.

The experimental S2 group were very keen to use the computer to enquire, and readily supplied it with questions. Three computer sessions were arranged.

In the second session one boy of PAT 82 reading comprehension readily copied kilometre-per-hour wind speeds from an encyclopedia in the library class. With teacher translation, the pupil entered them into the existing Beaufort database, thereby contributing the answer to his own question and recording the facts for others to use later.

The only child not capable of generating questions immediately was a boy of PAT reading comprehension percentile 39. He and another boy of PAT 33 were given help and further time. The latter succeeded. The former child, when introduced to procedural problem solving in Turtle geometry with LOGO, experienced instant success and was a class leader.

In session 3 the 'non-generator' was still not ready to ask questions. However, when asked what question he would choose to ask the teacher about the wind, he said, 'What speed does a hurricane go at?' He supplied his own part answer because he had heard the first researcher on wind speed tell the group at the last session. His part answer was '100 and something kph'. When asked where he could find out exactly, he replied the database computer. He readily wrote the question when told not to worry about the spelling (a weak area for him). The teacher translated it. When asked if he wanted to write more questions while waiting for a turn with the computer he replied, 'Yes, like you have done'. He produced six perfectly structured micro-PROLOG atomic sentences, substituting different wind types which he had remembered for the original 'hurricane'. His querying of the computer was equally successful. Usually he had difficulty in concentrating with traditional class pencil, reading and paper activities. However, he possessed a good memory for facts which he found interesting. His behaviour was usually erratic, noisy, immature and annoying to others, but when absorbed by an interest he was transformed into a serious, mature thinker and well-behaved child. Of course, not all subjects in the curriculum appealed equally — hence disruptive behaviour.

The questions written by most in the group were about the force or speed produced by a type of wind. These required the use of a variable x in the query. One girl asked several yes or no questions which required no variables and used the prefix 'does'. Two girls used an observation of the environment to query the wind classification.

The researcher with F2 attempted to work with a group of six, including the monitor, but found as time went on in the morning session that the more workable number was four. At the conclusion only two pupils were required. The database was fully queried, a food-chain was sketched out by hand and typed back into the word-processor for printing out. Much verbal communication was generated. The database was analysed successfully and synthesized by being represented in a hierarchical tree form. The original spelling of reiys (*sic*) and the incorrect version of the verb for plural atomic sentences eg 'sharks eats seals' were left as printed to observe whether the girls suggested that the designer change his grammar and spelling.

DISCUSSION

The difficulty with small group learning at a distance from the teacher (with the Form F2 pupils) highlighted the need for the choice of responsible, mature, knowledgeable pupil monitors and conscientious users. The difference between this and the learning that occurred within a class computing group which was set firmly within the framework of other learning experiences, was revealed by comparison with the S2 children.

The four F2 girls wanted questions answered, and they knew how to ask questions in micro-PROLOG after the monitor's teaching. The two girls who performed least well had lower reading levels; the less attentive had a percentile of 61 for listening comprehension and 65 for reading vocabulary. The other two girls, who worked very well together, showed patience, perseverance and logical thought in analysing the food-chain. They ignored any distractions and completed their task. No girls were observed to suggest corrections of the grammar or spelling of the program when the video was viewed. Perhaps the monitor had such a reputation in computer knowledge and mathematics that they assumed his English and spelling were beyond reproach!

It could be suggested that S2 PAT Reading Comprehension tests include reading of tables of data and graphs. These are a part of the reading and science curriculum. Perhaps the child who could not generate questions had a learning style not suited to declarative knowledge of the factual database. He would have had a cognitive style which suited procedural logic in a graphic medium. However, this theory was very quickly disproved when the same weak reader, behind others in his group, grasped the querying idea and leaped ahead of other group members in using the computer syntax. His leadership position earned so quickly with LOGO graphics was reflected in the language medium, but at a slower rate.

He had realized that here was a language which used fewer written words than normal to answer his questions. The formal reading comprehension of PAT and traditional searching through prose for an answer had placed this child in the 30s percentile. Yet this experiment has shown his logical thinking to be superior to those children who were highly placed by PAT testing. As a comparison his Listening Comprehension was 38, one point lower than his Reading; yet his ability to listen and perform logically has been measured by this experiment as superior to other pupils with higher formally-tested scores. The dividing factor is the print medium, and the amount of it.

Some children perform highly when confronted with print, while others are degraded or failed by it. New Zealand may have one of the highest levels of reading comprehension in the world, but by comparison mathematical ability is far behind, as revealed by the 1985 NZCER (New Zealand Council for Educational Research) research results from a mathematical survey of primary schools. Is it because, in the early school years, children are bombarded with print while learning to read, to the detriment of the thinking required in mathematics and science? Does this leave children with mathematical and scientific abilities with a lack of self esteem, because of their slow progress in reading and insufficient opportunity to display their latent abilities to their peers?

For a weak reader of short attention span, using a database to extract facts was appealing and generative of logical thinking. Communication with the computer needed written English. The weak reading boy saw the need to write in order to communicate with the computer. It was interesting too how quickly he spotted the ease of writing a question in 'computer language' and produced six sentences far more quickly than he had ever done when writing conventional prose.

The type of questions posed indicated the pupils' lack of observational and practical experience. Only one girl in the experimental group was taking wind readings with an anemometer. The group appeared to rely on the findings made by children in the control group, or on their memories. The environmental observations did not show up significantly in the questions.

I do not think that children are encouraged to question enough, especially in a practical, concrete operational, observational setting. Instead they are on the receiving end of questioning by teachers. They have very little practice at hypothesizing from a self-generated question which they can then test — which is at the centre of scientific processing. That is why practical experience of data processing contributes towards a technological education for an increasingly technological information processing society. Information is growing and changing at such a staggering rate that no one is capable of conveying or receiving it. Yet we all need to be given and shown the means by which information can be accessed. Albert Einstein once replied, when chided for not remembering his own telephone number, that he did not store such useless facts in his head when he could use a telephone book. Such a remark could be updated by substituting a database for the book, if facts are wanted.

CONCLUSION

The S2 and F2 students who used the databases were introduced to the concept of using a microcomputer to process data as an adult would use an expert system. Thereby the pupils participated in an application of logic in the real world.

Atomic descriptive sentences written in the SIMPLE syntax of micro-PROLOG were the bases of the student or teacher written science programs. The task was reasonably easy once the relationship of the two factors (individual items) was established. The pupils could, with help, query the information using SIMPLE syntax, but the MITSI version will overcome the difficulties of bracket use by providing a more acceptable question form, closer to English.

Programs were written for curriculum topics in science by a 12-year-old and a teacher, both self-taught. An 8-year-old added further information. There was no complex procedural programming. Extra data was added without disturbing the original program. The learner was in charge and used the computer as a tool, an adjunct to other learning.

All ability levels were represented in the research group. Not all those of high reading ability in S2 showed leadership qualities in logical thinking. Once some of the lower ability readers, motivated by scientific ideas, had had time to absorb the database concepts, however, they demonstrated greater application of their newly acquired knowledge 'generator'.The F2 group could understand Horn-clause logic to probe the intricacies of a hierarchically ordered tree of data, as expected from Piagetian theory, at the stage of formal operations. Their capable analysis and synthesis enabled greater opportunities and activities for learning for themselves and others when compared with the traditional 'project'. Unfortunately, for reasons beyond the researcher's control, not enough 'projects' were submitted by the teacher despite the best intentions.

Variables were accepted without difficulty as part of the language of the computer.

The greatest disadvantage of the research was in having only one computer. In the S2 experiment the students' questions and data were ready at a faster rate than the computer access time could cope with. With F2 only two students were usefully involved at any one time, those using the computer being under pressure from those waiting, therefore limiting discussion time. Even so, much communication took place when deciding the useful questions to type.

If a formal assessment of learning were undertaken each group in S2 should be about on par, as the Science unit had been piloted in other schools by the Department of Education. The computer group's additional progress can be explained by the application of further ways of processing information to aid memory, derive new information and to communicate in simple logic. Nearly all pupils queried the database at the concrete operational level. One pupil was noted to request information at a deeper level.

Further research might verify Papert's theory that logical operations mature at an individual rate. It might show that some adults achieve the formal operational stage through computer interaction based on logic programming. Realisation of their potential may be accelerated if they are self-motivated, working with a topic of personal interest and usefulness.

REFERENCES AND FURTHER READING

Codd, J A (1983), *Educational Evaluation and Critical Theory*, Paper presented at the Annual Conference, Philosophy of Education Society of Australasia, Massey University, New Zealand, 22-25 August.

Ennals, R (1983), *Beginning Micro-PROLOG*, Heinemann, London.

Ennals, R (1985), Using Micro-PROLOG for Classroom Historical Research, *Computer Education New Zealand*, August.

Howe, M J A (Ed) (1977), *Adult Learning*. Article by Hartley, J, and Davies, I K, 'Programmed Learning and Educational Technology', John Wiley & Sons, London.

Hunter, B, (1985), 'Problem-Solving with data bases', *The Computing Teacher*, May (1979)

Kowalski, R A (1979), *Logic for Problem Solving*, North Holland.

Mager, R F, and McCann, J (1961), *Learner Controlled Instruction*, Varian Associates: Palo Alto, California.

NZ Department of Education, Science Resource Unit: Level 2, Number 12, *Measuring the Wind*, Wellington, 1980.

Nolan, C J P (1984), *Evaluation of Microcomputers in (Special) Education*, Wellington,

O'Shea, T, and Self, J (1983), *Learning and Teaching with Computers*, Harvester Press Ltd.

Papert, S (1980), *Mindstorms*, Harvester Press, England.

Parlett, M and Hamilton, D 'Evaluation as Illumination' in Tawny, D (Ed) (1975), *Curriculum Evaluation Today: Trends and Implications*, London, Macmillan Co.

Pon, Kathy (1984), 'Databasing in the elementary (and secondary) classroom', *The Computing Teacher*, November.

Pressey, S L (1976), 'A simple device for teaching, testing and research', *School and Society*, No 23.

Robinson, J A (1983), 'Logic programming — past, present and future', article in *New Generation Computing*, p107-124, Vol **11** No. 2 Moto-oka, T (Ed).

7. Using PROLOG in the teaching of children with specific learning difficulties (dyslexics)

Rosalind Nichol and Jennifer Raffan
PEG-Exeter
University of Exeter
Exeter EX1 2LU
UK

PROLOG TOOLS WITH 11-14 YEAR-OLD PUPILS

Rosalind Nichol

Background

This study arose out of our interest in a pupil who could barely write his name, yet who was verbally brilliant. Subsequently we discovered he was attached to a special unit for children with Specific Literacy Difficulties (dyslexics) housed at the PEG-Exeter Project School. It is one of only four in the county. The school is a British 11-18 comprehensive for state pupils. The pupil concerned, a 13-year-old boy, was a member of the first class of pupils to whom we experimentally taught History using PROLOG in 1983. In the 1984-85 academic year, working with dyslexics became a discrete area of activity for the project. Our interest in the problem of dyslexia led to a separate British Government SCDC (School Curriculum Development Committee) financed study with which I have been involved since January 1986. I then became officially attached to the project, when I took over as the individual teacher of the dyslexics when the previous researcher emigrated to warmer climes.

The 7 boys involved in using PROLOG tools in the 1986-87 academic year were all of average to above intelligence (according to standard educational tests), and thus in the middle or top streams for their main curriculum studies. They were all timetabled weekly in the SLD Unit for individual tuition or in small groups of 2-3 on 'literacy skills', support work for their mainstream subjects. It was during part of this support time that we taught them using the PROLOG tools.

Using the toolkits DETECT, LINX and THE PLAN, the pupils wrote their own programs in a form of natural English. The focus of this work from the viewpoint of the Special Unit was to see if this approach could encourage or develop any literacy skills. An additional factor which quickly emerged was whether the tools stimulated the use of forward planning and associated cognitive skills. A subsidiary element was the fostering of the pupils' social and affective development, both through their own and other pupils' perceptions of them and their work. The teaching programme developed with the tacit encouragement of the Head of the Special Unit, who would have stopped pupils involvement if she felt they were not benefitting. She provided a yardstick of enlightened scepticism against which the project had to survive.

How do we work with the pupils?

They start off with a ready made program, GREENDIE for use with DETECT, or SEADOG when using LINX. The pupils later use the DETECT and LINX shells to write their own programs. We never begin programming with the adventure game shell, THE PLAN, as it is too complex. The GREENDIE program is a murder mystery which investigates the death of John Green, who is discovered one morning with a dagger stuck between his shoulder blades. SEADOG is a simulation which traces an Elizabethan voyage of piratical plunder to the Spanish main. It is based upon the exploits of Sir Francis Drake. We use these programs so that the dyslexics can see a working example of the kind of program they will in turn create. Working through an example helps them to acquire a model to emulate. Interaction with the program inducts them into the logical structure of programs written in DETECT or LINX. Having been through the example program, the pupils have also familiarized themselves with both the keyboard and the language of the shell's interface.

The next step was to decide upon the subject for their own program, and to begin planning it. Essential help was given in verbally planning and then recording on paper the main characters and features of their program. The program required the pupils to show links between the different clues in their own mystery (or database) so as to make the program usable. Another approach, used later, was to talk about a topic and feed in the information as we went along, thus reinforcing aspects of how the toolkit worked. Then we went on to more formal planning on paper. This was a crucial element in pupil development of programs. We employed two strategies, the complete planning of a program, or the development of it in stages as we progressed. We can argue that use of the toolkits involves a range of language skills in the 'overlearning' resulting from the high level of motivation to read and express ideas in writing and drawing a plan.

Figure 7.1 is the plan for a mystery set in the time of King Arthur, written by two 13-year-old boys. They built up the program from a range of books and pamphlets, and carefully planned the links between the different blocks of information. When they had written the program they tested it out on other pupils, and modified it so that there were sufficient clues for a user to solve the mystery. The planning, researching and writing of the programs involved more general skills, concerned with the organization and planning of thinking and the solving of problems. A crucial element was the researching, recording, analysing and structuring of information to enter into the program.

Through using the toolkits as a learning tool the programmer was strongly stimulated to learn in a variety of ways.

The surface syntax is easily understood by novice programmers with little or no experience of computers. In May I began working with the two 13-year-old pupils who later produced the CAMELOT program. By the third session they were confident and competent enough to enter their own material without supervision. They were able to see the logical pattern in the toolkit, and wonder how they could use its logical structure to express their own ideas. This led in the autumn term to them choosing to do the work on CAMELOT. They then progressed to writing a simulation upon the BLACK DEATH using the toolkit LINX.

After writing their first program the pupils can continue with the same toolkit or go on to another one — usually LINX or THE PLAN. LINX is used for writing games and simulations, THE PLAN for adventure games.

This is the stage we were at with the pupils I inherited from Jackie Dean in January — they were just beginning to change from DETECT to THE PLAN. THE PLAN is much more complex, as it requires the pupils to plan out their own micro-world, be it a castle or the human intestine. They people their micro-world with objects and creatures/ people, who can be involved in actions. The adventure game toolkit, THE PLAN, ties in very neatly with a cult of the age group, Dungeons and Dragons, and adventure games in general.

What language areas do the toolkits address?
Despite them not having been designed to deal with linguistic development, we intuitively feel that the tools help in the following areas:

1. Pronounced spelling problems — reversals, such as b/d, poor phonic skills, inability to discriminate between different spellings of a word according to the context, eg the spelling of you for yew (as in yew tree) or ewe (as in lady sheep).
2. Erratic handwriting — very poor presentation, which makes it difficult for others to evaluate their thinking.
3. Syntactic markers — weakness in noting syntactic markers, eg the endings of words like -ing, -'s, -ed.
4. Punctuation — weakness in handling punctuation.
5. Problems in sentence construction — they have difficulty in handling the structure of complex (or even simple) sentences, with sub-clauses. Sentence construction is basic for the presentation of thinking at a higher level.
6. Poor visual sequencing skills — eg inability to recognize common patterns of spellings and syntactic structures.
7. Information seeking skills — finding and use of appropriate research material, indexes, interviews, sorting out of key names and facts from written or verbal sources.

These factors in normal work result in a reluctance to commit any thoughts to paper and a slowness in reading. They are, of course, problems which achieve the level of self-fulfilling prophecies. As the pupils work in mainstream classes for much of their school time, their literacy problems are obvious to their peers. There is for some dyslexics a tendency to a low level of self-esteem.

The project in its work with the pupils has confronted one major problem, which is fundamental to its work. Should we concentrate on the development of their general language performance, or deal with the discrete areas listed above? Should we take an holistic approach or break down the linguistic process into a number of skills areas, which would be dealt with separately?

What do the pupils get out of working with the toolkits?
Each toolkit allows the pupil to concentrate on a specific thinking problem rather than follow a sequential procedure. Because of the interactive nature of the toolkits, the pupil's thinking is immediately visible: the toolkit allows instant modification in response to further thinking and reflection. The toolkits are capable of allowing the expression of powerful logical thought patterns. The individual pupils are immediately able to use them to explore a subject or topic or to create a story. THE PLAN is particularly interesting since, as the pupils develop their stories, they are forced through the use of actions to think both backwards and forwards about the consequences. One of the pupils commented that it was similar to his thinking in playing chess — with the difference that

Secrts

kingdom of Camelot

CAMALOT CASTLE

War plans

MY

Ma PS

Candle Holders

Hidden Chamber

Chest

Wall

Window

Tapastry

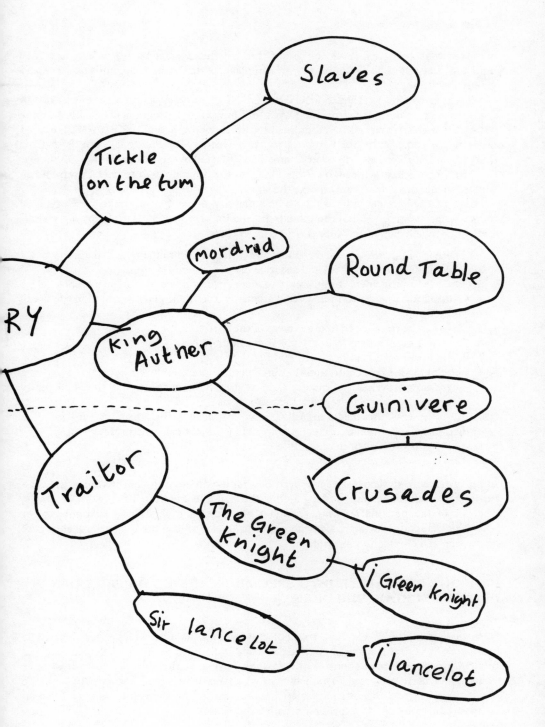

Figure 7.1

his ideas were being expressed on paper through the interactive use of language. My hunch is that there is an intensity of language which would be unusual in many mainstream lessons.

What is interesting is that DETECT and LINX are of particular use in subject areas in the main curriculum, for example a 14-year-old boy wrote a program BATTERY on the wiring of an electric circuit based on his physics curriculum, and the BLACK DEATH program has come out of the two boys' work in History. An additional point is that the thinking and problem solving is very immediate. Related to the writing of the programs is the fostering of oracy — through the discussion of the program with teachers, peers and an endless stream of visitors from all over the world.

For a teacher concerned with both the mastery of content and the developing of thinking and language skills, the toolkits have a lot of potential. The following claims, totally unproven, can be made for the PROLOG toolkits:

1. There is a higher degree of on-task activity than in traditional remedial approaches.
2. There is a more purposeful and accurate use of written representation.
3. There is improvement in the ability to identify, describe and sequence events.
4. Gains in maturation and self-esteem are made from their perceived skill in the use of the computer.
5. Skills can be transferred to other areas of the curriculum.
6. There is improvement in problem-solving ability.
7. There is improvement in planning skills.
8. Development of concentration/reinforcement of attention levels.
9. There is improvement in quality and structure of language, due to the opportunity to re-read, re-write, and re-work their programs.
10. Improvements are made in selling and syntactic skills, through the use of a dictionary, repetition of correct spelling and grammatical structures.
11. There is improvement in oral skills.
12. *They are made to think about how they think* — for perhaps the first time.

In our work with dyslexics we have been developing an environment in which they can express their thinking and understanding through the medium of toolkits or shells. Analysis of the possible learning outcomes of using such shells is a rich subject for psychological and educational research in the areas of cognitive development, peer interaction and curriculum innovation.

PROLOG TOOLS APPLIED TO SPECIFIC LEARNING DIFFICULTIES IN PRIMARY SCHOOL CHILDREN

Jennifer Raffan

Normal expectation is that junior school children will acquire and perfect their basic literacy skills before transfer to secondary school when the intellectual demands of the curriculum become paramount. Children who have specific learning difficulties have traditionally been subjected to remedial programmes which deal particularly with the acquisition of these skills, often in isolation from mainstream work. Increasingly it is seen as important to integrate remediation with adequate preparation for higher level study skills.

It is possible to define six areas in which help is needed:

1. Basic phonic work — children need to learn, for example, the phoneme/grapheme

correspondence, blending of letters and morphemes, and to acquire basic morphemic spelling rules.

2. Basic sight vocabulary — initial approaches to reading involve the acquisition of a limited sight vocabulary which becomes extended through subsequent reading and writing activities.
3. Written vocabulary — this is acquired over time as a product of phonic knowledge and acquired sight vocabulary.
4. The development of reading skills — from a basic mechanical level to higher-order reading skills with comprehension at all stages.
5. The ability to make written responses — eg to dictation, to creative stimulus, problem solving, the demands of different linguistic 'registers'.
6. The achievement of fluency — children need to derive information from written text and to be able to respond to it.

Most SLD children need sustained help in developing oral language skills, and it is implied in the foregoing analysis that that help precedes formal interaction with the written word. It is also important to note that there is a developmental perspective in each area and that concurrent progress is essential.

Logic programming in PROLOG does not represent an addition to the extensive repertoire of CAL techniques already available for assisting children to achieve basic literacy. We would argue that it offers an alternative and that it addresses the intrinsic difficulties that are peculiar to this group of children. Whatever the aetiology of the problem (and the theoretical literature is extensive and conflicting), the outcome is that these children have a variety of difficulties in forming and operating upon mental representations. This is most obvious in their inability to deal with the written representation of language, but at a more complex level we often find that they have difficulty in representing events or ideas and in comprehending the relationships between them. It would appear that the processes of analysis and synthesis are impaired so that remediation can most profitably be achieved with an approach which develops skill in these activities while giving opportunities for interaction with the written word.

Observation of secondary school children interacting with the PROLOG toolkits has shown a higher degree of on-task activity than traditional remedial approaches achieve. Children show

(a) more purposeful and accurate use of written representation,
(b) improvement in their ability to identify, describe and sequence events, and
(c) gains in self-esteem from their perceived skill in the use of the computer.

Pilot work with junior school children has shown the adaptability of the toolkits. Initially the children were involved in creating imaginary micro-worlds and structuring stories which took into account the constraints of those worlds. As a small-group activity (two to three children), there was the same enthusiasm as might be expected following any creative stimulus, and useful oral language development followed. The children recorded their ideas on the computer using a simple word-processing program, in drawings and wall pictures. When translated by the teacher, using THE PLAN, into a rudimentary program, it provided ample opportunity for remediation in the six areas identified above.

Children have also been introduced to the concept of retrieving information from a structured database where it is either available direct or as the result of implied knowledge. Using DETECT they have separately contributed to the database, structuring their own personal particulars so that it formed links with others by implication. This activity most directly addressed the problems involved in developing reading skills. Again, the computer activities were supported by concrete representation of the information in the form of a labelled network built up upon a visual display board (see, for example, Fig. 7.2).

A significant difficulty that SLD children have is the recognition of syntactic markers which denote, for example, tense or plurality. Normally remediation occurs in the course of reading aloud, either by self-correction or with intervention by the teacher. Inevitably the flow of ideas is interrupted, and comprehension is further disrupted. A program has been created using LINX to highlight a particular set of linguistic features. It is suggested that detailed comparative study will focus attention in a way not achieved in normal texts. Children will then be able to generate sentences of their own to conform with the pattern established within the 'shell'. In this case the activity of programming, it is hoped, will act as reinforcement of the concepts.

The adaptability of the toolkits to achieve programs suitable for younger children is already apparent. Observations of the behaviour of the younger children confirm that of the older children. It is yet to be shown whether there will be direct transference of skill achieved by the children in logical manipulation of information for programming purposes to the wider arena of reading and writing, and indeed what the relationship might be. But without any such claim or achievement we are satisfied that logic programming offers a highly motivating task which can be tailored to create opportunities for practice in the key areas of remediation.

Below is part of the information on 15 children attending the Learning Centre from 8 schools on 4 days of the week. It was entered as a DETECT knowledge structure by the children themselves, having discussed the relationships.

Adrian is in Class One.
They are fourth years in his class.
Mr Ash is the Headmaster at Adrian's school.

Simon is in Class Two.
He comes to the Learning Centre on Friday mornings.
He comes from Mr Ash's school.

Nigel comes to the Learning Centre on Friday mornings too.
He is in the same class as Adrian.
He is one year older than Simon.

Timothy comes to the Learning Centre on Tuesday afternoons and Thursday mornings.
He shares his lessons with Robert.

Robert goes to Borough School.
His class teacher is Mrs Barns.
Alec is at his school too, but they don't share a lesson.

Alec has Mr Hare for his teacher.
Mr Hare teaches fourth years.
Alec's second lesson is on Thursday afternoons.

Throughout the creation and subsequent use of the program the children were able to perform complex mental operations within its 'restricted' context of primitives and links.

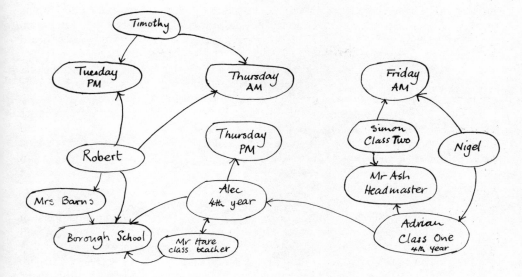

Figure 7.2 *Partial example of the diagrammatic representation of the information. Originally this was recreated as a coloured wall display.*

From the displayed information the children were able to reconstruct a timetable of classes and participants. Also they made an age-group graph and wrote descriptions of schools other than their own.

Part II: Teaching logic programming

Preface

Jonathan Harland Briggs

Part 1 demonstrates the wide range of curriculum areas that seem susceptible to exploration by PROLOG educational developers and researchers. It is important to note that, unlike many other 'educational' languages, non-mathematical areas of the curriculum find this approach equally accessible. Already the reader may have noticed that programming in PROLOG can take a variety of styles and directions, some preferring to make use of its procedural aspects, others restricting themselves to the purely declarative.

The 1980-82 project at Imperial College, led by Professor R Kowalski with Richard Ennals as the key researcher, focused on teaching Logic rather than PROLOG. This distinction has often been ignored both by those who have jumped on to the bandwagon, and those who have jumped out of its way. Professor Kowalski saw PROLOG as the first logic programming language but looked forward to more powerful ways of realizing 'logic as a computer language for children'.

Most current projects, and thus most of the chapters in this book, reflect the growing move towards viewing PROLOG as a tool rather than an end in itself. However, a number of key PROLOG projects have returned to consider the importance of PROLOG's antecedents in formal Logic.

Rosa Maria Bottino, Zahava Scherz and Richard Spencer-Smith have taken three different perspectives on the teaching of logic and logic programming. Rosa Maria Bottino uses PROLOG to emphasize a top-down approach to problem solving, presenting students with a large problem, and introducing concepts and ideas as required. Zahava Scherz uses a simplified concrete model of a logical reasoning system to introduce PROLOG programming. In contrast to both these, Richard Spencer-Smith teaches simple PROLOG in order to reinforce an introduction to formal Logic. Chapter 11 explores the ways in which we can teach PROLOG, and asks why we should teach PROLOG *per se*.

8. PROLOG experiences in classrooms: possibilities and problems — The 'PICO' project (PROLOG Information on COmputers)

Rosa Maria Bottino,
Istituto per la Matematica Applicata
Consiglio Nazionale delle Richerche
Via L B Alberti 4
16132 Genova
Italy

INTRODUCTION

This chapter is a critical analysis of the possibilities and problems involved in the introduction of PROLOG as a programming language in schools. Possibilities for using PROLOG relate to potential types of applications. The nature of PROLOG allows the teacher to achieve educational objectives through knowledge representation in a given domain; a logical approach to problem-solving; an introduction to the organization, construction and querying of databases; the development of skills related to reading and comprehension; and use of coded information. These PROLOG features enable PROLOG applications in areas like the Humanities, one of the curricular areas usually less influenced by new technologies and methods.

Moreover, it now seems increasingly important to give students an idea of current developments in computer science and future possibilities (eg applications of AI and fifth generation computing).

This chapter refers to a specific project (Bottino, Forcheri, Molfino, 1986) implemented in 1986 in Genoa. The project concerns the introduction of micro-PROLOG, a form of the programming language PROLOG implemented for micros, into higher secondary school classes. The project, based on the use of PROLOG for didactic purposes, is one of the first experiments in Italy of this type. It is related to earlier experiments in England and France. Others were subsequently carried out in Sweden, Belgium, The Netherlands, Australia, New Zealand and Israel.

This chapter analyses the project under the following headings, which are also the basis for general reflections: aims and objectives; content; support materials; results; problems and difficulties encountered. The project team consists of R M Bottino, P Forcheri and M T Molfino from the Istituto per la Matematica Applicata, who have worked in conjunction with three higher secondary school teachers, R Degli Innocenti, G Sissa and G Panunzio.

THE PICO PROJECT: AIMS, OBJECTIVES AND CONTENT

The aim of this project is to introduce students, through PROLOG programming, to knowledge representation in a certain domain. Knowledge representation takes the form of a program, which the students use to solve given problems. In this context PROLOG allows a declarative programming approach for information coding and retrieval based upon the structure of predicate logic.

Our idea is that students should solve a given complex problem by introducing the necessary elements of PROLOG when developing the program, rather than by teaching the language and then developing expertise through different small example programs.

Organization, coding and information retrieval capabilities were developed gradually to allow for a clear mental model of the problem under examination and of how an automatic system operates (du Boulay and O'Shea, 1978). The work was thus divided into four sequential stages. The first two do not require the direct use of a computer:

1. Information research using previously organized data, eg a folder of datasheets taken from an encyclopedia. Each sheet contains consistently structured data about different pieces of information.
2. Analysis and representation of new data not organized as in 1.
3. Translation of information contained in 2. into a PROLOG program (facts + rules). Querying of the program to solve given problems.
4. Summary.

In its first stage the project introduces students to the process of reading and extracting information, based on a sequence of queries. This is to familiarize them with the pattern of working in PROLOG.

The context is typical: written information is structurally presented in the form of datasheets from an encyclopedia (in our case it is a geographical encyclopedia where each sheet refers to a country of the world and the items on the sheet contain such data as population, capital, economic conditions, etc).

The students are given sheets on a number of countries in conjunction with a sequence of written questions which gradually become more difficult. The same sequence used in querying a PROLOG program is followed: atomic queries, compound queries, queries requiring variables, even though at this stage the use of variables is at an implicit level. This first part does not require prerequisites, it is used as an exploratory test to identify any conceptual difficulties the students may meet in the process of reading/retrieving information in a simplified context.

The second stage of the work deals with a completely new topic for the school students; the analysis and **organiz**ation of information related to a certain number of microcomputers in order to make a choice on the basis of given parameters (eg price, required configuration, etc).

The data is supplied to students in the form of illustrated advertising brochures of some microcomputers (eg Apple IIc, Atari 520 ST, Commodore 64, Olivetti M24, etc) and questions asked directly of retailers. Students are given an introductory explanation of the technical terms reported on the brochures (eg RAM, CPU, mass storage, etc). The information obtained from the brochures is then organized according to certain criteria (eg basic configuration, optionals and related prices which are indicated for every computer). Figure 8.1 shows how the information is organized during classroom experimentation.

The aim of this second stage is to develop skills in organising knowledge and formalizing a problem. Furthermore, forcing students to produce an explicit design before

	BASIC CONFIGURATION					OPTIONALS			
MICRO-COMPUTER	CPU marking	RAM 'N' bytes	MASS STORAGE supporting devices	VIDEO DISPLAY type	OPERATING SYSTEM	RAM 'N' bytes	MASS STORAGE supporting devices	VIDEO DISPLAY	PRINTER
ATARI 520 ST	MC 68000	512 KB	1 DRIVE 3 1/2"	Monochromatic	TOS	----	1 DRIVE 3 1/2"	----	XDM 121 XMM 801
APPLE IIc	65C02	128 KB	1 DRIVE 5 1/4"	Monochromatic	PRODOS	----	1 DRIVE 5 1/4"	----	IMAGE WRITER
APPLE MACINTOSH	MC 68000	512 KB	1 DRIVE 3 1/4"	Monochromatic	its own	----	1 DRIVE 3 1/2"	----	IMAGE WRITER LASER WRITER
COMMODORE 64	MOS 6510	64 KB	----	----	its own	----	1 DRIVE 5 1/4" CASSETTE UNIT	MONITOR 1702	PRINTER 1520 MPS 801
OLIVETTI M24	8086	128 KB	2 DRIVES 5.25"	Monochromatic	MS-DOS	128 KB 640 KB	----	COLOUR SCREEN	PRINTER 132
SINCLAIR ZX SPECTRUM PLUS	Z80	48 KB	----	----	its own	----	ZX microdrive expansion system	----	SEIKOSHA- -GP50S
SINCLAIR QL	MC 68000	128 KB	----	----	QDOS	128 KB 256 KB 512 KB	MICROFLOPPY DD-50 MICROFLOPPY DD-40	COLOUR SCREEN QL 14	QL-100

Figure 8.1 *Organization of some items of information related to a number of microcomputers. Students are then provided with tables showing the price of computers in the basic configuration reported and the prices of the various optionals.*

they implement a program can have a positive effect on their performance (Van Someren, 1985). In fact, the construction of a correct mental model can be facilitated by separating the fact retrieval and structuring stages from that of translation into PROLOG, thus favouring the understanding of the different levels into which this model is divided: real world, restriction to a specific domain of the problem under examination, formalization, coding.

In our third stage the information previously organized is translated into a PROLOG program. The following sequence was used to develop this work: writing of micro-PROLOG facts related to a certain number of microcomputers, program querying according to a 'classic' sequence — atomic queries, compound queries, queries using variables (Ennals, 1983), writing of rules to answer given queries, introduction of built-in arithmetical relations, writing of rules using arithmetical relations. Figure 8.2 shows some facts and rules of the program developed in class.

After having written the program, the students are asked to query it, by playing different roles. Worksheets are supplied, for example, posing a problem: purchase of one or more microcomputers, and a profile of the requirements and resources for, and purpose of, the purchase (money available, what it is to be used for, technical features, analysis of opportunities, etc).

The final stage is a summary of the skills developed during the other stages and can be tackled at different levels of complexity.

```
Atari-520-ST    basic-conf   MC-68000
Atari-520-ST    basic-conf   KB-512
Atari-520-ST    basic-conf   Tos
Atari-520-ST    basic-conf   monochromatic-display
Atari-520-ST    basic-conf   drive-1-3-inches
Apple-IIc       basic-conf   C6502
```

- -

```
Atari-520-ST    optional   drive-1-3-inches
Atari-520-ST    optional   XDM-121
Atari-520-ST    optional   XDM-801
Apple-IIc       optional   drive-1-5-inches
```

- -

```
Atari-520-ST    basic-price 1750000
Apple-IIc       basic-price 1865000
```

- -

```
MC-6800    is-a   CPU
KB-512     is-a   RAM
tos        is-a   operating-system
```

- -

x connected-to-printer y if x optional y and y is-a printer
x connected-to-mass storage y if x base y and y is-a mass-storage
x connected-to-mass storage y if x optional y and y is-a mass-storage
basic-price less y if x basic-price z and z less y

- -

Figure 8.2 *Some facts and rules of a program written by students. The names of the relations are translated into English for clarity purposes.*

In the PICO (PROLOG Information on COmputers) project, the introduction of the micro-PROLOG programming language occurs when a single articulated problem is developed, as opposed to several different examples. This favours the development of such skills as documentation, knowledge representation, identification of facts relating to a certain objective and planning of actions, which are fundamental for all problem-solving activities. According to my experience, it is more educational to write a single correct program of reasonable size, than to spend the same amount of time writing a number of programs which are so small as to be trivial. This favours learning of important general strategies, such as top-down methodology, debugging techniques, finding relations between problems and sub-problems, and so on (Bottino, Forcheri, Molfino, 1985).

Finally, the specific problem of choosing a microcomputer on the basis of set requirements is interesting for various reasons: it is attractive to students, it does not require previous knowledge acquired within the school context, it allows for the introduction of some elements of computer science which should be part of the core curriculum, and it enhances subsequent work with the computer and the formation of a correct model of its operation (eg difference between RAM and mass storage, etc).

CLASSROOM EXPERIMENTATION

The PICO project was fully implemented in a class of first-year pupils (aged 14-15) in a higher secondary school and partially implemented in a class in another secondary school. The type of work and methods used are not specific to a certain type of school, age range or pupil standard. Taking the example given, different levels of application can arise from the relative sophistication of the language employed.

From the methodological viewpoint, every stage of the project is structured using worksheets which introduce topics, concepts, ancillary information and recommended exercises which can be developed either with or without using the computer. This approach seems to be well adapted to the wide range of individual responses in relation to such non-traditional activities, even though part of these activities, particularly those requiring the use of the computer, are based on group-work. It is, however, important to provide space for individual reflection.

The use of worksheets tests the extent of learning, step by step, while highlighting differences in understanding and autonomy between students. On the one hand this allows for a targeted recovery and on the other hand it favours individual development and deep examination. The work sheets are divided into several didactic units, each developing one topic. Software tools are also a support to the worksheets.

The project was developed on an Apple IIc using micro-PROLOG and its SIMPLE front-end available from Logic Programming Associates (Clark, and McCabe, 1984). From the methodological and conceptual viewpoint, we tried to separate the concept of a PROLOG program (seen as a collection of statements setting out information) from the concept of operating on a program (modifying, displaying, saving, etc) (Cumming, 1986). This was done by developing the two topics through different units and by introducing them at different times.

This point is important in order to develop a clear mental model of a PROLOG system, but it is however critical for a beginner who often has an incomplete or wrong idea of the system.

The exposition of how PROLOG reaches goals and evaluates queries was based on examples at the blackboard without directly using the trace facility offered by micro-PROLOG. This was because the trace facility, because of how it is implemented, is confusing to interpret, especially for beginners. All the same we managed to give an overall idea of the problem at the level at which the language was introduced in our first experiment (lists were not introduced). The experiment was conducted within a normal school context; for example, the class of students was not pre-selected and the hours they were taught were those of their normal timetable.

The work was introduced within a humanities course and was developed in cooperation with the two humanities teachers. Classroom experimentation was monitored by the author. The experiment was evaluated during its course and the evaluation was based on a direct analysis of class work and of the worksheets filled in. At the end of the project the technical competence acquired by every student was ascertained by a final test. The conclusions which may be drawn are of the qualitative type since an experiment in only one class is too limited for a quantitative analysis.

It was observed that the preliminary work done in the first stage proved to be helpful in the following stages, both for developing a critical sense during analysis and organization of information, and for an introduction to the concept of information retrieval based on a number of queries. At the end of the experiment most students could write simple facts and rules in micro-PROLOG and could formulate 'is' and 'which' queries.

Problems were caused by: the writing of rules where the conclusion is implied by more than one condition, particularly when using arithmetical relations; compound queries and queries requiring more than one variable; and syntax difficulties.

Concerning syntax difficulties, it was observed that the following apparently non-justified constraints imposed by syntax were confusing for the students: the difference between capital and small letters, not only in variables but also when using such commands as 'list' and the fact that when a program is listed, the variable symbols shown in rule definitions were not in general the same as those used when the rule was typed in. These factors add a layer of syntactic difficulty to the conceptual difficulties already arising from operating with variables.

Some students also used the English version of micro-PROLOG, which did not create serious problems. This proved that students of this age can use PROLOG directly without requiring the simplified syntax offered by SIMPLE. It allows for the use of mnemonic variable names, and eliminates such problems as confusion between infix and prefix notation and limited space for working memory. This helps surmount a major problem which arose during the classroom experiment: the limited storage space available. In our experiment this led to the restriction of the database on which to operate. Limited memory is a major restrictive factor when dealing with a problem which requires the representation of a volume of knowledge.

In conclusion, in spite of the difficulties listed above, the experiment yielded, in general, positive results. The students who worked hard could at the end master the language quite well, sometimes being able to carry out personal investigations and related information processing. In some cases students who had difficulties with normal school subjects showed good skills development during the project.

On the basis of the results of this experiment and detailed analysis of the research data gathered during classroom experimentation, the worksheets and related procedures will be evaluated and modified for a second period of experimentation next academic year.

CONCLUSION

The PROLOG programming language can be used efficiently for educational purposes. In particular it develops logical-deductive reasoning, organization of knowledge and a logical approach to problem-solving. Introducing this language within the school teaching context is a task which encounters some difficulties. These are both conceptual difficulties requiring the development of a correct mental model of how a PROLOG system operates, and syntactic difficulties. In this context it is very useful to have gained experience through experimental data, which on the one hand highlights the possibilities offered by the language and on the other, contributes to identifying critical points, difficulties and their causes.

ACKNOWLEDGMENTS

I would like to thank the teachers, R Degli Innocenti and M G Cottica, who made the classroom experimentation described in this chapter possible. Several methodological and didactic remarks and suggestions derived from an accurate analysis of the work which was made with them during the course of the experience. R Degli Innocenti prepared the material for the first stage of the project.

REFERENCES AND FURTHER READING

Bottino, R M, Forcheri, P, and Molfino, M T (1985), *Computer Science Literacy in Secondary Schools*, Proceedings of 37th CIEAEM, Leiden, The Netherlands.

Bottino, R M, Forcheri, P, and Molfino, M T (1986) Teaching with PROLOG, *Pegboard* Vol **1**/1, pp12-18.

Clark, K L and McCabe, F G (1984), *Micro-PROLOG: Programming in Logic*, Prentice-Hall.

Conlon, T (1985), *Start Problem-Solving with PROLOG*, Addison-Wesley.

Cumming, G (1986) 'Logic programming and education: Designing PROLOG to fit children's minds', *Pegboard* Vol **1**/1, pp34-46.

Du Boulay, B and O'Shea, T (1978), 'Seeing the works: A Strategy for teaching interactive programming', *Working Paper No.28*, Dept of Artificial Intelligence, University of Edinburgh.

Ennals, J R (1983), *Beginning Micro-PROLOG*, Ellis Horwood, Chichester.

Van Someren, M (1985), 'Beginners' problems in learning PROLOG', *Memo No 54*, Dept of Social Science Informatics and Dept of Experimental Psychology, University of Amsterdam.

9. Learning with PROLOG — a new approach

Zahava Scherz
Department of Science Teaching
The Weizmann Institute of Science
Rehovot
ISRAEL 76100

Oded Maler and Ehud Shapiro
Department of Mathematics
The Weizmann Institute of Science
Rehovot
ISRAEL 76100

Current applications of computers in education fall into two main categories: computer science oriented instruction and computer-aided learning (CAL). Courses in programming, databases, algorithms and their computer science topics are related to the first category. The use of software for teaching specific subjects is associated with the second category. The existence of these categories, that seems to be a result of a premature gap between those who program the computer and those who want to apply it to education, is a possible reason for the feeling of disappointment related to the contribution of computers to education.

We claim that an effective use of computers in school will occur when students and teachers learn not only to operate a computer but also to apply high-level programming language techniques in their course work. We believe that in the near future the active use of the computer in the classroom will be an integral part of all lessons, as reading, writing and arithmetic are today. This will probably change the quality of future teaching and learning and will contribute to students' intellect. As Olson (1985) pointed out: 'It is important to consider how intellect will be altered by the growing reliance on computer technologies.'

In the light of the above, in this chapter, we would like to introduce a project for teaching PROLOG as a computer language for students and teachers. Additionally, we will describe our programme for teaching PROLOG as a first computer language. We will discuss the advantages of PROLOG in general, and our approach in particular, for integrating computers into the school curricula.

PROLOG is a declarative language which enables the description of objects and the logical relations between them, using logical statements — *facts* and *rules* which are interpreted by the computer as programs. The actual execution of a PROLOG program is done by *queries*, given by the user, in order to initiate the program to solve the problems concerned. The solution is carried out on the computer, using logical deduction mechanism, by the PROLOG interpreter. PROLOG interpreters are now available on some microcomputers with slight differences in their syntax. The version that was used in our project, called Wisdom PROLOG (Safra, 1984), is based on Edinburgh-PROLOG and is implemented in both Hebrew and English languages on personal computers under MS-DOS.

WHY PROLOG?

This section addresses two cardinal questions of this chapter: 'Why teach PROLOG as a first computer language?' and, 'Is there any unique contribution of PROLOG to education?'. We will discuss these questions using four arguments.

First, PROLOG provides an opportunity to practise some aspects of logic in a stimulating way on the computer. The field of logic that was presented in the past by ancient languages like Greek and Latin, and by the Euclidean Geometry, is believed to have made a major contribution to the development of logical reasoning and scientific thinking (Anderson, 1980). Programming in logic seems to have many of the intellectual benefits of studying Logic with the advantage of its potential execution on the computer. Although PROLOG, as a materialization of abstract concepts, contains some restrictive features that are not inherent in logic, it is a sufficiently good approximation of the ideas behind logic for many purposes. Furthermore, it seems to have the benefits of creating deductive reasoning without a rigorous understanding of the complicated theory of pure Logic.

Second, unlike other computer languages which are oriented towards numerical operations, PROLOG processes logical inferences, and therefore can be a medium for representing logical information taken from the area of physical and life sciences, as well as social sciences and linguistics. Many educational psychologists and educators have claimed that internalization of subject-matter by the learner happens while presenting it using 'organizers' such as frames and schematic concept maps (Ausubel, 1979; Novak, 1971). The act of programming different information drawn from varius subject areas in PROLOG provides a means of formalization for the content using an axiomatic language. Thus, the learner who programs in PROLOG can use a declarative style to describe relationships between the relevant concepts in the subject matter.

Third, many computer scientists believe that PROLOG-like languages will become dominant in the future (Feigenbaum and McCorduch, 1983). Most of our students today, who will be the citizens of tomorrow, are likely to become users (or programmers) of artificial intelligence tools based on logic languages. These students will probably benefit more from learning the basis of logic programming than conventional languages like BASIC, Cobol, Fortran, etc.

Fourth, PROLOG is a very powerful high-level programming language, yet it is easy to learn, friendly and close to natural-language — especially the implementations designed for school use. PROLOG provides an easy and open framework for building knowledge bases and inherently gives answers to questions which cannot be so directly manipulated in procedural languages.

HOW TO TEACH PROLOG TO THE NOVICE STUDENT

Earlier attempts to teach PROLOG to non-programmers and novice users have been made by researchers at Imperial College in London, and related groups (Clark and

McCabe, 1984; Ennals, 1984; Briggs, 1984; Conlon, 1985). In this chapter we introduce a new approach for teaching PROLOG. In contrast to the Imperial College approach, we start from the propositional level of logic programming, and base it strongly on fundamental concepts for teaching Logic. In designing the course we did not assume any previous knowledge of programming languages, nor computer literacy. However, we are aware of the fact that many of our potential students may have been previously exposed to other programming languages like BASIC and might have some difficulties caused by the gap between the two.

DESCRIPTION OF THE PROGRAM

A box and its manager
The course starts with the description of an empty box, into which one can insert objects and from which they can be removed. We present the student with the goal of making the box function as intelligently as possible. Initially, the box and the objects are graphically represented, but it is soon replaced by a symbolic, verbal representation. In order to personify the PROLOG interpreter we introduce a simple-minded manager who mediates between the user and the box. This manager is implemented by a very simple menu-driven PROLOG shell that enables the user to insert statements to the box, to take them out, to ask questions and to get a listing of the box's contents (see Fig. 9.1).

```
Hello, welcome to WISDOM PROLOG.
Help (you can choose the following):
          insert.
          remove.
          question.
          contents.
```

Figure 9.1 *The Prolog Box Menu*

The user can interact with the manager to create his own list of objects in the box (Fig. 9.2). The user can ask about the presence of objects in the box by using queries. For example, a query such as:

? apple.

is regarded as representing the sentence 'Is there an apple in the box?', to which the computer will respond 'Yes' when referring to the database created in Fig. 9.2.

This initial experience with objects eases the understanding of negation in Logic and PROLOG.

The obtuseness of the manager, which is initially expressed by his inability to recognize spelling mistakes, is our first example of the rigidity of human-computer dialogue. The fact that the manager cannot discriminate between meaningful objects and meaningless ones, treating both as strings of characters, is a good example of the nature of formal Logic and of computers. We also introduce the principle that one cannot remove from a box an object that has not been inserted before. This 'empty box assumption' is analogous to the 'closed world assumption' used in database theory, and is very intuitive when we speak

```
        what do you want?
insert
        insert what?
apple.
        insert what?
pear.
        insert what?
orange.
        insert what?
end.
        What do you want?
remove.
        remove what?
pear.
        remove what?
end.
        what do you want?
question.
        what is your question?
apple.
        yes.
        what is your question?
pear?
        no
        what is your question?
end.
        what do you want?
contents.
        apple.
        orange.
```

Figure 9.2 *Simple interaction with the Prolog Box*

about boxes and objects. Therefore a request to remove the object 'pear' from the box content in Fig. 9.2 would be answered by:

   there is no pear in the box.

The propositional box

After the student has practised the manipulation of objects using the computerized box manager, a new idea is suggested: that of picturing the human mind functioning like a box. Here knowledge consists of collections of information items residing in the brain. These information items can stand for beliefs, facts, hypotheses, opinions, etc, and can be manipulated in anyone's personal box through processes such as learning, forgetting and answering questions. The basic idea is to impose knowledge on the computerized box by inserting propositions which are believed to be true.

In order to introduce these syntactic restrictions of PROLOG we stage a negotiation process with our 'manager'. The first condition stipulated is that no spaces are allowed within single words in a sentence. The words should be either typed without spaces or connected to each other using underscores (Fig. 9.3).

```
one__plus__one__is__two.
elizabeth__is__the__queen__of__england.
the__sun__shines.
life__is__beautiful.
school__is__hard.
the__tree__is__green.
the__tree__is__tall.
```

Figure 9.3 *The propositional PROLOG Box*

Queries about such propositions are still regarded as questions about the existence of 'objects' in the box. However, from this point on, the notions of truth, proofs and knowledge start appearing implicitly and explicitly in the teaching material, as explained below.

The inflexible manager analogy continues to demonstrate the limitations of computers as compared to humans. The manager cannot tell correct sentences (according to general knowledge) from incorrect ones. He is ready to insert both into the box. He is ready to accept contradictory facts as well. He will not answer affirmatively questions about propositions that are known to be true but have not been entered previously, and will ignore semantic identities among syntactically different sentences.

Conjunctive queries

After the students have practised manipulation of statements and queries we introduce conjunctions. This is another step forward towards giving the computer an intelligent capability. Conjunction is usually demonstrated in natural language sentences using the word 'and'. Conjunction in Logic means a propositional statement that is true if, and only if, both its components are true. By using the current notation, the manager cannot differentiate between a conjunction and its conjuncts. Inserting the conjunctive sentence in its present form does not guarantee positive answers to its clauses and vice versa. For example, inserting the conjunction:

the__tree__is__green__and__the__tree__is__tall.

does not imply positive answer to the queries

? the__tree__is__green.

and

? the__tree__is__tall.

The manager needs a special symbol in order to distinguish the conjunction symbol from other strings. This need for a conjunctive connective is satisfied by allowing the use of a comma between the conjuncts. For example, one can insert the two statements above as a conjunctive query:

? the__tree__is__green, the__tree__is__tall.

which is understood as asking whether the tree is both green and tall. The manager's response will be:

yes.

The semantics of conjunctive queries is straightforward within the box paradigm. Using one query, we just ask whether two or more objects are inside the box. The same syntactic principles that led to the introduction of the conjunction connective are used later for the introduction of the disjunction and implication connectives.

Rules, or introducing deduction

The implication concept which is the basis for deduction is also introduced using natural language. We informally show the student deduction using the logic structure called modus ponens. As expected, the manager cannot operate deduction when the implication sentences are given in a human-like 'if-then' format. As in conjunction, a special connective is needed.

The semantic of rules is then introduced using examples such as 'It is cloudy if it rains'. In our special syntactic notation the symbol ':—' serves as the word 'if'.

it__is__cloudy:__
**   it__rains.**

by adding the atom

it__rains.

to the database we can ask the query:

? it__is__cloudy.

and get

yes.

as an answer.

Our box now contains two kinds of objects: those that are 'really' there, and those that 'look as if' they are in the box, depending on the existence of other objects. From this point on, it becomes clear that space and work can be saved, and a more intelligent behaviour can be gained, by creating rules based on few objects that were 'really' inserted in the box in order to deduce the existence of other objects.

Reasoning chains are quite intuitive, and are very simply explained in our propositional PROLOG, without the burden associated with explaining full PROLOG proof mechanism. For example, by adding the rules:

farmers__are__happy:—
    plants__are__growing.

and

plants__are__growing:—
    it rains.

to the above database, one can ask the query:

? farmers__are__happy.

and get the answer

yes.

Disjunction and alternative rules

Disjunction, which means the use of the logical relation 'or', is introduced and explained in a similar way to conjunction. The word 'or' in our syntax is replaced by the notation ';'. For example,

? the__tree__is__green; the__tree__is__tall.

means a query that asks whether the tree is green or tall. Soon afterwards, the option of writing alternative rules with identical heads is introduced. This is done by showing the equivalence between both methods, eg the rule

abraham__is__happy:— abraham__is__in__love;
abraham__is__rich.

is identical to the set of rules:

abraham__is__happy:— abraham__is__in__love.
abraham__is__happy:— abraham__is__rich.

Alternative rules are pointed out to be preferable considering PROLOG proof mechanism, which is discussed later on.

Unary predicates for describing object properties

The limited intelligence of the box and its manager up to this stage is further discussed. One conclusion is that this is attributed to the way it treats propositions — as a single string of characters. The fact that the manager cannot identify common properties among statements which, from our point of view, are similar, is a major barrier for more human-like behaviour. After some examples of natural language sentences which have the same pattern, the student is told how to translate them into a concise formal notation. This translation includes removal of words such as 'is' and other 'cosmetic' features of human language (see Fig. 9.4). The main advantage of these notations lies in the use of variables, which is introduced next.

English	PROLOG
The tree is green.	green(tree).
The tree is tall.	tall(tree).
The dress is green.	green(dress).
The leaves are green.	green(leaves).
Socrates is greek	greek(socrates).
Adam is a male.	male(adam).
Eve is a female.	female(eve).

Figure 9.4 *Translation of English sentences into PROLOG*

Variables

Although the concept of variables in PROLOG is different than in other programming languages, it is closer to variables in algebra and therefore can be intuitively understood better. Variables in PROLOG appear in queries, are existentially quantified and refer to an unknown entity. Variables in our program are demonstrated through natural language words that denote an unspecified object: 'who', 'something', 'a person', 'one', etc. After showing these words, we pose a problem to the student to find 'who is green' according to the database in Fig. 9.4, ie for which individual is a fact about his greenness contained in the box. After showing the impractical solution of asking queries which are virtually propositional about each potential individual, we express our wish for queries of the form:

> ? green(who).

But how can one tell the unspecified individual 'who' from the possibly distinct individual 'who'? As always, a syntactic agreement with the manager is achieved: words starting with a capital letter or with an underscore are treated as variables, while other words or numbers are regarded as constants, eg

> ? greek(__who).
> ? green(X).

The manager's response to the first query will be

__who = socrates.

The response to the second query will be:

X = tree.

The manager's response to such existential queries is explained using a very informal description of unification ('matching') and substitution. This discussion is concluded by a repeated note about the meaning of negative answers in PROLOG, as a result of possibly missing or misspelt information, and by an explanation of the way to acquire multiple solutions to such queries, using the notation (;).

? green (X).
   X = tree. ;
   X = dress. ;
   X = leaves. ;
   no.

Variables can be used for conjunctive queries as well. Conjunctive queries without shared variables act as two separate queries. Shared variables add to the expressive power of the language, and are the basis of almost any useful PROLOG program. This concept is quite easy to explain using unary predicates. Referring to our original database one can ask queries with unshared variables such as:

? male (X), female (Y).

and get an answer;

X = adam.
Y = eve.

or queries with shared variables such as:

? green (X), tall (X).

and get the answer:

X = tree.

At this point we lifted any restriction about the number of arguments in a predicate, and thus concluded our introduction to PROLOG.

Binary and unary predicates for describing relations among objects
Unary predicates that were useful for describing propositions about properties of objects

are not sufficient for representing other classes of propositions. These as yet uncovered propositions describe certain relationships between two or more entities, eg;

father(abraham, isaac).
father(isaac, jacob).

The students are taught how to express such sentences by letting a predicate stand for the relation, and letting the related objects be represented by the argument in the parentheses. The first sentence, therefore, can be verbalized as 'Abraham is the father of Isaac'.

Queries in full PROLOG are not different in principle from unary queries, but they start demonstrating the real power of PROLOG in using one fact as a basis for answering different queries, eg:

? father(abraham,__son).
 __son = isaac.
? father(__father, isaac).
 __father = abraham.
? father(__father,__son).
 __father = abraham
 __son = issac. ;
 __father = issac
 __son = jacob.

Note that binary relations are the starting point in most books, and are the core of Ennals' (1984) book for children, whereas in our approach they are introduced fairly late, after the student has passed through the development of PROLOG from propositional to unary and then to full PROLOG.

Variables in facts and rules
Universal quantification is informally introduced using words like 'everybody' or 'all'. Our agreement with the manager requires him to refer to variables appearing in facts or in heads of rules. This enables the insertion of facts like 'everybody likes beans' into the box, yielding a positive answer to each similar query about individuals that like beans.

likes(X, beans).

The use of universal quantification in rules is a bit more intuitive. For example:

likes(X, beans):— mexican(X).

The introduction of full pure PROLOG is concluded by comprehensive examples of facts, rules and queries, stated in natural language, PROLOG, and an intermediate logical-natural language.

At this point we abandon the box and its manager, and continue with full PROLOG interpreter programming, using lots of examples taken from everyday life and from school subject matter.

PROLOG IN THE CURRICULUM

We end this chapter by describing one very simple example of using PROLOG for programming classroom teaching material. The example is taken from a junior-high science course, dealing with properties of elements.

The students are assumed to know that elements can be classified as metals and non-metals according to some properties such as luminosity, electrical conductivity in the solid state, melting point and boiling point. Let's concentrate in this example on two alkali metals, sodium and potassium, and two non-metals, the halogens chlorine and bromine. The basic relations, described as facts in PROLOG, are:

```
element(sodium).            white(sodium)
element(potassium).         white(potassium).
element(chlorine).          yellow__green(chlorine)
element(bromine).           brown__red(bromine).

conducts__electricity(sodium).     shines(sodium).
conducts__electricity(potassium).  shines(potassium).

melting__point(sodium, 98).
melting__point(potassium, 64).
melting__point(chlorine, —100).
melting__point(bromine, 7).

boiling__point(sodium, 892).
boiling__point(potassium, 760).
boiling__point(chlorine, —35).
boiling__point(bromine, 59).
```

Using the above facts we continue the program by adding rules. A metal and non-metal can be defined by the following rules:

```
metal(X):—
   element(X),
   conducts__electricity(X),
   shines(X).
non__metal(X):—
   element(X),
   not(metal (X)),
      X/ = carbon,
      X/ = silicon.
```

(/ = means not equal).

The rule definition of non-metal is a good opportunity to introduce the students to negation in PROLOG. Negation in PROLOG is identified by the predicate 'not' which means that if 'X' is true then 'not X' is false, and if 'X' is false then 'not X' is true.

Other rules can be written for the definition of the physical state of the element at room temperature:

```
physical__state (X, solid):—
   room__temperature(__room__temperature),
   melting__point(X,__melting__point),
   melting point > __room__temperature.

physical__state(X, liquid):—
   room__temperature(__room__temperature),
   melting__point(X, __melting__point),
   melting__point < __room__temperature,
   boiling__point(X, __boiling__point),
   __boiling__point > __room__temperature.

physical__state (X, gas):—
   room__temperature(__room__temperature),
   boiling__point(X, boiling__point),
   __boiling__point < __room__temperature.

room__temperature(25).
```

This small program can be developed to include many elements, and many more rules (eg rules about metaloids, inert gases, number of electrons etc).

Here are some examples of interactive queries the user can ask when loading the above described PROLOG program:

```
? physical__state(chlorine, X).
   X = gas.
? physical__state(X, solid).
   X = sodium. ;
   X = potassium.
? non__metal(X).
   X = chlorine. ;
   X = bromine.
? non__metal(X), liquid(X).
   X = bromine.
```

CONCLUSION

The program described in this chapter is now being taught in an experimental course to 10th grade students and to their teachers. Work is still being carried on towards developing a teaching approach to more advanced PROLOG programming techniques using list processing, recursion and PROLOG proof theorem. Implications and conclusions concerning the course implementations and its impact on the cognitive abilities of the students will be described in a later chapter.

REFERENCES AND FURTHER READING

Anderson, J R (1980), 'Deductive reasoning', in *Cognitive Psychology and its Implications*, Freeman and Company, 296-325.

Ausubel, D P (1968), *Educational Psychology: A Cognitive View*. Holt, Rinehart and Winston, Inc., New York.

Briggs, J (1984), *Micro-PROLOG Rules!* PEG-Exeter School of Education, University of Exeter, EX1 2LU.

Clark, K L, and McCabe, F G (1984), *Micro-PROLOG: Programming in Logic*, Prentice Hall International, Englewood.

Conlon, T (1985), *Start Problem-Solving with PROLOG*, Addison-Wesley.

Ennals, J R (1984), *Beginning Micro-PROLOG*, Ellis Horwood Ltd.

Feigenbaum, E A and McCorduck, P (1983), *The Fifth Generation*, Addison-Wesley.

Kowalski, R A (1985), 'Predicate logic as programming language', *Proc. IFIP*, North-Holland, May, 5-8.

Novak, J D, Ring, D J and Tamir, P (1971), 'Interpretation of research findings in terms of Ausubel's theory and implications for science education', *Science Education*, **55**, 483-519.

Olson, D R (1985), 'Computers as tools of the intellect', *Educational Research*, May, 5-8.

Robinson, J A (1979), *Logic Form and Function. The Mechanism of Deduction-Reasoning*. Edinburgh University Press.

Safra, S (1984), WISDOM PROLOG, Department of Mathematics, The Weizmann Institute, Rehovot, Israel.

10. Teaching logical analysis with PROLOG

Richard Spencer-Smith
Dept of Philosophy
King's College
Strand
London WC2R 2LS
UK

This chapter doesn't have much to say about PROLOG *per se*; it's more about one conception of how to teach PROLOG together with Logic. It relates to a project funded by the University Grants Committee, at the Department of Philosophy at King's College London, to develop a course for undergraduates combining Logic and PROLOG. Part of the research involved in developing our course must concern the best way to interleave the subjects, but the approach I would initially favour involves the students receiving a fairly thorough grounding in Logic before coming to PROLOG. I believe this should have advantages both for philosophy students — for whom the learning of Logic is fundamental — and for students of Computer Science — the obvious recipients of a PROLOG course.

But why bother? Computers can offer some help in checking exercises in formal Logic — but why bother combining the study of Logic with a computer language? If the question came from someone teaching Logic to philosophy undergraduates, as well it might, I would answer roughly as follows.

Philosophy students sometimes come away with the mistaken impression that Logic is purely formal, as if it were a game played with uninterpreted symbols, with no application to real inference and analysis. One way to correct this is to set questions which are not wholly formal, which exercise their grasp of the basic concepts, rather than simply testing their ability in the manipulation of formal rules. Another way, though, is to get them to do some PROLOG, since by doing this they can see logical analysis being put to work in a very direct way. In part, what I say below is an attempt to elaborate this answer.

One of the difficulties with teaching Logic to humanities undergraduates is that many are not used to working with a formal language — they're not used to being rigorous about syntax. This can both prevent them properly understanding inference, the rules of which are defined for expressions of the formal language, and impede their grasp of the semantic concepts — for instance, the distinction between predicative and referential expressions. What's important here is not the particular syntactic manifestation that such a distinction takes (whether the predicates go in prefix or infix form, etc), as that the students grasp *some* system of formal syntax.

Learning Logic in the context of PROLOG can help here in two ways. One way is that a machine running PROLOG requires syntactic rigour of the user — consistency of notation, respect for the difference between predicative and non-predicative expressions, insertion of connectives, and so on. Working with a computer language like PROLOG means that students can discover for themselves the importance of these matters. The formulation of a definition in first-order notation, for example, can be checked by writing it as a PROLOG program, and seeing whether the machine can make the appropriate inferences using it. Not only will the logical content of the definition be tested, but also, at a more basic level, its syntactic well-formedness.

The second way PROLOG can help is that a program can encode a grammar for elementary Logic in a very perspicuous way. Here is a truncated version of the definition of a well-formed formula (wff), written in SIMPLE micro-PROLOG.

wff(A)
wff(B)
wff(—X) if wff(X)
wff(X & Y) if wff(X) and wff(Y).

This is just a notational variant of the rules of structure which any student beginning Logic should be familiar with. But because it is now realized on computer, it can be brought to life, and so its significance can be explained to students in ways previously unavailable.

I will mention two of these ways. They reflect the fact that the same encoding of rules in a declarative program may, if the control readings are right, both generate instances of the concept it defines, and check examples to see if they instantiate that concept. First, it can be used to illustrate how an infinity of facts about well-formedness can be captured by a recursive definition. Just ask it which things are wffs. The illustration is very crude and repetitive, of course, but even so it provides a graphic way of showing, to someone new to the idea, how an infinity can be condensed into a form which a finite being can master.

Secondly, the program can be used as the basis of exercises in which the students refine and extend the grammar: what is it for a wff to have the overall structure of a conjunction; when is one wff the negation of another; when is one wff a sub-formula of another, and so on. Even the simplest case, extending it to pick out just the atomic wffs, must at least get one to think about what it is for a formula to be atomic.

The preceding discussion serves to illustrate the two levels at which PROLOG can enhance the learning of Logic — both at the level of using a logical system, and at the level of theorizing about it. At the beginning of the course, as here envisaged, the students will primarily learn how to use Logic, in analysis and inference. Correspondingly, they will be exposed to computers as users of programs, programs which will both check exercises, and generate examples when need be.

But since these programs will be written in PROLOG, the students will not simply be passive recipients of the software, as in a more traditional CAL approach. As the wff definition shows, they will at a later stage be able to understand, modify and extend aspects of the programs. This can only be good for their grasp of the logical concepts involved, which should be deepened by going over them from a new angle. But it is also important for their understanding of PROLOG. If they have already been exposed to a tutoring program with a modicum of sophistication, they will be in a good position to appreciate how complexity and flexibility of behaviour can arise by the combination of separate clauses, any one of which taken in isolation — as in the examples above — may seem rather simplistic.

This brings me to my second example. When students are first taught the tree method (Hodges, 1977), it can help them to be led through a number of cases of tree construction. How many examples each student requires will depend on his or her ability. The tree method, applied to an argument, can be described as a top-down search for a consistent counter-example to it: top-down because it looks at the overall structure of each component wff, ie for the connective with widest scope in it, and breaks it down to simpler cases on that basis. We take the premises together with the negation of the conclusion and search for a consistent set of atomic states of affairs which would render those sentences true. Consider:

A v B, C —> B, — C, So: A

Is this valid? We search as follows:

$$
\begin{array}{c}
\textbf{A v B} \\
\textbf{C—>} \quad \textbf{B} \\
\textbf{—C} \\
\textbf{—A}
\end{array}
$$

$$
\begin{array}{cc}
\textbf{A|} & \textbf{|B|} \\
| & |\ | \\
| & |\ | \\
\textbf{—C} & \textbf{B}
\end{array}
$$

A consistent counter-example is provided by a branch which does not close: —C, —A, B, ie C false, A false, B true. We can check this result by supplying these values to a truth table, ie:

A B C A v B, C—> B, —C, So: —A
F T F T   T   T   F

The truth-table method, by contrast with the tree method, provides a bottom-up search for a counter-example, ie, it assigns semantic values to the basic units, and then works up to the values of the complex whole. The two approaches are of course in agreement — it is possible for the premises of this argument to be true yet the conclusion false.

For some reason students often find the top-down method harder to apply than the more laborious truth table method. It would therefore be advantageous to have available a tree-tutoring program, one which could take them through a limited number of trees, prompting them in the construction of a tree, and providing a limited help facility. The program would be written as a combination of a number of discrete modules. Each module would encode a specific set of rules, and have a clearly defined function — a module to check input expressions for well-formedness, one for the tree rules, one for the truth-table rules, one to hand the results from the former to the latter, and so on. By such a simple combination of quite simple units, one can achieve a program with some explanatory value, as I hope is suggested by the above illustration. Moreover, when the students come to study PROLOG, here will be an example of a structured, modular program, the behaviour of which they are already familiar with.

I don't regard the tree method as something to be taught in place of natural deduction techniques (Newton-Smith, 1985), but as something intermediate between semantic and proof-theoretic techniques, and which therefore can be taught alongside both. Viewed as above, it is a semantic technique. Viewed in a different light, it involves the syntactic manipulation of formulae. The same holds true of its extension to modal Logic. It can be regarded as a search for a refuting semantic diagram — in Hughes' and Cresswell's (1968) sense — where this typically involves 'opening a window on a possible world'. Or it can be regarded as a simplified proof procedure, involving sub-proofs containing reasoning about an arbitrary possible world.

The tree method has some very attractive features. In some respects it is easier to learn and apply than natural deduction, because it only involves the decomposition of formulae into simpler formulae. Its simplicity makes it attractive from the programming point of view, in that it should be relatively easy for students to understand and reconstruct a proof-checking routine in this form. Moreover, in the case of predicate Logic, it provides both a simple way to present the semantics of the quantifiers, and a readily comprehensible illustration of the lack of a full decision procedure — the lack of a positive test for invalidity. The relevance of such an illustration to a course of Logic and computing is quite apparent.

It is also very useful in preparing students for the full rigours of natural deduction, because there is a natural correspondence between the rules of tree construction and introduction and elimination rules. Sometimes students have difficulty with natural deduction because they don't see the obvious — the fact that, for example, a conjunction in the premises means that an &- elimination is likely to be required at some point in the proof; that a conjunction in the conclusion is likely to require an &- introduction at some point. Because the tree method works top-down (or from the outside in) on the components of an argument, it can get the learner to see how the structure of the premises and conclusion determines the kind of rules that are likely to be employed.

But the tree method is not a substitute for natural deduction. The difference is this: the tree method is a means for *checking* the validity of an argument; by itself, it is not a means of *constructing* an argument. This difference reflects the fact that the tree method is primarily a means for checking the consistency of a set of sentences — and, as far as that goes, it doesn't matter in what order you apply the rules of tree construction; whereas in producing an argument you have to proceed by a sequence of inferential steps that lead from the premises to the conclusion. Here the order is crucial; you may not, for example, be able to apply an introduction-rule until you have made some appropriate eliminations. One thing Logic is about is sharpening people's conception of how to reason, about how to move validly in thought from some assumptions to a conclusion — not just which argument forms are deductively valid. The difference can be brought out very sharply in cases where the conclusion of the argument is not given in advance — quite a natural occurrence.

I want to illustrate this point with something which may strike you as rather a toy example. I hope to convince you that the example is not frivolous, and that there are many points of theoretical interest which it instantiates — there are at least four that I can think of. The examples can be found both as popular puzzles and as exercises in courses in problem-solving — but have been more thoroughly elaborated by the logician Raymond Smullyan in a series of books (Smullyan, 1978).

In Smullyan's terminology, they concern the land of knights and knaves. Knights are *honest* — their honesty consisting in their always telling the truth. Knaves are correspondingly *dishonest*: they always tell falsehoods. There is a further category of being, the normal, who sometimes tell the truth, and sometimes do not. With these basic ingredients one can set many problems by varying the circumstances. For example, let us assume that we are in a land of only knights and knaves, and we encounter two of the locals — lets call them '*a*' and '*b*' — and *a* informs us: 'At least one of us is a knave.' What can we deduce about the nature of *a* and *b* on the basis of this information?

I shall try to bring out the sort of theoretical issues which lie behind this kind of problem. First, then, there is *natural deduction*. When people reason informally about these examples — before they're taught any formal rules of inference — their reasoning may nevertheless exemplify such rules as disjunctive syllogism, *reductio*, and so on. (This facilitates the teaching of introduction and elimination rules — you can show that you are systematizing and making explicit inferential rules that they actually follow.) And, more importantly in this context, the rule of assumption: suppose he's a knave, what follows? Success here depends on something which is absent from the tree method — the ability to make assumptions, draw out their consequences by reasoning with them, and discharge them if they produce inconsistency. The solution to the problem is not given in advance, so you have to reason your way towards it, ie construct an argument which has the solution as its conclusion. Since there is no set of premises plus conclusion, the tree method is not readily applicable.

The ability to generate and reject assumptions, I believe, is something central to good problem-solving technique. Typically, when you are set a problem you are presented with a certain amount of information. You reason with that information as far as you can, but usually it doesn't get you to the solution. So at this point, if the problem-solver is to progress, he or she must conjecture hypotheses, and try them out — see whether they are consistent with what is known or assumed so far, and reject them if not, or hold on to them as consistent if not yet reduced to absurdity. For example, we find the procedure of conjecture-and-elimination of hypotheses equally indispensable to the solution of the kind of cryptic arithmetical problems used in Newell and Simon's studies (1977). What addition does the following encode?

$$\begin{array}{r} \textbf{DONALD} + \\ \textbf{GERALD} \\ \hline \textbf{= ROBERT} \end{array}$$

As with the knights and knaves, you are presented with a certain amount of information, you must formulate certain general principles which govern this topic, and then you will have to generate hypotheses — in this case, about possible values for the letters. The procedure of conjecturing and refuting hypotheses is made formally precise in the natural deduction rules for assumption and discharge.

The second point about knights and knaves concerns the nature of *definition*. A grasp of the logical structure of definitions is an important preliminary to logic programming. Firstly, there are definitions which are more or less of a philosophical ideal — those having the form of the universal closure of a bi-conditional. Then, where bi-conditionality is unattainable, partial definitions are possible, as Carnap recognised with his Reduction Sentences. For example, the reduction sentences for solubility might be:

(∀x)(Immersed (x)—> (Dissolved(x)—> Soluble(x)))
(∀x)(∀y)(Same-kind(x,y)—> (Soluble(y)>
Soluble (x)))

From the point of view of philosophy, the students can be briefly introduced to such important issues as extensionality, dispositions, natural kinds and even verificationism. From a formal point of view, they can practise quantificational reasoning by proving, say, that sample *b* is soluble given that it is the same kind as sample *a*, which was immersed and did dissolve. And finally, having carried out such inferences themselves, they can get the machine to do them — by writing the reduction sentences as PROLOG rules. They can be introduced to logic programming by little more than a switch in notation (modulo the equivalence of P—>(Q—>R) with (P&Q)—>R). They will have the satisfaction of seeing that a machine can actually perform the same sorts of inferences as they have learnt as natural deduction rules.

With such a basis, it is not hard for the students to come up with a partial definition of an honest knight — the schema:

(1) (∀x)(x says A —>) (knight(x) —> A)).

Having formulated such principles, the solutions to knights and knaves exercises can be written out as explicit natural deductions. Of course, the proofs tend to be more long-winded than their informal counterparts, because all the assumptions that are being appealed to are made explicit, eg the definitions of knights and knaves. This is a useful exercise for students both of philosophy and of programming. For example, it's important in philosophy to be able to discern the assumptions being appealed to in the course of an argument.

This brings me to the third point about these examples. While traditional Logic courses emphasize the analysis of the structure of single sentences, they usually do not develop the analysis of whole problems, eg the logical analysis of a mini-theory about the world, or a theory about a mini-world. The simulation of micro-worlds is a technique sometimes employed in AI, eg in the TEACH files of the PROLOG system. The knights and knaves examples involve a simulated micro-world, and a full analysis of it involves not just the partial definition of certain key concepts, but also a recognition of the different logical statuses of such principles, eg the distinction between principles which are analytically true of our micro-world:

(∀x) — (knight(x) & knave(x))

(of anything which speaks), and principles which state contingently true generalizations — of the land of knights and knaves:

(∀x)(knight(x) v knave(x)).

It is important to distinguish a principle like (1) from something which might be confused with it:

(2) (∀x) (x says A —> (A —> knight(x)))

Whereas (1) partially defines what it is to be an honest knight, (2) states a truth only so long as only knight and knaves are present. It is false when normals are present, for they may also speak truly. Further 'empirical' generalizations may be discovered *en route* to or as a result of solving a particular problem — for example, of the land of knights and knaves:

(Vx)— x says (knave(x))

— no-one can say of himself that he is a knave. This principle is useful when a problem presents what might be called a disguised liar sentence, eg:

a says (knave(a) v —2 = 2).

It is here that the policy of making principles explicit, and sensitivity to the different status of (1) and (2), can be seen to pay off. If the student properly investigates this example, he or she will realize that a contradiction is involved, and that one or more assumptions must be at fault. Either they were misinformed — *a* didn't say that either he was a knave or 2 is not identical to 2 — or the assumption (in force up to now) that only knights and knaves are present must be mistaken.

Mention of liar sentences brings me to the last, but definitely not least, of the points about these cases. This is that they provide a natural lead in to philosophically important principles concerning *meaning* and *truth* — for example, the schema that relates meaning and truth conditions (a variant of Tarski's Convention T):

(Vx)(x means that A —> (true(x) <—> A)).

The generalization they discover, that if we assume that there are only knights and knaves around, no-one can say of himself that he is a knave, is transformed into the logical fact that, if we assume the principle of bivalence, no sentence can say of itself that it is false. So if we present such a sentence:

(a) a is not true,

which is to say:

a means (—true(a))

this easily combines with the above schema to produce a contradiction. In my (so far limited) experience of teaching this material, students find the move to these more abstract examples far more difficult to work with. By coming at it through the more concrete cases about knights and knaves, it should be possible to render intelligible the workings of these more abstract schemata.

So I return to my original question: why combine Logic and PROLOG in a single course?

First, then, what's the point of learning PROLOG via Logic? In coming to logic programming via Logic, the declarative style of programming should be that much easier to grasp (especially for those used to imperative languages). Having got a firm basis in logical techniques and concepts, the students can concentrate on programming principles. For example, the SIMPLE wff program mentioned earlier, besides revising the syntax of propositional Logic, introduces the students to lists, list processing, and recursive definition. Moreover, there are those aspects of program structure which go beyond their purely logical content, eg the order in which you place conjuncts, or the clauses of a recursive definition, makes no logical difference, but can have a significant effect on the operation of a program.

Secondly, there is the question of more concern to philosophers: what's the point of adding the PROLOG material to a course on Logic? The answer I have tried to develop emphasizes PROLOG as a means of consolidating the student's understanding of Logic, as well as showing how logical analysis can be applied in practice. But there is another more controversial answer: that with the increasing prominence of inter-disciplinary areas like cognitive science, and the increasing interest of, say, philosophers of mind in AI, there is some intrinsic merit in extending the analytical tools taught to philosophy undergraduates to include some from computer science. If there is anything in this answer then the kinds of programs philosophy students could benefit by going on to study would be (for example) those which provide simple illustrations of the problems involved in modelling cognitive processes artificially.

To conclude, I will mention briefly a program of roughly this sort, used by Johnson-Laird (1983) to illustrate his theory of mental models, but which also illustrates what I have been saying about the use of assumptions. It's a program for producing and updating a database about spatial relations by converting information in propositional form into a simple 2-dimensional array.

Information — eg:		Representation:
A right-of B		B A
C right-of B		— — — — — —
D before A	conjectured	
E before C	extension:	B A C
D right-of		D E
	contradiction	

— so we need to distinguish what is information, and what is conjecture. If a revision consistent with the information is possible, the program should update the database accordingly:

$$\text{B|} \quad \text{C|} \quad \text{A|}$$
$$\text{E|} \quad \text{D|}$$

For Johnson-Laird, the database managing program provides a simple illustration of the recursive revision of a mental model (Johnson-Laird, 1983). It also illustrates the idea of making conjectures which go beyond the information you are given, and which may need to be revised in the light of subsequent information[1].

[1]Based on a talk at a conference organized by Steve Torrance and myself, at King's College, London. The Conference, on PROLOG and its Relevance to Philosophy, was held on 25 October, 1985. I would like to thank Steve for discussing aspects of this talk.

REFERENCES AND FURTHER READING

Hodges, W (1977), *Logic*, Penguin, Harmondsworth.

Hughes, G E, and Cresswell, M J (1968), *An Introduction to Modal Logic*, Methuen & Co, London.

Johnson-Laird, P (1983), *Mental Models*, University Press, Cambridge.

Newell, A (1977), 'On the analysis of human problem-solving protocols' in Johnson-Laird, P, and Wason, P (eds) *Thinking*, University Press, Cambridge.

Newton-Smith, W (1985), *Logic*, Routledge, London.

Smullyan, F (1978), *What is the Name of this Book?*, Prentice-Hall, Englewood Cliffs.

11. Why teach PROLOG? The uses of PROLOG in education

Jonathan Harland Briggs
Kingston College of Further Education
Kingston Hall Road
Kingston-upon-Thames
and
School of Education
Exeter University
UK

INTRODUCTION

This chapter gives an overview of the possible uses of PROLOG in education and training. Much is being claimed for the possible benefits of its use in schools and colleges. How it is used materially affects what is gained. This chapter lists some of the possible tasks with which the student may be involved and then suggests the possible benefits of each task.

PROLOG has been used in education since 1981. It was suggested in 1980 by Kowalski that 'logic could be used as a computer language for children'. Since then projects have used PROLOG in education in (at least) the UK, Israel, Australia, Denmark, Canada and France.

Before examining some of the possible benefits of using the language it is important to examine how it can be used; the ways in which the students can be involved with the computer and what is being taught. There are eight different uses that can be outlined:

1. Programming in PROLOG.
2. Logic programming.
3. Using an application.
4. Using an application shell.
5. Implementing an application shell.
6. Using an expert system.
7. Using an expert system shell.
8. Implementing an expert system shell.

There is no doubt that many of these tasks can be overlapped but they can be seen as different and separate.

The first two of these tasks are concerned with using PROLOG as a programming language. PROLOG represents two different styles of programming: declarative and procedural. It seems likely that teaching one style rather than the other will produce different results.

PROLOG PROGRAMMING

Computer programming is already taught in many other programming languages. Despite the wide range of languages and dialects available, they are all designed to run on only one sort of computer. Whoever manufactured the machine, the internal computer architecture is basically the same as that described by Von Neumann. Programming a Von Neumann computer involves writing a sequence of instructions or procedures in a form that the computer will understand. Existing computer languages, including BASIC, Pascal, LOGO, etc, are procedural languages.

PROLOG is also a procedural computer language. It has imperative features such as READ, PRINT, ADDCL and DELCL.

A program is of the form:

A   if   B and C and D

This can be read procedurally as:

To do A   first do B then do C then do D

Most programs written in BASIC or LOGO could be rewritten into PROLOG:

check (PERSON is a girl) if
** newline and**
** print (is PERSON «yes/no» ?) and**
** read (ANSWER) and**
** match (ANSWER yes) and**
** print (How old is PERSON?) and**
** read (ANSWER2) and**
** less (ANSWER2 17)**

LOGIC PROGRAMMING

Some of the projects using PROLOG as a programming language have adopted an alternative style of programming: logic programming. A logic program is a logical definition or description of a problem. Formal Logic provides a language or syntax for describing knowledge. It allows knowledge to be expressed in many different ways. To simplify representation for and use by a computer, PROLOG restricts statements to the following form, known as Horn-clauses:

A if B and C and ...

Facts and rules can be expressed in this way. A fact can be considered as a rule without any conditions, and for simplicity PROLOG allows the 'if' to be omitted.

A logic program is 'used' to answer questions or queries. The simplest form of query will check to see whether a fact can be derived or proved from the facts and rules making up the knowledge base. A more complex query will allow answers to be extracted from the knowledge.

PROLOG sees questions as goals that have to be proved, shown to be satisfied by facts and rules within the knowledge base. The method by which PROLOG searches the knowledge base, its inference mechanism, is very simple:

- PROLOG proves a goal if there is a fact (a rule without conditions) about the goal.
  or
- PROLOG proves the goal if there is a rule with the goal as its conclusion by attempting to prove each of its conditions.

Programming in Logic was the aim of the 'logic as a computer language for children project'. This project taught that sub-set of PROLOG that would allow children to express facts and rules about a subject area without concern for the other extra-logical features of the language. The 'inference model' was not explicitly taught and no attempt was made to alter the behaviour of the PROLOG programs that were produced.

EXPERT SYSTEMS

Expert systems are computer programs that in some senses capture some of the knowledge of a human expert, allowing the computer to perform tasks that might be expected from that expert. They are being used commercially to provide advice, diagnose faults and select appropriate courses of action.

Although some interest has been shown in using expert systems in education and training, relatively few systems are regularly being used at present. Few of the commercially available systems are appropriate for education, concentrating on topics such as legislation and regulations.

There are three uses of PROLOG in relation to expert systems. Students can use expert systems developed by their teachers or other outside experts, they can be involved in the design of systems using tools written in PROLOG, or they can use the language to implement the tools themselves.

Using Expert Systems

PROLOG is only one of the computer languages used to implement expert systems. It is difficult to argue that a completed system in PROLOG is superior or inferior to one written in Pascal or LISP. The increasing use of PROLOG is due to its wide availability on a range of popular hardware and the ease with which systems can be written.

Many expert systems are not developed using any of these languages directly. Instead, they are written using 'expert system shells': expert systems from which the domain knowledge has been removed.

Using Expert System Shells

There are a number of popular expert system shells available in the UK including Xi, ES/P Advisor, APES, Crystal and HULK. Each shell comprises a suite of programs that help users represent their knowledge, ask questions and obtain explanations. They differ in the range of facilities they provide, how flexibly they can represent knowledge, and in their appearance. Some, like APES and ES/P Advisor, provide interfaces to PROLOG so that additional features can be added.

It is too early to predict the effect of these commercial tools on education and training. Already, however, there is some evidence that commercial users who have tackled expert systems using these shells, have found that they have been forced to re-examine much of what they thought they knew about their expertise.

At Kingston College of Further Education, the author is involved with a project to consider the implications of using expert systems in the further education curriculum. This project involves the design and implementation of a number of new expert system shells. These will be simpler than their commercial equivalents, each illustrating only a small number of the range of features of their larger counterparts.

Implementing an Expert System Shell

The final use of expert systems in education would be to encourage students to implement their own expert system shells. Unlike many other programming languages, it is straightforward in PROLOG to write programs that manipulate other programs. This feature is being exploited by programmers writing expert systems and expert system shells. To illustrate this, it is often suggested that advanced students of PROLOG use the language itself to implement a simple PROLOG interpreter:

> **prove (goal) if fact(goal)**
> **prove (goal) if rule (head if conditions) and**
> > **same-as (goal head) and**
> > **prove-all (conditions)**
> **prove-all (NIL)**
> **prove-all (first .. rest) if**
> > **prove (first) and**
> > **prove-all (rest)**

An expert systems programmer will need to alter the behaviour of this basic PROLOG interpreter, adding questions to the user or explanation facilities.

Because a simple interpreter is so simple to construct, the programmer can first design the particular language in which the 'expertise' is to be coded. This does not have to be PROLOG.

The ability to design new languages and write simple interpreters for them led the implementers and users of micro-PROLOG (a version of PROLOG, the first specially designed for school microcomputers) to offer a selection of different surface syntaxes in which micro-PROLOG could be programmed: SIMPLE, DEC, MITSI etc.

Applications

Programs written in PROLOG are not restricted to expert systems and expert system shells. A range of other, perhaps more familiar, applications can be implemented. The potential uses of these applications in schools and colleges closely mirror those already outlined for expert systems: using applications in their own right, implementing 'application shells or tools', and using these tools to implement new applications.

A spreadsheet or word-processor written in PROLOG need not differ greatly from that used by most secretaries. It would probably operate more slowly. It could have additional 'expert' features but these are not automatic consequences of choosing PROLOG as the implementation language. PROLOG could also be used to write educational software but once again there are no intrinsic reasons why this would be better than those programs being used at present throughout the country.

APPLICATION SHELLS

The work of the author at Exeter University School of Education is concerned with using PROLOG to help teach History, other Humanities subjects and the teaching of pupils with specific learning difficulties (dyslexics). The approach adopted by the project team has been to use PROLOG to implement simple tools or application shells that provide a programming environment in which teachers and students can explore historical processes and ideas by designing and writing 'programs'.

Using an Application Shell
Each shell concentrates on a particular type of application area and so far tools have been developed to allow students to write adventure games, simulations, detective databases and to handle structured information. Application shells are similar to expert system shells. Instead of a framework for handling expertise, the shell will provide a structure into which the student or teacher can enter knowledge. The shell will then provide access to that knowledge, either answering questions or manipulating the knowledge to provide simulations.

The focus of the Exeter project is to encourage children's thinking. The computer gives them models within which they can explore the processes of problem-solving within particular domains or more generally.

Implementing Application Shells
PROLOG was chosen as a suitable language for implementing 'application shells' because of the ease with which it is possible to write programs that manipulate other programs. As already seen with expert systems, it is straightforward to develop a language with which to describe knowledge for a particular application and then to write an interpreter to manipulate that knowledge in a particular way. The other main advantage of using PROLOG is that it is sufficiently high level to allow a prototype to be designed and implemented very quickly. As an example, one of the Exeter programs, LINX, allows pupils to explore decision-making by providing a framework into which they can enter a network of possible decisions and consequences. The basic structure is extremely simple:

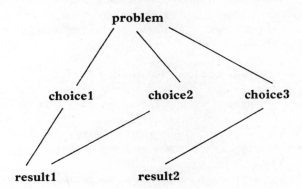

The resulting simulation can be made more sophisticated by allowing consequences to be delayed or combined. The 'application shell', LINX, consists of procedures that allow pupils to enter, examine and alter such information, and an interpreter allowing them to 'run' the simulation.

THE BENEFITS OF PROLOG

The claims for PROLOG are legion: improving logical thinking, teaching advanced computing, or changing the face of education. It is clear from the wide range of uses outlined above that it is unlikely that all students presented with PROLOG will benefit in the same ways.

There do seem to be some implications of introducing the language in schools and colleges:

1. Giving awareness of advanced information technology.
2. Teaching the concepts of formal logic.
3. Providing an environment for structuring knowledge.
4. Passing on expertise.
5. Teaching a particular subject.

Some will be easier to justify than others.

Awareness of Advanced Information Technology

It is apparent that advances in computing and information technology need to be assimilated by education. Within a computer science course a wide range of computer languages may need to be introduced to indicate the range and diversity of approaches to computer programming. Advanced computing students could also benefit from the opportunity to use PROLOG as an implementation language, implementing applications or expert system shells.

More widely appropriate, there are moves to give all students an appreciation of computers and computing. In this context, expert systems represent a departure from the 'traditional' numerically biased applications of computers and may have deep significance for future contacts between pupils and expertise.

Teaching the Concepts of Formal Logic

Using PROLOG cannot be automatically equated with learning about Logic. Often applications of PROLOG are taught so that the concepts of formal Logic are obscured. Conversely, it is possible for 'logic programming' to be the main focus for a course that will then build on this foundation to include expert systems and applications. Indeed, in Israel, a project to teach logic programming starts by introducing some of the concepts of formal Logic.

Providing an Environment for Structuring Knowledge

Logic programming, using expert system shells and using application tools, can all be seen to have one common benefit. They each provide an environment in which the students can describe their subjects and then modify and refine this description. It may be important to some teachers that this is within the context of formal Logic but many expert system shells and application shells will use different ways of representing and manipulating the knowledge.

This ability to manipulate knowledge is not shared by many other programming languages or pieces of educational software. It has been the aim of many teachers to write programs about their own subjects as a powerful aid to their teaching. This often proves impossible because of the large amount of computing knowledge required to code the system. This becomes an even greater problem if students are expected to write programs. For example it is undesirable for History or Geography students to have to learn computer programming before applying this to their own subjects.

Using logic programming tools or expert system shells, the student is able to write 'programs' without learning about computer programming. To make full use of this style of use, a wide range of these tools have to be written. At present there are few programmers with this expertise.

Passing on Expertise

There is much controversy as to whether an expert system is a suitable medium in which to pass on expertise. If the students are able to examine and modify the knowledge within the system, this may supplement the ability to have their questions answered and help them construct high-level models of the area of expertise.

Certainly, involving a novice within a team of experts constructing an expert system provides an environment in which the novice can acquire much expertise. This has been noted by computer scientists working on commercial expert systems projects who have reported that their understanding of the new area at the end of the project has far exceeded their expectations.

A number of projects have suggested that alternative expert tutoring systems could be written which would use similar knowledge bases but, instead of providing advice, would explicitly teach the area of knowledge. This requires the system to have teaching expertise in addition to knowledge of the subject domain. To date, the areas tackled have been extremely small and well defined.

Teaching a Subject

Can PROLOG help teach subjects such as History? Underlying many of the problems for which PROLOG is often offered as a solution is its ability to help teach about a particular subject. This chapter has attempted to show that teaching people about PROLOG and teaching with PROLOG may be very different.

Given teachers who are keen to involve their students with their subjects, PROLOG provides a range of tools and approaches that may help them tackle particular topics. In many instances it offers a different kind of human-computer interaction to that already offered by other computer packages. This does not imply that PROLOG is automatically better than the alternative approaches.

Using PROLOG to introduce logic programming principles, using expert system shells or using tools tailored to a particular subject domain, offer the teacher new ways of helping their students structure their knowledge. If appropriate tools are used this may indeed help students make sense of what is being taught.

CONCLUSIONS

PROLOG has been in the educational arena only a few years. Educational acceptance of computing in general has been slow and there is reluctance at present to accept that innovation in information technology has not been halted but in many respects is accelerating. PROLOG has been seen by many people but understood by few. It will take some time before the full implications of this style of programming and the importance of the new tools that can be written become fully apparent.

Before deciding that PROLOG is the solution it is important to decide what the question is. It is possible to use the language across the curriculum, to investigate the use of expert systems in training and to use it as a powerful way of thinking about problems. It is also possible to ignore some of the power of the language and to use it as if it were BASIC or COBOL.

The aim of the author's work at both Kingston and Exeter is to test out the claim that the most important aspect of PROLOG's use in education is as a medium for producing knowledge engineering environments so that students can explore the structures of the subjects they are learning. PROLOG is therefore seen as an implementation language, the first of a range of powerful declarative tools with which even higher-level tools can be written, providing new ways of thinking about knowledge.

ACKNOWLEDGEMENTS

The author's work exploring the implications of expert systems in further education is funded by the Further Education Unit of the Department of Education and Science. The work at Exeter University School of Education is supported by the Nuffield Foundation.

I would like to thank Zahava Scherz, Ari Hann, Jorge Aage Jensen, Karsten Bogh, Chris Tompsett, Jon Nichol, Paul French and Derek Brough for their comments about this work.

Part III: Expert systems and knowledge-based tools

Preface

Jonathan Harland Briggs

Expert systems are computer programs which perform some of the tasks of human experts: providing advice, diagnosing diseases, fault finding or helping analyse or modify a complex product or process. They have increasingly become the focus of attention as large and small companies see their potential attractions. By the end of 1986 most of the UK companies with household names, such as British Telecom, British Gas and Shell UK Ltd. had established 'expert system groups' to examine their uses within their organizations. In addition a rash of small consultancies has emerged to satisfy the burgeoning demand for expert systems advice.

An expert system is an accumulation of knowledge or expertise about a particular subject, usually written down in the form of rules. This makes PROLOG an ideal medium for implementation of an expert system. Together with this knowledge is a program or 'inference mechanism' that will manipulate the knowledge in particular ways. Many such inference mechanisms are being packaged together with appropriate windowing software, but without domain specific knowledge, as expert system shells. Among these we find that Xi, ES/P Advisor and APES have been judged suitable for exploration by educational researchers and developers.

Expert systems have a number of other distinguishing characteristics. They ask questions in order to supplement their knowledge, and they can explain their reasoning.

Included in Part III are contributions from a number of pioneering projects that begin to explore educational applications of expert systems. In addition, Chapter 14 is an account of PEG-Exeter's developments which integrate some of the features of expert systems into more general knowledge-based tools.

12. An intelligent knowledge-based system as an aid to chemical problem-solving

David Bateman
Centre for Educational Studies
King's College
552 King's Road
London SW10 0DA
UK

A research project is in progress investigating the potential of one type of knowledge-based system in schools. It is funded by a studentship from the Information Technology in Education Programme of the ESRC. The project is supervised by Dr J Harris at the Centre for Educational Studies, King's College, London.

THE PROJECT

Three activities form the basis of this study. The first of these is the construction of a knowledge-based system. It is proposed that such a system can be constructed using hardware and software tools available in schools. The system will be capable of solving problems in the specified domain, of providing information about the domain, and of providing explanation of solutions to problems it has solved. This chapter deals with this element of the study.

The second activity is to observe the interaction between this system and pupils who are engaged in chemical problem-solving. Observation of the interaction between tutors and pupils engaged in chemical problem-solving forms the third activity. The purpose is not to make any judgements about the two types of interaction, it is instead to form a careful description of them. It is proposed that the human dialogue will contain episodes of passive tutoring, ie, when the pupil takes control of the dialogue for the purpose of asking for information and explanation. It is further proposed that pupils will be able to use the software for the same purpose. Analysis of the two types of interaction will provide evidence relating to these proposals.

KNOWLEDGE REPRESENTATION

A knowledge-based system must embody a good representation of its domain if it is to be of use. The top-down expert system approach to formalizing knowledge starts with a problem in the domain. In the domain of physical separating techniques in chemistry one typical type of problem is:

How do we separate a substance from a mixture?

A typical top-level rule to allow this type of problem to be solved is:

> **evaporation separates a pure substance from a binary mixture if**
> **the mixture is a solution and**
> **the pure substance is a solid**

The conditions of this rule are then defined by other lower-level rules or facts:

> **a binary mixture is a solution if**
> **the mixture contains a solid and**
> **the mixture contains a liquid and**
> **the solid is soluble in the liquid**

Using an expert system shell such as APES, which is written in PROLOG and runs on a 16-bit RML Nimbus microcomputer, the process of describing such rules in a formalized way can be quite rapid for the experienced user. The predicate logic of PROLOG is the formalism for this representation. Such a system will solve problems of a given type and provide explanation in terms of a trace of the rules used for inference.

One difficulty with this approach is in recognizing the constants and variables and the relationships between them, even in this tiny domain of only two rules. A more fundamental difficulty with this approach is that the meaning of many of the terms in the domain is not explicit and need not be for the system to successfully solve problems. For the pupil, however, the meaning of such terms as 'pure substance' and 'mixture' is vital to a proper understanding of the process of evaporation and hence to any educational function for the system.

A bottom-up approach offers a way of enriching the representation and providing the user with explicit descriptions of objects which comprise the rules. There are several stages in converting knowledge from natural language representation to a predicate logic representation.

The first stage involves the identification of the representational primitives upon which understanding of the domain depends; this is often the specialist language used to discuss the domain. Other examples from the two rules given include the terms 'solution', 'solid' and 'liquid'. These objects can be classified during the second stage, the example given so far forming a group concerned with matter. Other groups in this domain include properties, apparatus and processes. Within these groups the objects are either individual, eg 'water', or generic, eg 'pure substance'.

The third step involves the definition of the representational primitives. In this stage the relationships between the terms are described. For example there is a type relationship between generic objects in the same group: 'pure substance' is a type of 'substance'. In the fourth step the definitions are set out as a semantic network. This gives clarity to the representation. The representational primitives form the nodes in this network and the relationships form arc labels. A small portion is shown in Fig. 12.1 with the nodes ringed and the arc labels boxed.

This portion only shows binary relationships in which the arrows show the direction in which to read the nodes and link labels. It is possible to have three or more representational primitives linked by one relationship (Fig. 12.2). In this case numbers on the arcs indicate the order of the nodes.

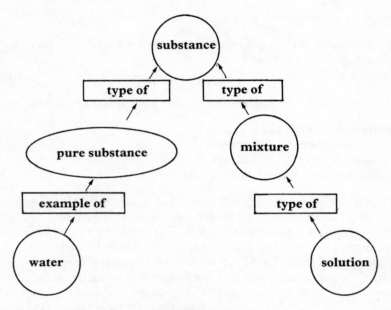

Figure 12.1

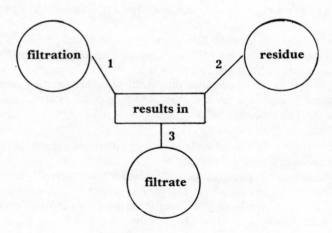

Figure 12.2

On its own this network does not allow for the solving of problems. It can be extended, as done by Deliyanni and Kowalski (1979), to include rules. In this extension the nodes can include variables as well as generic and individual representational primitives. Chemical rules of the type described earlier can now be included after being rewritten slightly to clearly identify constants and variables (preceded by an underscore):

evaporation separates __puresubstance from __mixture if
    __mixture is a solution and
    __puresubstance is a solid

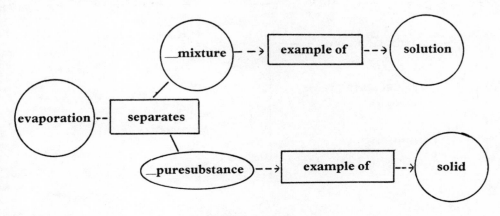

Figure 12.3

The single line link indicates a conclusion to a rule and a double line indicates a condition. All of the chemical knowledge derived from the top-down and the bottom-up approaches can now be combined in a homogeneous formalism. Further, there is a simple mapping between link labels and predicates and between nodes and arguments which facilitates the coding of the network in PROLOG.

THE KNOWLEDGE-BASED SYSTEM

The proposed system is nearing completion. It offers pupils four initial options which may be repeatedly selected in any order or combination. Pupils may select problems or describe their own. They can attempt to solve problems by selecting a technique or constructing a sequence of techniques. They may ask the system for information such as the physical properties of a substance. The fourth option is an explanation facility.

This software offers an environment in which pupils can work on a problem rather than describe their own knowledge. The difficulties encountered therefore were centred around designing an appropriate interface for query and explanation rather than for constructing a knowledge base.

In order to pose queries to a knowledge base the user must solve a series of problems. This series has been described (Norman, 1984) as four stages of user activity, namely: intention, selection, execution, and evaluation. The user must have some intention before being able to proceed. The second problem is how to select from the possible options the action which is most likely to lead to the intended outcome. These first two steps occur without the user touching the keyboard and are essentially thoughts about what to do. Having selected an action, this action has to be executed and the result evaluated in terms of the original intention.

The interaction is menu-driven. This greatly limits the flexibility of a PROLOG system but eases the burden of selection and execution. Currently the sort of interaction outlined below is possible if, for example, the pupil wishes to know if sulphur dissolves in water. The boxed option should be chosen in each case.

| select-prob | solve-prob | helpful-information | helpful-explanation |

— — —information about — — —

physical state

solubility

If this menu contains a list of predicates we may not convey the nature of the relationship to the user. Even a longer description does not guarantee understanding. For example, 'physical state' may be as unclear as 'state'. Selection will depend on successful mapping of the user's intentions on to the menu items. Picking the 'solubility' option results in:

is soluble in

This question template may help to convey to users the format of a possible question.

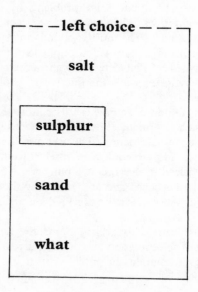

— — —left choice — — —

salt

sulphur

sand

what

In this menu 'what' is a selection for an unknown and allows PROLOG 'which' queries to be evaluated.

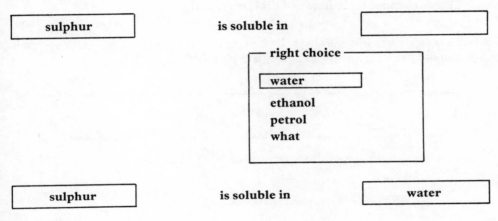

NO

Hopefully, the user has found out the required item of information. The user is returned to the original menu at this point. From here she/he may request explanation of the information obtained. The left and right choice menus could have included an item such as 'other'. Selection of this would allow substances unknown to the system to be used. This has not been implemented because the query-the-user system in APES is linked to the explanation system, the use of which is generally slow.

A further enhancement would be generalizing the system to *n*-ary predicates instead of restricting it to binary ones. However, as the number of arguments increases the question templates become less clear.

The explanation available from APES seems to match the covering law model of explanation. This involves some proposition to be explained which can be related to some hypothesis, theory, general covering law, or, in PROLOG terminology, to a rule. If the conditions of the rule hold true then the original proposition has been shown to be correct.

There are of course other types of explanation. Empirical studies of explanation in science lessons have been limited but some categories have been identified. Brown (1981) describes three types of explanation which encompass his own categories as well as those of Smith and Meux (1970) and Hyman (1974). Type 1 covers the use of generalizations and specific instances, type 2 relates to functional explanation and type 3 refers to serial explanation. Brown's own categories are as follows: Type 1 is a reason-giving explanation which offers reasons for, or causes of, the occurrence of a phenomenon, eg Why is filtration used to separate sand from sand and water? Type 2 is an interpretive explanation which clarifies, exemplifies or interprets the meaning of terms, eg What is filtration? Type 3 is a descriptive explanation which describes a process or structure, eg How is filtration carried out?

Interpretive explanation would be a valuable addition to the APES shell. The nodes in the semantic network are the objects which may have an interpretive explanation. This explanation would be made of the relationships between the node of interest and all the other nodes to which it is connected.

There is an assumption that the use of generalizations or rules as used in APES necessarily leads to understanding.

'The explanation in the form of the rule is self evident.'

(Hammond and Sergot, 1985)

It seems unlikely that this will always be the case for our students. Suppose the system is explaining why some separating technique is applicable (Fig. 12.4).

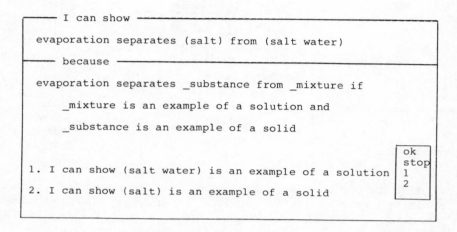

Figure 12.4

As well as wanting to know why the conditions are true, the user might want a justification for the rule used, perhaps in terms of the differences in physical properties on which these techniques ultimately depend.

A final aspect of the use of APES concerns the way in which a knowledge-based system can produce multiple solutions to problems. This is of interest when the solutions are different or when they are the same but arrived at via different solution pathways. If the user can be made aware of these alternative explanations and provided with a mechanism for moving between them, a more responsive explanation system would result.

REFERENCES AND FURTHER READING

Brown, G (1981), *Explaining: Studies From the Higher Education Context*, SSRC.

Deliyanni, G, and Kowalski, R A (1979), 'Logic and semantic networks', *Communications of ACM*, March, Vol **22**, No3, p184.

Hammond, P, and Sergot, M (1985), *APES User Manual*, 1st edition, pp 2-13, LBS Ltd.

Hyman, J R (1974), *Teaching: Vantage Points for Study*, Lippincott Press, New York.

Norman, D A (1984), *Four Stages of User Activities*, Conference Papers for INTERACT '84, Elsevier Science Publishers.

Smith, B O, and Meux, M O (1970), *A Study of the Logic of Teaching*, University of Illinois Press.

13. Knowing what the student knows: a use of APES in science education

Nancy Law, Jon Ogborn and Denise Whitelock
Dept of Science Education
University of London Institute of Education
Bedford Way
London WR1H 0AL
UK

A PROLOG program contains a description of a 'world', and running the program generates consequences which follow from the facts and rules in that description. Consider what might be told to a PROLOG program in the case of one thing supporting another: for example, a book resting on top of a table. Some simple rules about the general notion of support might be:

1. An object which is supported must rest on another object.
2. If things are piled on one another, the lower ones support those above them.
3. All supports require sufficient strength to sustain that which they support.

We can capture this 'real world' picture in a small PROLOG program shown below.

```
X rest-on Y if
            X on Y
X rest-on Y if
            Z on Y and
            X rest-on Z
X supports Y if
            Y rest-on X and
            X strong-for Y
X supported if
            Y supports X
```

However, how does the deductive capability of PROLOG manifest itself when employed in the expert system shell APES? The salient features of the APES shell are demonstrated if we engage in a dialogue with our program and ask whether Mary is supported. The program has no knowledge about a person named Mary but has been given a set of rules about support which should be applied in order to deduce an answer to our query. In fact, the system replies with two questions:

1. Is Mary on anything? and
2. Is Mary's support strong enough for her?

With this extra information which is then added to the database, the system can confirm that Mary is supported and will also explain how it reached that conclusion.

> **which (X : Mary on X)?**
> > **Answer is chair**
> > **Answer is end**
> **Is it true that chair strong-for Mary? Yes**
> > **= = = Yes, I can confirm Mary supported why**
> **To deduce Mary supported I used the rule**
> > **X supported if Y supports X**
> **I can show chair supports Mary stop**
> **Execution terminated**

If we add another rule to the database, which elaborates upon our general notion of support and suggests that the floor is the ultimate support since it appears to be very strong and cannot break, and then consider whether Dave who is sitting on a stool holding a pile of books is supported, we are again asked whether the stool is a strong enough support for Dave. Even when the reply is a negative one to this query, the program still confirms that Dave is supported by reasoning that the floor supports Dave, as is shown below.

> **which (X : Dave on X)?**
> **Answer is stool**
> **Answer is end**
> **Is it true that stool strong-for Dave?**
> **which (X Y) : X on Y)?**
> **Answer is (Mary chair)** .
> **Answer is (books Dave)**
> **Answer is (Dave stool)**
> **Answer is (stool floor)**
> **Answer is end**
> > **= = = Yes, I can confirm Dave supported why**
> **To deduce Dave supported I used the rule**
> > **X supported if Y supports X**
> **I can show floor supports Dave.**
> **Execution terminated.**

This is an answer we would not have expected since we had previously stated that the stool could not support Dave, let alone Dave plus a pile of books! Therefore, our program demonstrated that a common-sense description of support was not accurate enough to convey the subtlety implied by this notion, and revealed flaws in our less-than-rigorous definition. However, the description can now be modified since the interaction with APES has provided clues as to where our descriptions were incomplete or invalid and will also quickly provide feedback about the appropriateness and reliability of any new representation which is constructed.

We have demonstrated PROLOG's query-the-user facility employed within APES, which enabled the database to expand and acquire more facts, which can in turn be manipulated by the system's inferencing rules. Explanation features are of particular interest to researchers in the field of education, for reasons discussed in the remainder of this chapter. The dialogue between computer and user can be recorded and noted; APES will also report what it has been told in a given session, as in the example below:

list dialogue
You told me that Mary on chair
You told me that books on Dave
You told me that Dave on stool
You told me that stool on floor
You told me that chair strong-for Mary
You told me that floor strong-for X if X rest-on floor
You denied stool strong-for Dave

Two important questions now need to be answered:

1. Why should science educators be concerned with representing such problems as support and movement in a non-scientific way?
2. How can the pertinent features of an expert system shell be of use in such a task?

There is a growing body of research interested in pupils' intuitive ideas about science and there have been a considerable number of investigations which support the view that pupils have their own conceptions about natural phenomena.

A variety of studies has been conducted in such areas as dynamics, heat, light, and many others (Gilbert and Watts, 1983). Although proof of existence of these prior beliefs is abundant, it is often difficult to fit a descriptive pattern to the results obtained, and the mismatch between pupils' understanding of science and formal science can persist even through to undergraduate level (McDermott, 1983). However these 'alternative conceptions' are so strongly taken for granted that they are often not made explicit, and need to be purposefully teased from individuals in situations where they feel it is both possible and reasonable to explain things which normally need no explanation.

Therefore, our current research interests lie in attempting to elicit and formalize in a computational model pupils' own thinking about dynamics which can capitalize upon the explanatory and query-the-user facilities of APES. The idea is to bring tacit knowledge into the open, knowledge which otherwise could dominate thinking without the person even being aware of the process. That is, if pupils' common-sense notions about dynamics can be brought out using this tool, in a way in which the consequences of holding incomplete knowledge or an inadequate rule system will cause the system to reach invalid answers or to ask unreasonable questions, then this combination could give rise to a new level of pupil awareness about their own ideas and could help to provoke a reconsideration of their current ways of thinking. The concept area of dynamics is particularly appropriate, since Newtonian dynamics does indeed require a fundamental shift in the basic concepts used to understand the work.

This work is at present at a very early stage, with more to show by way of ambitions than achievements. The example of 'support' is purely illustrative: other thinking we hope to capture would involve ideas of what makes things move, what makes them fall, what stops them moving or falling, and so on. The planned research has two essential dimensions: first, to explore the idea of formal representations of informal ideas and second, to explore the idea of using PROLOG as a mental 'scratch pad' used to externalize and so make available for scrutiny thoughts and theories about processes.

REFERENCES AND FURTHER READING

Gilbert, J K and Watts, D M (1983), 'Concepts, misconceptions and alternative conceptions: changing perspectives in science education'. In *Studies in Science Education*, Vol 10, pp.61-98.

McDermott, L C (1983), 'Critical review of research in the domain of mechanics'. In Delacote, G (Ed) *Research on Physics Education: Proceedings of the First International Workshop, La Londe les Maures*, Edition du CNRS, Paris.

Part IV: Pupils and cognition

Preface

Jackie Dean
Education Department of Western Australian Government

In order to determine how people learn we need to examine cognitive structures and processes, the roles of language and social interaction, and the situations within which learning occurs. People learn best when they perceive that what they are learning is relevant to them, when they are so involved in a task for its own sake that their motivation is intrinsic, and when they are able to control and organise their learning, ie when they can be active learners in pursuance of goals which are significant to them.

Computer technology provides us with a unique opportunity for extending children's learning. The computer's high status among children, its ability to give instant feedback, its demand for precision and the variety of its functions and responses ensure that we have many advantages when we teach using computers.

The crucial question is: which software tools are most appropriate for teaching and learning with computers? The answer is: those which empower children, and which enable them to express and extend their knowledge. Looked at in relation to how people learn, PROLOG seems to be currently the most suitable medium for enhancing our students' thinking processes across a broad spectrum.

Why is this? Briefly, PROLOG's structure is compatible with what we know about how people learn. Its primarily declarative nature makes it readily accessible and understandable. As Winograd (1975) says:

> 'Much of what we know is most easily statable as a set of declaratives. Natural language is primarily declarative, and the usual way to give information to another person is to break it into statements. This has implications both for adding knowledge to programs, and communicating their content to other people.'

Cohen (1977) also points out that current models of semantic representation of knowledge include a network model, with the links between the nodes representing many different relationships. As PROLOG statements and rules can be represented as semantic networks, they can be said to reflect one of the semantic structures inside the mind.

PROLOG predicates can be viewed not only as relationships between objects, but as categories defining different types of information. The PEG-Exeter PROLOG tools, in particular, encourage this approach (eg facts in DETECT, choice in LINX). This emphasis on category reflects what Cohen has called people's 'strong spontaneous tendencies to organise items into categories and sub-categories, and to use imposed groupings of this kind to aid recall'. The Exeter PROLOG tools strengthen these natural tendencies by making them explicit: the tools require that data be divided into named categories. In using these tools pupils learn to employ coherent organizing principles which accord with cognitive tendencies they already possess.

PROLOG's flexibility also enables us to design and/or amend PROLOG front-end tools to suit the needs of learners. In this section Cumming and Abbott describe how they have done this with MITSI (Briggs, 1984) by extending, for example, its explanatory facilities. The PEG-Exeter project has also designed several PROLOG toolkits to enable their pupils to explore different forms of knowledge representation within the Humanities (Dean, 1986). These toolkits give pupils access to specific knowledge structures which both reflect and support the thinking processes involved in using them. Pupils across the ability range are catered for by the insertion of supportive features (eg templates, helpful error messages).

Another factor crucial to understandability and ease of use is the language in which the computer interacts with the user. This language should be congruent with natural language if cognitive confusion is to be avoided. PROLOG's in-built predicates (eg **list**, **delete**, **add**) are immediately comprehensible to users.

As every teacher knows, and as Cumming and Abbott (1986) have pointed out in relation to children learning PROLOG, the teaching methodology used affects pupils' learning. They found that a top-down teaching approach was more successful in terms of PROLOG learning outcomes than was a bottom-up approach. Similarly, the PEG-Exeter team's experience has been that children across the ability range could cope successfully with the task of structuring and creating databases using, for example, the PROLOG toolkit DETECT (Dean, 1986, pp96-108 and 125-131). The Exeter pupils' success can be attributed to a large extent to a teaching strategy which included:

- provision of a model in the form of an exemplar database which they first explored.
- the setting of a real goal-based task embedded within the curriculum (eg pupils analysed an historical situation and represented it as a database).
- giving the children access to top-level organizational structures to aid cognitive clarity (eg tables for categorizing information and diagrams showing the logical links between discrete blocks of data).
- insistence on planning sessions.
- reduction of programming instructions to a minimum — preferably one sheet.
- pupil interaction with peers; both the PEG-Exeter and Southampton PROLOG projects have found that peer collaboration and peer tutoring had a positive effect on learning (see Chapter 15, pp167-175.)
- interaction with the computer: pupils entered, tested and amended their data until they achieved a working program.

The structure of any learning task is thus crucial to effective learning. However, the very nature of PROLOG enables it to supply learners with a coherent, logical framework, a consistent structure, within which to represent their knowledge. It forces users to make clear distinctions between different types of data, to order information consistently, to express themselves precisely and to make explicit logical connections between different pieces of information. In this way PROLOG toolkits both enable and enforce logical coherence. PROLOG also fosters the development of metacognition by requiring pupils consciously to structure their thinking and clarify their language as they take control of their own learning.

REFERENCES AND FURTHER READING

Briggs J H (1984), *Micro-PROLOG Rules!* Logic Programming Associates Ltd, London.

Cohen, G (1977), *The Psychology of Cognition*, Academic Press.

Cumming, G, and Abbott, E (1986), 'It's the teaching strategy that matters, even if the language is PROLOG', *Australian Educational Computing*, July.

Dean, J (1986), *PROLOG: a New Tool for Learning and Understanding History*, Unpublished MEd dissertation, University of Exeter.

Winograd, T (1975), *Frame representations and the declarative/procedural controversy*, in Bobrow, D G, (ed) *Representation and Understanding: Studies in Cognitive Science*, Academic Press.

14. PROLOG tools in education

Jon Nichol, Jonathan Briggs, Jackie Dean, Rosalind Nichol, Kevin O'Connell, Jennifer Raffan, Martyn Wild
PEG-Exeter (Prolog Education Group)
School of Education
University of Exeter
Exeter EX1 2LU
UK

INTRODUCTION

'What's this load of ******* crap?'
'Don't ****** well ask me.'
This was an interchange a visitor overhead between two 12-year-old special education needs pupils in 1983. They were grappling with a program written in PROLOG to illustrate Viking exploration and trade. The program asked the pupils to use TSIMPLE, a version of PROLOG for 8-bit micros, to query a database on Viking trade. The database contained information on Viking ports, sailing times between them and their relative geographical directions, and goods produced and traded at each. The teacher asked the pupils to record on a map and table the progress of a Viking trader, represented as the printout from the PROLOG program (see Fig. 14.6 on p.163). The complexity of the query structure required to ask questions illustrated the difficulty of using PROLOG programs as a normal element in lessons. An advanced working knowledge of algebra would have aided the two confused pupils, and the fact that they did not know the difference between North and South did not help.

How, in the subsequent three years, have we attempted to bridge the gap between the difficulty of applying PROLOG in forms like TSIMPLE to children's learning, and our current use of PROLOG as a normal element in the education of mainstream pupils and those with special educational needs and specific learning difficulties (dyslexics?).

Underlying our work are a number of premises.

PREMISES

We believe that PROLOG use must grow out of the everyday curriculum of individual schools and teachers. To do this, it must meet teachers' perceived needs. Therefore PROLOG must complement the existing curriculum, and be an improvement in terms of learning outcomes from present provision. To satisfy this criterion, PROLOG must provide both teachers and pupils with powerful tools with which to develop their understanding of topics/problems. These tools can be both domain specific, and of general application. PROLOG tools enable both pupils and teachers to write their own programs *in English*. The tools differ widely in their external forms, but share common structural features based upon predicate logic. The value of PROLOG-based teaching and learning may lie at the deeper level of knowledge-handling frameworks, which contain both particular and unique features. This approach ties neatly into the current emphasis in educational computing on learning with, as opposed to about and through, computers.

LEARNING WITH COMPUTERS

The use of the computer as a learning device is most commonly seen through the adoption of data-processing packages, spreadsheets and word-processors. In relation to educational curriculum development it is already being applied in first class authoring software. For example, there is the mathematics material produced by ITMA, and the excellent innovatory authoring software produced by the Computers in the Curriculum Project, King's College (Chelsea), in particular their Dynamic Modelling System for scientific applications and mathematical use within the Humanities.

PEG-Exeter has taken a similar line through the production of a number of domain-specific authoring programs, based upon the logical structure of a discipline's sub-domains. These content-free intelligent knowledge-based tools enable pupils to express their understanding of aspects of a subject. PEG-Exeter has developed the following PROLOG shells:

Area	Authoring Program	
Historical enquiry	DETECT	For handling discrete blocks of text, accessed through key subject words.
		DETECT allows the discovery, questioning and processing of evidence, the framing of new questions and the formulation and testing of hypotheses.
		Example Programs *GREENDIE* — a murder mystery based on Collingwood's John Doe investigation.
		BOGBOD — an investigation into an Iron-age body found in a peat-bog, based on the School's Council History 13-16 Project, Tollund Man investigation.
		MOUNDIG — an archaeological dig into a Viking burial mound on the Isle of Man.
	PLACES	For processing information which appears in the form of coherently structured lists of data; in this case place-name information.
		Example Program *CREDPLAC* — an investigation into local place-names around our project school.

Mental recreation	THE PLAN	An adventure-writing toolkit. It allows pupils to create their own imaginary world, or recreate a historical reality, inside the micro, which they can then explore.
Causation	LINX	For writing simulations or other programs involving decision-making and a branching structure of enquiry, for example, the classification of information as in the identification of types of historical evidence.

Example Program
SEADOG — the recreation of an Elizabethan privateering voyage to the Spanish Main.

Expert Systems	APES	This program enables us to write 'knowledge programs' which contain the knowledge of an expert. Such programs can interrogate the user, and respond to the user's questions. The user can add information to the program, and thus establish a dialogue with it. APES is a commercially available expert system available only on 16-bit micros, from Logic Programming Associates.
	MITSI	For teaching Information technology. A simplified front-end to PROLOG to make it accessible to non-computer science users.

It is at present testing the following new shells:

Area	Authoring Program	
Enquiry	NAMES	For analysing information about personal names, such as place and date of origin, meaning of terms.
Information processing	TRADES	For dealing with information about trade.
Linguistic structures	SLOTS	Provides support for building, checking or processing structured knowledge. Applied to simple sentence description of scenes and Latin sentences.
Expert systems	ADVISOR	Textual advice is triggered according to specified constraints. An example of use is a program for the planning of essays.

What are the possible educational advantages of using PROLOG in the education of children?

CAN PROLOG SERVE BROAD EDUCATIONAL GOALS?

Perhaps the two fundamental educational aims underpinning all teaching are:

1. The development of conceptual understanding in pupils.
2. The fostering of metacognition, which subsumes the crucial area of metalinguistics.

Within these broad educational goals are curriculum goals specific to the various subject domains, with the exception of literacy.

1. The development of conceptual understanding
Children writing computer programs can exercise thinking skills beyond the range of normal activity, and can force a deeper investigation of concepts. This is in line with Vygotsky's notion of a zone of proximal development, with the computer filling the role of mediator, thus accelerating independent functioning (Vygotsky, 1978). An obvious example of this process in action is the use of PROLOG tools by pupils with specific literacy difficulties. Using DETECT, LINX and THE PLAN, these pupils have produced programs containing several pages of text each — text which has been reworked and refined many times to allow the program to work most effectively. This they are clearly unable to do when handwriting. Also, children as young as nine have written functioning logical rules using THE PLAN. For example, in an adventure set inside the human body, the adventurer is attacked by white blood cells in the liver. A 9-year-old boy (VRQ 105) wrote this rule specifying the conditions the adventurer had to meet before s/he could kill the attackers:

((kill blood-cells) (WITH blood-cells HAVE
sword)(REMOVE blood-cells PRINT (The blood
cells lie dead before you))

This demonstrates a clear grasp of the concept of conditional rule-writing, a grasp which had not previously been apparent (because the learning environment at school is rarely structured to foster or elicit this kind of thinking?). The thinking induced by this child's use of THE PLAN illustrates the truism that the medium, form and context of the learning experience are crucial in accelerating conceptual development.

> 'Just as adults have been able to solve complex problems with computers that they were unable to do before, so children should be able to go beyond their current developmental capabilities with computer assistance. Human-computer intelligent systems will serve to extend and ultimately to reorganise what we think of as human imagination, intelligence, problem-solving skills, and memory.'
>
> (Pea, 1984, p18).

2. Metacognition
Metacognition is the ability to reflect upon, and exercise control over, one's thought processes. People acquire power and control over their thinking when they are able to step back, reflect upon and discuss their own mental processes. Children can be enabled to do this by interacting with content-specific PROLOG programs which require planning, reflection, deduction, hypothesizing and verification, and also by using content-free PROLOG tools which enable them to plan, research, order and enter their own data. The general principle behind having children order and represent their knowledge like this is to give them insight into knowledge structures and allow them to model this knowledge (Dean, Nichol and Briggs, 1987). Children will thus be enabled to develop an awareness of their thinking processes, which is essential to gaining heightened control over them. Each PEG-Exeter authoring tool embodies a particular structure. This structural coherence means that each tool can reflect the logical structure and the appropriate enquiry strategy for a particular area or problem. Its underlying structure must be made obvious to users so that they can conceptualize the problem and make sense of it. Within the logical structure of each tool users can express their factual, conceptual and affective knowledge. These tools allow users to concentrate on the logical structure of the problem on hand rather than on the programming, for the reasons explored in the first section of

this chapter. The question of metacognition raises the issue of *transferability*. If the writing of programs based on predicate logic enables a common pattern of thinking to emerge in relation to the metacognitive logical thinking involved in analogous areas, it would be interesting to see if there is a transfer of skills from one area to another.

METALINGUISTICS

Pupils' use of both PROLOG CAL programs and content-free tools requiring children to enter their own data, aid metalinguistic development. Because it requires logical, precise and unambiguous language, the computer forces children to reflect on and refine their linguistic usage. Where programs such as Castle Builder (see Fig. 14.7 on p.164) are written for other children's use, the writers take great care over the precise meaning of the language involved. Such reflective and controlled use of language constitutes a powerful vehicle for thought. Although all computer languages require precise and explicit language of the users, PROLOG's declarative nature allows powerful rule-and-goal-based thinking to occur.

Winograd (1975) lists several built-in advantages of declarative over procedural languages, such as: understandability, learnability, accessibility, communicability. He asserts (p189):

'Much of what we know is most easily statable as a set of declaratives. Natural language is primarily declarative, and the usual way to give information to another person is to break it into statements. This has implications both for adding knowledge to programs, and communicating their content to other people. Quite aside from how the eventual program runs, there may be important advantages in stating things declaratively, from the standpoint of building it and working with it.'

Across the curriculum this declarative approach is thus linguistically more appropriate in terms of knowledge representation than is the imperative approach of procedural languages.

PROLOG can be used in the teaching of subjects across the curriculum. PEG-Exeter's work has been predominantly in the areas of Humanities and Literacy. Our main goals for the Humanities area apply across the curriculum. We aim to develop both 'know-how' and 'know-that' knowledge in children, with the emphasis on process learning.

Can PROLOG's potential for fostering metacognition and conceptual growth be realized in practice? There is no concrete non-anecdotal evidence to date. However, the experience of the PEG-Exeter project group suggests that PROLOG can be a valuable tool in achieving these goals ('can be' rather than 'is', as the benefits to pupils of any tool use depend crucially upon the teacher, upon the context and upon the teaching strategies employed).

How can we introduce powerful PROLOG tools into the curriculum?

STRATEGY

PEG-Exeter has evolved a number of strategies and ideas for introducing PROLOG shells into the classroom. Our aim is to give children these PROLOG tools to extend their thinking and literacy skills in different areas of the curriculum. We have adopted a pragmatic, bottom-up approach to the evolution of PROLOG software and related teaching materials. The bottom-up approach involves an intensive approach. We concentrate resources in one or two centres and classrooms, the lessons of which can be applied more generally. Ideas and approaches evolve in the course of a normal teaching programme within a number of schools. On this we base the general application of such software in the school curriculum. This pattern of curriculum development is based upon the model of commercial publishing, as opposed to state supported teams of innovators.

For example, at present we have one team member looking at PROLOG's use in the teaching of Latin, working with one form of 12-year-olds. Another team member is developing strategies for teaching Special Educational Needs pupils at a primary centre. A third is examining the use of PROLOG in a Humanities course for 11-12-year-olds, and as a tool in the teaching of GCSE History. A fourth is serving as the liaison teacher in three primary schools. A fifth is developing initial and in-service teacher training courses. Each developmental point benefits from cross-fertilization between a number of factors. These we consider essential for making the PROLOG tools generally available. The factors are:

1. *A computer science research base.* This provides the technical knowledge to turn teachers' ideas for using logic-based tools into classroom reality. The computer science base has to be in close touch with the educational needs of the development team. We have two computer scientists working part-time on the project, one on the mainstream applications, the other in the SLD area.

2. *Industrial support and liaison.* Without the support of the providers of PROLOG, and the willingness of computer manufacturers to make PROLOG available on their machines (Research Machines and Acorn), dissemination would not be possible.

3. *Classroom experience,* both in computing and subject domains. The project is based upon practising teachers who try out and develop ideas which relate to mainstream curriculum development. This experimentation occurs within the social milieu of a network of schools to which the project team members belong, and upon whose support it relies. Four team members are involved in classroom applications.

4. *Educational research.* There has been a constant infusion of ideas from the academic and educational research community. The team has paid close attention to ideas on cognitive development, peer interaction and group processes, and factors producing successful curriculum innovation. These findings feed into the teaching and in-service and initial training strategies which we develop and their associated resource materials. The team is based in Britain's second largest educational training establishment. Within the School of Education, there is a constant cross-fertilization of ideas between PEG and similar research and development projects in the areas of LOGO, Mathematics Education, TVEI (Technical and Vocational Education Initiative) and CPVE (Certificate of Pre-Vocational Education). We also draw upon the expertise of other educational computing institutions and bodies, such as the Herts Advisory Unit, HABET (The Historical Association Body for Educational Technology) and the international network of developing experience through the PROLOG Education Group. This produces a biannual journal, which contains papers and reports from interested workers around the world. The PEG team at Exeter is made up of two academic educationalists, a full-time research student and two school teacher fellows.

5. *Resource Production.* In order to make its ideas more generally available the team has been able to draw upon professional publishing advice, and has the service of a Manpower Services Commission resources team. This is a government-funded project which aims to train the unemployed in new areas.

In relation to personnel, there is doubling up of function in some areas.

1986/87 — PATTERN OF DEVELOPMENT AND DIFFUSION

What are our structures for the implementation of our ideas concerning possible PROLOG applications? In applying its curriculum development work more generally, PEG-Exeter has applied itself to two general issues: strategies for breaking down barriers to innovation and change inside schools and the development of related in-service and initial training courses. Our general aim is to develop PROLOG shells as cross-curricular tools which can become everyday elements in the pupils' learning. From 1984/6 we pioneered a number of these shells, and in 1986/87 we are active in the following areas:

● Improvement of the shells for use in junior schools and with SEN and SLD pupils. This involves improving the interface, so as to enable the pupils and teachers to program or query their programs in as near natural language as possible. We are also writing an Educational Expert System Shell for 16- and 32-bit micros (EXPRESS — Exeter PEG Expert Systems Shell). ADEX is a prototype for this project.

● Use of the PROLOG tools and PROLOG in the project secondary school:
1. As a central element integrated into the teaching of Classical, Historical and Religious Studies (CHRS) to classes of 11-12 year-olds.
2. As an occasional element in the teaching of English, Geography and History to other forms.
3. PROLOG programming as a major element in the teaching of Latin. The LEA seconded teacher who is liaising the primary project is running this experiment.
4. The PROLOG tools as the main element in a weekly one-hour lesson for each of seven 11-14-year-old SLD pupils (dyslexics) attached to the school's SLD unit, and with Mark, a fourth-year GCSE pupil.
5. Employment of the PROLOG tools in the Special Educational Needs Department. (NB There is a Special Unit for SLD pupils, and a separate Special Educational Needs Department in the school.)
6. Use with SEN pupils within the mainstream classroom. This enquiry will see if SEN pupils within our mainstream classes can achieve the same success as SLD pupils have achieved. We are working with a group of pupils, identified from the evaluation of the progress of our last year form of pupils taking Classical, Historical and Religious Studies.

● Primary school project, involving 10-11-year-old pupils in three feeder schools for our project secondary school, an 11-18 mixed comprehensive. This project deals with both mainstream, SEN and SLD pupils. The children are being introduced to the PROLOG tools and expert systems. In each school we have a 16-bit micro, and software. This enables us to work with small groups of children. There is one full-time LEA seconded teacher, a part-time research assistant (an experienced primary teacher) plus an ESRC research student working on this project. The aim is to introduce an experienced teacher into the primary environment as a catalyst to work alongside the existing staff. This form of in-school in-set is aimed to break down the barriers to innovation which centralized in-set patterns seem to have found impenetrable.

● A small-scale schools curriculum development committee project for the use of PROLOG in the education of SLD (specific learning difficulty — dyslexic) children in junior schools. This project is based at a Devon junior school. The project is working upon a language-writing PROLOG tool, which will complement the other tools already produced.

● Teacher training — the development of courses for the introduction of the micro into the normal school curriculum. The project will deal with both initial training and in-service. We have already mounted courses for teachers in the three primary schools and for initial trainees. A major thrust of this project will be an examination of the implications of expert systems and other knowledge-based tools. The teacher training project will build on the findings of MAPOL at Moray House College, the Expert Systems and Teaching Practice Project at Sussex University and the Expert Systems and Industrial Training Projects at Kingston College of Further Education. We will also draw upon the fund of experience at the School of Education developed during the Teacher Education Project. One full-time LEA seconded teacher is servicing this project.

● Dissemination of the PROLOG tools and associated materials to 30 pilot schools for testing.

● The development of PEG-Exeter as an information centre and service for the growing PROLOG in Education community. Within the School of Education we have established a PEG centre, which will serve as a base for PEG.

In July 1987 PEG held its second international conference at Exeter, which drew together findings from the international body of educational researchers in the field of PROLOG in Education. Figure 14.1 shows the intermeshing of the different groups involved in the PEG-Exeter Project.

In relation to this research and development programme, we are addressing a number of specific issues:

1. The bottleneck in introducing the computer into the normal curricular provision of a school. In moving from phobia to fluency, both staff and pupils have to acquire a sufficient range of skills and develop attitudes which will make the medium a realistic vehicle for learning. What kind of induction course can best break through this bottleneck?

2. A similar bottleneck in introducing experienced teachers and teacher trainees to the micro.

3. The problem of special educational needs pupils, ie those who do not read for pleasure and find difficulty in writing. The difficulty is that they switch off when we try to do any serious literary-based work. This means that we have some ten pupils out of thirty who are getting little out of their teaching. These children cover the special educational needs group. Can we get them to work as successfully as the dyslexics?

4. Strategies for successfully using 3-4 micros with 30 children in a conventional teaching environment. At present this is the most likely environment for the use of computing within subject areas in schools.

5. The transition from the primary to the secondary sector of education.

6. The introduction of expert systems programs and programming into both the school environment and the field of initial and in-service training. The idea of an expert system shell which teachers and pupils can use to write their own programs containing experts' knowledge is very attractive. The use of such programs in the learning process is very seductive, with the vision of each pupil having access to a surrogate teacher via the expert system program.

How are we turning our general ideas into practice?

PEG-EXETER, 1986/87

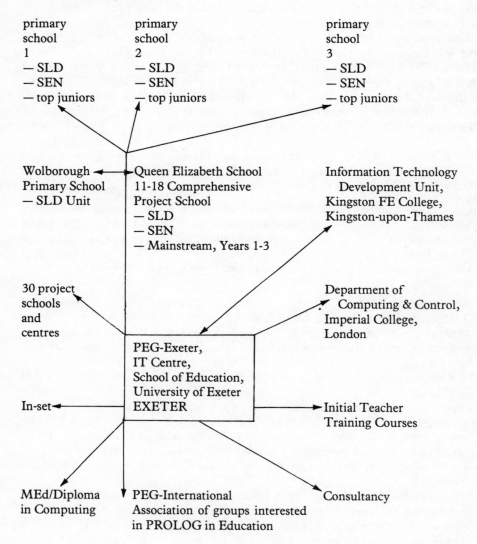

primary
school
1
— SLD
— SEN
— top juniors

primary
school
2
— SLD
— SEN
— top juniors

primary
school
3
— SLD
— SEN
— top juniors

Wolborough
Primary School
— SLD Unit

Queen Elizabeth School
11-18 Comprehensive
Project School
— SLD
— SEN
— Mainstream, Years 1-3

Information Technology
   Development Unit,
Kingston FE College,
Kingston-upon-Thames

30 project
schools
and
centres

Department of
   Computing & Control,
Imperial College,
London

PEG-Exeter,
IT Centre,
School of Education,
University of Exeter
EXETER

In-set

Initial Teacher
Training Courses

MEd/Diploma
in Computing

PEG-International
Association of groups interested
in PROLOG in Education

Consultancy

Figure 14.1

THEORY INTO PRACTICE

There are four elements involved in the introduction of PROLOG into the classroom in our work, and a fifth, teacher training, related to it.

1. PROLOG programming.
2. Learning through PROLOG CAL.
3. The use of powerful PROLOG tools, shells.

4. Expert systems programming.
5. Teacher training.

PROLOG programming

From 1982 to 1984 we developed documentation to enable both pupils and teachers to write their own simple PROLOG programs. The results were encouraging, both for teachers and pupils but, in terms of everyday use in the learning process, of limited value. The problem can be stated simply — to write a PROLOG program of any sophistication requires a long-term logic programming course. Programs consisting of simple inputs of data rules were of limited application in children's learning of school subjects.

PROLOG CAL

We can use CAL written in PROLOG to teach specific issues, such as local Saxon settlement and voyages of exploration and discovery. PROLOG CAL's main function is to provide models for pupils and teachers to write their own programs using the shells. For each area we develop specific PROLOG CAL programs. For example, for teaching prepositions to specific learning difficulty pupils we have a cat and mouse simulation which incorporates the words we want the children to learn. Having mastered cat and mouse they can move on to writing their own programs which incorporate the concepts we want them to learn.

PROLOG Tools — Shells

We are using the tools extensively in our mainstream and SEN and SLD teaching. Each shell is introduced through the medium of a piece of CAL written using the shell. The following examples of uses of the shells in the SLD and SEN area show our ideas in operation. PROLOG tools have given SLD and SEN children hope, enjoyment and a sense of progress and reward from their schooling. These pupils have gained a real sense of achievement and pride in their work, perhaps for the first time, both in their mainstream learning and in language work in the SLD and Special Needs Units of our secondary and primary project schools. It is the opportunity for interaction with both the teacher and fellow pupils that provides a rich medium for the oral development of thinking. An example of such interaction has been observed in the rich dialogue between a group of three children, Louise, VRQ 130+, Paul, VRQ 80, and Dominique, VRQ 98. The group was chosen for containing the two extremes of special educational needs pupils, Louise and Paul. They are writing a program which will help fellow pupils choose the site of a castle.

SEN, SLD and mainsteam pupils using the toolkits have found them to be a liberating force. They are an interactive writing device which gives children a structure to the resolution of their thinking, and allows them to carry on a dialogue with the written word. The students can see their ideas and thoughts take a coherent shape on paper. For example, Fig. 14.2 is Louise's plan of part of a voyage based on the *Odyssey*, written as an 11-year-old during her first-year Classical, Historical and Religious Studies course. In general, pupil thinking occurs in an accessible form previously denied to fellow pupils. The gains have been clear in literary and organizational skills, and there has been a marked growth in individual self esteem and other personal and social qualities.

Two cases, Bryan and Mark, illustrate the point. Bryan is a first year in the form taking the Classical, Historical and Religious Studies course. He is a verbally intelligent pupil, with limited literary skills — testing shows his performance to be average. He is classified as a pupil who receives special educational needs support. The opportunity to write his

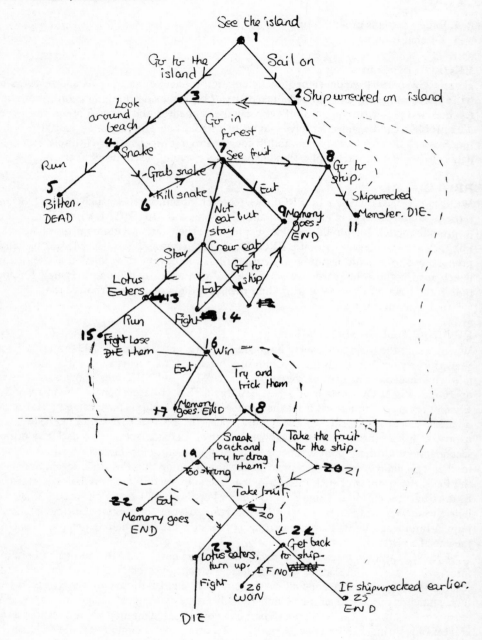

The Network of Our
Computer Program

Figure 14.2 Louise's Plan

own program using LINX, our simulation shell, on *The Voyage of the Argonauts* produced a carefully planned and extensive piece of work (see Fig. 14.3). It covered fifteen sides of an exercise book and it took four hours of continuous typing to enter it using the LINX shell. As we typed, we enjoyed a growing feeling of excitement and anticipation, because at each stage when I tested the program it worked perfectly. He had written it in the form of an adventure book. The program taxed Bryan's literary and thinking skills to the full. Subsequent to developing this program, Bryan has embarked on a number of similar activities in both Humanities (Classical, Historical and Religious Studies — CHRS) and his special needs work. There has been a marked change in both his attitude and performance.

Mark, one of our specific literacy difficulty pupils from the school's special unit, is an even more extreme case. The opportunity to produce work which enables him to sort out his ideas, and express them clearly, has resulted in a high degree of fluency in using the toolkits. He has produced a number of programs which contain carefully worked out information (see Fig. 14.4). The highly motivated 'over learning' involved in the process of refining the structure, content, spelling and grammar of his programs seems to have led to major progress in his literary skills. There has also been a quite remarkable change in his attitude to both school work and his peers through the success he has achieved in using the toolkits.

Mark has voluntarily returned to work with us in the first year of GCSE, the examination course for the 14-16 age range. At present he is writing a simulation based upon decisions of a diplomat, the British Consul in Sarajevo, at the outbreak of the First World War. Figure 14.4 shows his outline plan for the simulation. It is multi-branching and deals with a plethora of complex inter-meshed issues. Using textbooks, monographs and other aids, he is entering and fleshing out his simulation week by week.

Expert Systems
The project is continuing to develop an expert system shell, using the computer science expertise of Imperial College and Kingston FE College's Information Technology Development Unit. A major aim is to get pupils to write their own expert systems. An idea of the use of an expert system shell in this way can be seen with our current work with 12-13-year-old pupils on the choosing of a site for a castle (see Fig 14.7). The pupils have to prepare the information to enter into the computer, using the site judging table to help them. The program will represent their expert knowledge, which others can use to help choose the site of the castle.

TEACHER TRAINING

The teacher training element is a crucial factor in the dissemination of the PROLOG tools and their use in everyday learning. In our primary school project we introduced the teachers to the shells through three half-day courses. At present both the teachers and children in the three schools have embarked upon projects using the shells. The support teacher works in the schools for three half-days a week, tutoring both the teachers and the pupils. Within our mainstream school we are providing instruction and support for interested staff, and already have the shells being used as a regular element by SLD department staff. We have also been experimenting with the introduction of PROLOG shells to teachers through a two-day module which is part of a diploma/ masters in computing course. Course members were asked to write a program for use with pupils or produce a specification for a new shell. Twenty out of twenty-two course members

```
((start egypt))
((position egypt))
((choice voyage east 2))
((choice voyage west 3))
((choice 2 west 5))
((choice 2 south 6))
((choice 2 north 4))
((choice 3 north 7))
((choice 3 east 8))
((choice 8 (sail south-west against the wind) 14))
((choice 8 (sail south-east in direction of drifting wood) 10))
((choice 10 turn-back 9))
((choice 10 sail-on 11))
((choice 11 turn 15))
((choice 11 go-on 16))
((choice 15 (sail in daylight) 19))
((choice 15 (sail at night) 20))
((choice 212 (sail to the green hill) 22))
((choice 212 (wait there) 21))
((choice 6 weapons 12))
((choice 6 food 13))
((choice 12 land 16))
((choice 12 (sail on) 17))
((choice 21 fight 25))
((choice 21 turn 24))
((choice 20 fight 22))
((choice 20 run 23))
((text egypt (Thousands of years ago : all of northern Africa is : believed to have consisted of : a fertile plain roam
((text river (The river Nile ran fast : through a long narrow valley between cliffs : and then as it neared its outlet ,
((text story (the story so far : : You and your mother have been put in a coffin : and sent to sea by the king : : the
((text 11 (You wait : Then you see a ship sail through : But then rocks fall on the ship : That makes you more deter
((text voyage (You set sail with 50 of the strongest men : : You sail for two weeks to the north : : Look on your ma
((text 2 (You sail east : You send two men for water : you never see them again : You loose two endurance points :
((text 3 (You sail west for one week : : You find land : You send six men for food and water : they all return safel
((text 19 (The king sees your ship : He takes his men and takes you and puts the rest in prison : Then he puts you i
((text 5 (You sail west and see land : : You stop and get water : you send 2 men for water : they both return safely)
((text 4 (you sail north : you are in the middle of a war : would you like to fight or to run)))
((text 7 (you sail north : you run out of food and water : : YOU ALL DIE)))
((text 6 (You sail south thinking about home : But your ship has run aground on a reef : You have to throw stuff
((text 14 (You sail for weeks : You are forced to turn back : but , you run up on a reef : you have to throw someth
((text 10 (You see a coast : You do do not land but sail on : You see the clashing rocks : Which way do you want to
((text 9 (You sail away from the reef (the clashing rocks) : You need food : You see land ahead : You land and get
((text 16 (You land : All your men go searching for food : The natives kill some of your men : : You run to your b
((text 15 (You find 5 people : You help them on board : You get 2 endurance pieces or 10 gold pieces : : You can c
((text 211 (She gets the keys off the guard and lets you all out : She gets you your weapons : You thank her : She c
((text 212 (If you want to you can tell them to sail to the green hill : and wait for our signal : : or : : You can tell t
((text 8 (You sail in a great circle : You sail north with the wind)))
((text 20 (You reach land at night : You are spotted by a guard : He sets the alarm going : All the men go to their
((text a (You wait)))
((text 8 89))
((text 12 (You have just thrown your weapons over-board : You drift off the reef : You need food : You have the
((text 13 (You have just thrown the food : over-board : You drift off the reef : You need food and water badly)))
((text 18 (You sail to an island : Your men get off on to the shore : arrows fly everywhere : : You run back to your
((text 161 (You look up at a spear : As it misses you pick it up : and then throw it : You feel a sharp pain in your
((text 17 (You sail on until you see : a rocky coast)))
((text 21 (You set off : : YOU FIND THE FLEECE : : But , you find it guarded : by a dragon with seven heads : Y
((text 22 (You men send two men to hide the ship : while the rest of you swim ashore : Then you split into twos :
((text 26 (A few of the king ' s men are still alive : They attack you and kill you : : THE END)))
((text 25 (Each person distracts a head : for you : You walk around to climb on it : and STAMP IT TO DEATH)))
((text 27 (The king's men close on your tail : You grab the fleece and carry on : leaving 2 dead men : : He (the king
((text 271 (The dead rise to fight you : They kill most of your men : You throw the dead into the sea : Where our
((text 272 (THE GOLDEN FLEECE TAKES YOU ALL HOME AGAIN : : You hear your dad Zeus calling you for
((text 24 (you die - text to be added - tough)))
((text 20 (YOu come at the night : You are spotted by a guard : he sets the alarm gong : All the men go to their bat
((text 23 (You turn to run : YOu run up a sand bank : You are stuck until high tide : You are now surrounded by t
((link egypt river))
((link river story))
((link story voyage))
((link 5 11))
((link 19 211))
((link 211 212))
((link 13 18))
((link 18 10))
((link 16 161))
((link 17 10))
((link 22 26))
((link 25 27))
((link 27 271))
((link 271 272))
```

Figure 14.3 *Bryan's program — first lines of text only.*

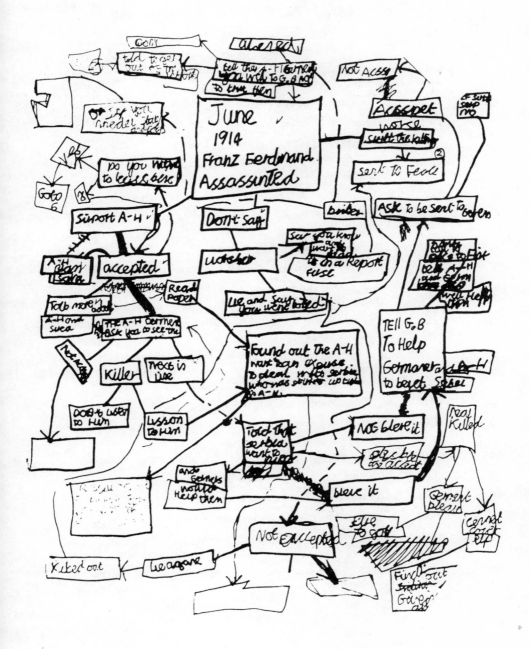

Figure 14.4 *Mark's plan.*

completed their assignments, one pair making a joint submission. Seventeen wrote programs using the shells, two used micro-PROLOG to write their own programs and one produced a specification for a new shell. Figure 14.5 shows the range of applications they developed.

Number	Shell	Subject/Program
1.	DETECT	Humanities. Egyptian Civilisation
2.	DETECT	English/Humanities. Murder — a detective exercise
3.	DETECT	English/Humanities. Robbery — a detective exercise
4.	LINX	Mathematics. The Use of PROLOG to Create a Tree Search For Mathematics — work with quadrilaterals
5.	LINX	Mathematics. A Diagnostic Mathematical Adventure Game
6.	LINX	Outdoor Education. Planning and embarking upon a canoe expedition
7.	LINX	Outdoor Education. Safety Rules
8.	LINX	Geography. Mapwork discovering about a village
9.	LINX	Geography. Outdoor Education. Mapwork, day expedition on Dartmoor
10.	LINX	Science — Homeopathy. Program for diagnosing homeopathic cures for headache
11.	LINX	Biology. A program which asks the pupil to pretend to be a piece of food in the body, and see what might happen to you as you go through the digestive process
12.	LINX	Biology. Plant propagation
13.	LINX + DETECT	Biology. Working on the body
14.	LINX	Chemistry. Analysis of metals (prototype expert system)
15.	LINX	General. Car fault diagnosis
16.	PLAN	Archaeology. Tutankhamun's tomb
17.	PLAN	Geography. Mapwork, choosing a route
18.	micro-PROLOG	Program for analysing family relationships
19.	NEW SHELL	Shell to help students choose Higher Education courses

Analysis By Subject

Number	Subject
1	Archaeology
1	Careers
3	Biology
1	Chemistry
2	English/Humanities
1	Genealogy
1	General (car maintenance)
3	Geography
1	Humanities
2	Mathematics
2	Outdoor Education
1	Science (Homeopathy)

Figure 14.5

Viking Trader

It is a spring day in AD 930. A Viking trading ship, a knorr, has landed at the mouth of your valley on the Isle of Man. Your valley is one day's sailing time away from the Viking port of Dublin, Ireland. Dublin is to the South-West. The knorr has brought with it certain supplies your farming families need. The trader buys hides and grain from you to exchange for the goods he sells. He is keen to build up trade with your community.

The trader can tell you many things about his trading. He can answer your questions about:

(a) What goods he can supply.
(b) Where these goods come from.
(c) How the goods can reach your valley from the places where they are grown, caught, made or traded.
(d) The directions in which he has to travel to get from one port to another.
(e) How long the journeys take between ports.
(f) How he travels — by ship or land.

The *computer* represents the memory of the Viking trader. To ask it questions, follow the instructions on pages 1-2.

Contents

Figure 14.6

COMPUTER INSTRUCTIONS
QUESTIONS YOU CAN ASK THE TRADER

The trader can answer questions about: What TRADE GOODS he can bring; the places he can go to get TRADE GOODS; the TIME it takes on journeys; the DIRECTIONS between places; whether the places are LINKED directly, and if so, whether by sea or land. Type in your *questions* exactly as shown below:

Simple questions about TRADE GOODS
What goods can the trader supply?   Type in:

which (x trade-goods includes x)

What kind of iron-goods   can he supply?
         copper-goods
         silver-goods
         glass-goods
         bone-goods
         furs-Russia
define type of goods — for example, type in:

define bone-goods

Where can he get a certin kind of good from? Type in:

which (x x supplied good)
eg **which (x x supplied pottery)**   good = name of good

What kind of goods can he get from a certain place? Type in:

which (x place-name trades x)
eg **which (x Dublin-Ireland trades x)**

Questions about TIME on a journey
How long does it take to go from one place to another?

- between two places **which (x (place-name1 place-name2) time x)**
  next to one another

- between two places **which((x y z X Y)(place-name1 x) time y**
  far apart **and (x z) time X and (z place-name2) time Y)**

- between four places **which ((x y z)(place-name1 place-name2)**
  (leave out last **time x and (place-name2 place-name3) time**
  section for three **y and (place-name3 place-name4) time z)**
  places)

and so on, up to as many unknowns as you want, using
(x y z X Y Z x1 y1 z1) where each x or y, etc is an unknown.

Questions about DIRECTIONS between places
What direction is one port from another, where directly linked?

which (x (place-name1 place-name2) direction x)

What direction is one port from another, where indirectly linked?

**which ((x y z) (place-name1 place-name2) direction x and
(place-name2 place-name3) direction y and (place-name3
place-name4) direction z)**

What direction is one port from another, where indirectly linked, and you do not know
the names of the ports in-between?

**which ((x y z X (place-name1 x) direction y and (x z)
direction X and (z place-name1) direction)**

Note: x and z are unknown place-names, y X Y unknown directions.

Questions about LINKS between places
Which places are linked by sea?

which((x y)(x y) linked-by sea)

Are two places linked by sea?

does ((place-name1 place-name2) linked by sea)

Which places are linked to place-name1 *directly?*

which (x place-name1 linked-to x) or
which (x x linked-to place-name1)

Complex questions about TRADE GOODS
What goods can the trader get from more than one place?

2 sets   **which ((x y) place-name1 trades x and place-name2**
of   **trades y)**
goods

3 sets   **which ((x y z) place-name1 trades x and place-name2**
of   **trades y and place-name3 trades z)**
goods

4 sets   **which ((x y z X) place-name1 trades x and place-name2**
of   **trades y and place-name3 trades z and place-name4**
goods   **trades x)**

eg   **which ((x y z) Dublin-Ireland trades x and**
        York-England trades y and Truso trades z)

Figure 14.6 *(cont)*

and so on, up to as many goods as you want.

Where can the trader get the goods in a list from?

2 places: **which((x y) x supplies good1 and y supplies good2)**

3 places: **which((x y z) x supplies good1 and y supplies good2 and z supplies good3)**

and so on, up to as many goods as you want, using (x y z X Y Z x1 y1 z1) where each x y z is an unknown place.

THINGS TO DO

(1)   On rough paper draw up a list of the things you would like from the trader. Then put into boxes those things he can sell you and the places they are from.

GOODS	PLACES	GOODS	PLACES

(2)   The trader talks about voyages to buy white-bears, silks and jewels and millstones. Work out how he could make these trips:

	ISLE	TO	TIME	DIREC-TION	SEA/LAND	TO	TIME	DIREC-TION	SEA/LAND
white-bears									
millstones									
silks & jewels									

(3)   How might Ottar the Viking trader have travelled to Alfred's court at London, and what might he have bought and sold at the ports on the way?

(4)   Tell the story of a Viking voyage to Vinland *or* Truso as if you were with the Viking trader. Mention:

ship/getting ready/goods/money/directions/weather/crew/sailing/
voyages/ports/business/people you meet, etc.

(5) Use what the trader tells you to draw your own map of the Viking world — see below.

THE VIKING WORLD

'____' One day's journey

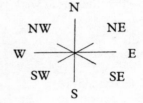

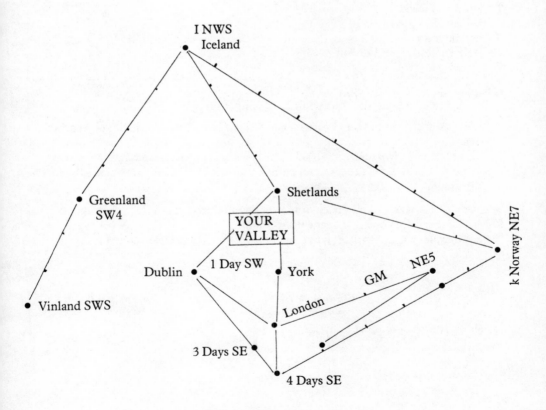

Figure 14.6 (*cont*)

MAINTOWN CASTLE — A COMPUTER SIMULATION

The computer can be an expert about the five possible sites. A user can question the expert before s/he makes a choice of site. The computer's expertise or knowledge will be what you tell it. How do you write the program?

For each site you have to tell the computer if that site is good, fair or bad on each of the points. You also want the computer to be able to tell the program user the reasons for the site being good, fair or bad on each point. So, when you put the program in, you will tell it to remember that reason.

How do we go about writing this program as a form?

The first thing is to work out a list of points on which to judge each site. Your list of reasons is:

1. Hill
2. Near water
3. Near road
4. Hidden
5. Blocks invasion
6. Near the town
7. Supply of wood
8. See enemy
9. Escape route
12. Help route — from London

Then you have to judge the site on each of the points. For each point you can say if it is good, fair or bad.

For example, judging site A on point 1, you might say:

Site A is a good hill site because it is a small steep hill on which you can build a castle.

Site A is not a fair site — it is a good site because it is on a steep hill.

Site A is not a poor site for a hill point because it is on a hill. Don't be silly, look at the map.

You would also want to tell the computer what to remember, so that when the user has finished s/he can see how it has made its decisions.

For example, you might want it to remember for the first decision on point 1:

Site A is a good site because it is on a steep hill.

Figure 14.7a *Maintown — possible routes of attack.*

The Defence of Maintown

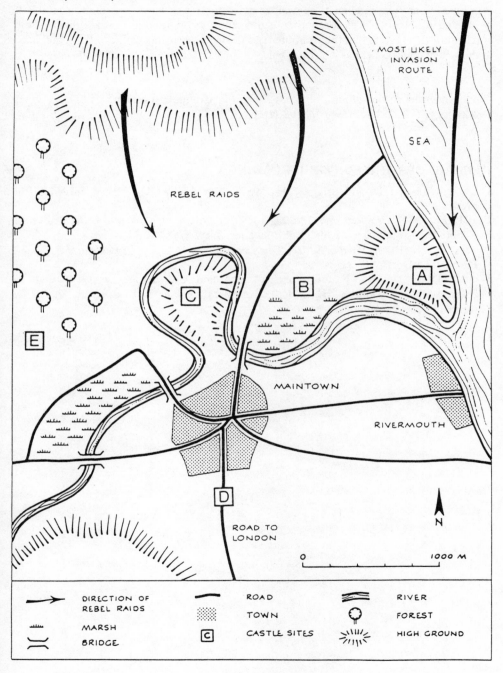

Figure 14.7b

CONCLUSION

Pupil use of powerful intelligent knowledge based tools to develop their understanding of issues and problems places computing at the centre as opposed to the periphery of the curriculum. It suggests that the computer as a device for learning can take the same place in the school environment as it already holds in the world of work.

[*Note: An earlier version of this chapter appears in* Programmed Learning and Educational Technology, *Vol.24, No.2 (1987) pp108-116.*]

REFERENCES AND FURTHER READING

Dean, J, Nichol, J D, and Briggs J H (1987), *Why Prolog?* The Open University, in press.
Pea, R D (1984), *Prospects and Challenges for using Microcomputer in schools*, Technical Report No.7, Bank Street College of Education, New York.
Vygotsky, L S (1978), *Mind in Society: The Development of Higher Psychological Processes*, Harvard University Press.
Winograd, T (1975), 'Frame representations and the declarative — procedural controversy', in Dobrow, D G (ed) *Representation and understanding: Studies in cognitive science*, Academic Press.

15. Peers, problem-solving and programming: projects and prospects

Christopher O Colbourn and Paul Light
Department of Psychology
University of Southampton
UK

INTRODUCTION

In recent years there has been a lively research interest in social processes involved in young children's use of microcomputers. Following a brief consideration of the factors precipitating this interest we shall describe some empirical studies designed to contribute to our understanding of such processes and also draw some conclusions about the educational use of microcomputers in the curriculum with specific reference to the use of the PROLOG programming language.

Within developmental psychology, one of the most conspicious contemporary trends has been the increase in interest in social aspects of children's development, and especially in the role of social processes in children's cognitive development (eg Hinde, Perret-Clermont and Stevenson-Hinde, 1985: Richards and Light, 1986). The facilitatory effects of both adult-child and child-child interaction have received attention but the influential work of Doise and colleagues in Geneva (eg Doise and Mugny, 1984; Perret-Clermont, 1980) has given particular impetus to the study of the role of child-child interaction in stimulating the development of logical thinking.

During the same period, the microcomputer has become relatively commonplace in the classroom, and the realization of its educational potential has come to be seen as an important issue (see Sage and Smith, 1983). Among the many facets of this issue, the social dimension has an important place. Whereas some years ago the potential of the computer in the classroom was discussed largely in terms of the *individualization* of the curriculum (see O'Shea and Self, 1983, for a review of such ideas), more recent proponents of microcomputer use in education have emphasized the computer's capacity to stimulate active *collaboration* and *discussion* between children (eg, Fletcher, 1985; Hawkins, 1983; Hoyles, Sutherland and Evans, 1986).

In practice not least because of resource limitations, young children's microcomputer use very frequently takes place in the context of collaborative groups (eg Jackson, Fletcher and Messer, 1986). Also, at primary and middle school level, it is not unusual for children in such groups to be undertaking microcomputer tasks unrelated to the other activities going on in the classroom at the time. This in itself opens up the possibility of conducting rather highly-structured experimental studies of learning in this context without at the same time departing too radically from the normal conditions of microcomputer use in the classroom.

Our own research interests in this area stem from a series of experimental studies of peer interaction as a factor in learning and problem-solving. In these studies, children, usually in the age range 8-12 years, were pre-tested individually on a task and then assigned at random to either an individual or a paired practice condition. About a week later they were post-tested individually. Using this experimental design we were able to establish that under some circumstances children's performance on certain problem-solving tasks was significantly better following paired co-operative practice than following individual practice. However, this was the case only for children who at the outset already showed some grasp of the appropriate strategy, and peer facilitation only occurred when steps were taken to prevent one or other of the children in the pair from wholly dominating the interaction. In this chapter we will very briefly sketch the directions of our current work using examples from rather different areas. Finally, we shall discuss some of the possibilities for future work on these topics from our own perspective.

PEER INTERACTION AND PROBLEM-SOLVING

The studies alluded to at the end of the previous section, on individual progress in problem-solving following paired versus individual practice, have been extended fairly directly into studies of microcomputer-based problem-solving activities.

The initial studies in this series used 'physical' versions of the classic 'Tower of Hanoi' problem (Glachan and Light, 1982), while later published studies included a microcomputer-based version of the 'Mastermind' code-breaking game (Light and Glachan, 1985). The results of the 'Mastermind' experiments showed that the degree of progress on the task shown by children depended on verbal interactions characterized by a substantially greater number of proposals and counter-arguments during the practice phase. More recent studies using microcomputer-based problem-solving tasks (of the 'set piece' type, including the 'Tower of Hanoi') have extended these findings to indicate that 'structured' interactive practice, where 'dual-key' control of the microcomputer by the pair of children was mandatory, was associated with better post-test performance. However, this effect only applied to the more capable children who were able to achieve optimal performance at post-test, and was limited to those trials used in the training sessions. There was no evidence of the children learning a general solution to the problem as proposed by Simon (1975), and this has potential implications for teaching problem-solving to which we shall return a little later. The result, that there was no general effect of peer interaction, but one dependent on enforced collaboration via software design, is of potential interest for educational computer applications in the classroom.

In a recent study (Light, Foot, Colbourn and McClelland, 1987) we picked up another aspect of the peer interaction effect — that of friendship in working groups versus an arbitrary allocation to groups. The importance of the first type of allocation for group and individual progress has been suggested by teachers. In a small-scale study we approached this issue empirically. Two classes of 11-year-olds were asked by teachers to nominate preferred working partners. This information, together with scores on a cognitive abilities test, were used as the basis for constructing four single-sex trios of 'self-selecting' children (ie, trios in which participants had included one another in their nominations) and four single-sex trios of 'arbitrarily allocated' children (ie trios whose members had not nominated one another).

During four 20-minute sessions held on successive days, the trios were introduced to the QUEST database software package (see, eg Freeman and Tagg, 1985), using a prepared geographical database. The groups were given worksheets with instructions and graded exercises, and a 'teacher' was on hand to provide support. It was emphasized that the trios should only key in *agreed* entries. The sessions were recorded on video-tape from which a qualitative analysis of the group interactions was carried out.

The 'self-selected' trios (who, their teacher confirmed, had considerable experience of working together previously) tended to show more positive and supportive patterns of interaction, and were somewhat less demanding of 'teacher' interventions than their 'arbitrarily allocated' counterparts. The arbitrary groups made significantly more careless minor errors (which nevertheless brought group-computer interaction to a halt) in keyboard entries which may well relate to their higher demand for 'teacher' interventions. Overall, the girls made greater use of the worksheets, made fewer substantive errors, and showed greater positive attitudes to collaborative microcomputer work than the boys. Such sex differences are interesting in the light of concern about gender stereotyping of school computer use (eg, Hawkins, 1984). We found rather similar sex differences in a study of peer interaction and micro-PROLOG use which is outlined below.

PEER INTERACTION, PROLOG AND LEARNING ENVIRONMENTS

While the studies discussed so far have been focused on aspects of logical problem-solving as an activity, and microcomputer *use* as a medium, we were not capitalizing on the argument that the microcomputer offers more than just a different medium for learning, it offers new and qualitatively different possibilities as a learning *environment*. There is a very long history of arguments for the educational benefits of experience with powerful symbolic systems such as Mathematics, Logic etc (see, for example, Bruner, 1966; Vygotsky, 1978). Those who have developed such arguments more recently (eg Papert, 1980; O'Shea and Self, 1983; Pea and Kurland, 1984; Ennals, 1984) have emphasized particular forms of computer programming rather than the kinds of tasks discussed above. The intellectual benefits claimed for programming (largely discussed in terms of increasing the children's reflective awareness of what they are doing) are not dissimilar from those claimed for peer interaction. On this basis we conducted an initial exploration of the interplay between peer interaction and the acquisition of elementary micro-PROLOG programming skills in a classroom setting (Colbourn and Light, 1987; Light, Colbourn and Smith, 1986, 1987).

This project involved regular weekly teaching sessions over a three-month period, where children worked through a range of materials, with teacher-support, designed to introduce them to the use of the SIMPLE front-end program to micro-PROLOG. The context of the work was essentially the first-year Humanities curriculum of a secondary school. Exercises ranged from building and searching small historical databases, 'solving' and writing mystery stories, to using and developing elementary 'expert systems'. Most of the materials were developed or adapted from other projects (eg Ennals, 1984; Nichol and Dean, 1984; de Saram, 1985) with valuable support from those involved. The key variable in the teaching sessions was the organization of the children into working groups, each of which consisted of eight children. In some of these groups the children worked one to a machine, in some two to a machine, and in some they worked four to a machine. Towards the end of the project a number of sessions were selectively recorded on video-tape and assessments made of social interaction patterns in the groups. We also explicitly assessed each individual child's knowledge of micro-PROLOG, and attitudes towards school computer use.

The results of most interest here concern the relation between progress in learning PROLOG and the organization of working groups. In a paper-and-pencil test of

PROLOG knowledge there were no reliable differences between children from different size groups. Overall, the level of knowledge was quite variable across both children and exercises. Particularly weak areas were the syntax and semantics of PROLOG sentences involving a molecular structure (ie atomic sentences linked by *and*) and/or SIMPLE *which* queries, especially those involving 'variables'. The children's knowledge was better on the basic language 'utilities', constructing atomic sentences, and the SIMPLE *is* query, with the caveat that use of variables and molecular sentences caused problems even in these contexts. However, a more intriguing finding came from a re-test of a proportion of the children using a microcomputer-presented version of some of the test exercises. This allowed us to assess the children in their working groups. Children working in the 'individual' condition produced similar performances on both tests, but those children working in 'pairs' and 'fours' showed a significantly better second test performance. On the basis of an analysis of interaction patterns and discourse from video-tapes of the second test sessions, we do not believe that this finding was merely due to the superior performance of one group member, but due to a genuine exchange of ideas and resolution of arguments within the groups.

Apart from the last result mentioned above, it seemed clear that the peer facilitation effect, characteristic of our earlier 'controlled' studies, was not manifest in this 'classroom' study. However, analysis of the video-taped teaching sessions showed that although the children in the 'individual' condition each had their own microcomputer to work with, they interacted fairly freely with other children in the class who were engaged in the same types of activities. From this point of view we might conclude that it was peer interaction rather than microcomputer provision which was important in this study.

PROLOG PROGRAMMING AS A FOCUS FOR EDUCATIONAL COMPUTER USE

Other aims of our study of micro-PROLOG in the classroom included an examination of the usefulness of the programming language for educational use, and any influence its acquisition might have on more general problem-solving abilities along the lines of the argument outlined at the beginning of the previous section. For reasons that are not uncommon in applied research, we made little progress in fulfilling these aims. As testified to by many reports in the recent issue of *Pegboard* (Spring 1986), the development of such teaching programmes requires considerable involvement by the school teaching staff and/or full-time researchers over a reasonably long time period. Nevertheless, we should like to make two points here concerned with PROLOG usage by children (and adults for that matter).

The PROLOG implementation
The first point is concerned with the implementation of the language used. As is the case in many projects and schools, limited resources forced us to utilize a small-microcomputer version of the language (ie Sinclair Spectrum PROLOG). Such implementations necessarily have relatively primitive 'support' facilities and error messages are, to say the least, cryptic. Although there are user facilities to expand these messages, this tends to be at the expense of space for programs and data. Such problems are not, of course, unique to PROLOG on small microcomputers. It was clear that the above features of the PROLOG implementation used by us caused a very large number of requests for teacher intervention. Interestingly enough it was the girls who spent significantly more time

consulting the teaching materials and keeping notes on their work than the boys, so solving some of their difficulties. However, all the children had considerable problems with editing and debugging their 'programmes'. This is often seen as inevitable, and one answer is to provide powerful programming environments with lots of user support including automatic or semi-automatic program debuggers (eg Hasemer, 1984). Such solutions currently require substantial hardware, but even improved language design (eg Green, 1980; Coker, 1984) and 'direct manipulation' types of programming environments (eg diSessa, 1986; Hutchins, Hollan and Norman, 1986) seem likely to improve matters considerably. Already microcomputer-based PROLOG programming environments with a number of these features have appeared, although predictably they demand more sophisticated hardware than many schools currently own. However, the experience of one of us (CJC) in teaching symbolic programming (using LISP, SOLO, and PROLOG in a variety of primitive and relatively sophisticated programming environments) to university students for the purposes of cognitive modelling exercises, leads us to conclude that such interfaces are likely to have a beneficial impact on novice programmers (and, probably, on nearly all novice users).

The topic of programming environments can also be addressed via the nature of the PROLOG programming involved. A number of research groups in this area have adopted a 'toolkit' approach (eg Briggs, Dean and Nichol, 1985; and the Leicester-based SPIRAL project). This involves the development of specific-purpose PROLOG front-ends which allow children to represent particular forms of knowledge within a subject domain while providing a gentle introduction to aspects of logic programming. However, Cumming (1986; see also Chapter 18 in this book) has argued in favour of more limited front-end programs (ie in the sense of retaining the essence of PROLOG, like SIMPLE and MITSI) that are easily tailored to children's mental models of the task in which they are engaged. Our own interests have favoured the latter approach for reasons we shall outline in the final section of this paper. To conclude this section we shall briefly raise the matter of logical problem-solving behaviour with and without 'symbolic' programming facilities.

Logical problem-solving behaviour

Psychologists have made an extensive study of human reasoning and have reached the general conclusion that we are not particularly good at solving logical problems for much of the time (eg Evans, 1982). However, more recent empirical research has pointed to several factors which seem to enhance performance on propositional reasoning tasks, such as a thematic content to a problem (eg Wason, 1983), use of an *availability* heuristic (ie judgements made on the basis of information retrieved from memory; see eg Pollard, 1982), and presence of a *pragmatic reasoning schema* (eg Cheng and Holyoak, 1985). Such findings have been taken to refute the view that people typically reason in accord with formal logic, and support the notion that domain-specific knowledge and sets of generalised context-sensitive rules (pragmatic schemas) are utilized in reasoning (eg Johnson-Laird, 1983; Cheng and Holyoak, 1985).

Much of this research has focused on adult subjects, and studies of conditional reasoning in children have largely been in the Piagetian tradition of the development of formal reasoning abilities. However, this was challenged in a penetrating analysis of the reasoning tasks used (Donaldson, 1978), and the emphasis shifted to explanations in terms of domain-specific knowledge. In view of Cheng and Holyoak's (1985) evidence for the use of more generalized knowledge structures in reasoning, we very recently examined this notion in 10-year-old children. Using a type of selection task (eg Wason and Green, 1984) expressed as a 'tricking' game and concerned with a story about buzzing and non-buzzing bees in a hive, we found that a significantly greater number of the children could solve the Modus Tollens problem (ie *not q* → *not p*) when it was presented as an 'authorization' schema (ie a rule about which bees should be inside the hive at a particular time for a particular reason), than when it was presented as a formal rule about a state of affairs (ie a rule about where particular bees were). Considering that the problem context was fabricated, it is unlikely that the children were familiar with it, and therefore we suggest that they were using a generalized reasoning schema concerned with authorization, the general principles of which were familiar to them from everyday life.

The relevance of these findings to children's use of PROLOG for problem-solving and reasoning tasks should now be clear. It is also worth noting Kahney's (1983) observations that some novice programmers, using the database-manipulation programming language SOLO, often encountered a mismatch between their 'real-world' knowledge of the problem domain and their programming knowledge, to the detriment of problem solution. They sometimes initially adapted an inappropriate mental model of the program solution required for a particular 'real-world' problem they had been set.

Thus the notion of 'logic as a programming language for children' (eg Ennals, 1984; Kowalski, 1984) needs to be viewed from the perspective of appropriate problem contexts so that we can capitalize on, and further develop, pragmatic reasoning schemas in pupils. This leads us to our final section on a possible context for further work in the application of PROLOG programming in education.

PROSPECTS

We have reported a variety of studies in the chapter which we believe are relevant to the concerns of researchers and educationalists active in the area of PROLOG and microcomputer use in education. They have all involved a fundamentally *experimental* approach, which is characterized by the systematic manipulation of variables thought to be of interest. This approach does place many limitations on the researcher and has never really established its value in the field of educational research. However, it seemed to us that the relatively segregated nature of much contemporary microcomputer use in schools provided a valuable vehicle for effective applied experimental studies of children's problem-solving behaviour and learning. Such studies are still badly needed (eg Sage and Smith, 1983), although we appreciate that the educational prospects for PROLOG use need to be considered in a wider sense.

As mentioned earlier, one of us has been involved in teaching PROLOG (and other languages) in the context of cognitive modelling projects in several university-level courses on cognitive psychology. The introduction of elementary artificial intelligence (A1) tools and techniques to psychology students has been observed to be beneficial to their appreciation of theoretical issues. Although much work on suitable programming environments for such teaching has been done (eg Hasemer, 1984; Kahney, 1983), no reports of the success of this enterprise, in terms of psychological appreciation, have come to our attention. Colbourn (1984) offered a brief justification for teaching aspects of AI programming to psychology students, and Kareev and Avrahami (1985) made a preliminary report of a similar type of course for 14 — 15-year-old school children. It has also been suggested that even younger children, say 11-year-olds, as used in our earlier PROLOG study, would both cope with and be highly motivated by a course looking at 'how their minds work' using PROLOG programming exercises (C Solomon, personal communication). We found earlier, much to our surprise, that the children used in our earlier project were highly motivated by PROLOG 'programming' despite their main previous computer experience being of games involving dynamic colour graphics. Thus we are prepared to believe that 'building minds' in PROLOG would also be motivating. The choice of PROLOG as the medium for this exercise can be justified primarily on the grounds of its combined declarative and procedural semantics which have already made it an important programming language for AI researchers and cognitive psychologists alike. Such a course for children needs very careful design to avoid giving the wrong impression of both AI and our knowledge of the underpinnings of human cognitive psychology, although it would appear to us to be a very promising prospect.

REFERENCES AND FURTHER READING

Briggs, J, Dean, J, and Nichol, J (1985), 'Toolkits for naive users'. *Proceedings of the 2nd International Conference on Artificial Intelligence and Education*, University of Exeter, 2-3 September 1985.

Bruner, J S (1966), 'On cognitive growth', In J S Bruner, R R Olver, and P M Greenfield (eds). *Studies in Cognitive Growth*, New York: Wiley.

Cheng, P W, and Holyoak, K J (1985), 'Pragmatic reasoning schemas', *Cognitive Psychology*, **17**, 391-416.

Coker, M (1984), 'Creating a "good" programming language for beginners', in M Yazdani (ed), *New Horizons in Educational Computing*, Chichester: Ellis Horwood.

Colbourn, C J (1984), 'Moulding minds with modern machines,' *Educational and Child Psychology*, **1** (2 & 3), 40-46.

Colbourn, C J and Light, P H, (1987), 'Social interaction and learning using micro-PROLOG', *Journal of Computer Assisted Learning*, **3**. In press.

Cumming, G (1986), 'Logic programming and education: Designing PROLOG to fit children's minds', *Pegboard*, **1/1** (Spring), 34-46.

de Saram, H (1985), *Programming in micro-PROLOG*, Chichester: Ellis Horwood.

diSessa, A A (1986), 'Notes on the future of programming: Breaking the utility barrier,' in D A Norman and S W Draper (eds), *User Centred System Design: New Perspectives on Human-Computer Interaction*, Hillsdale, N J: Lawrence Erlbaum.

Doise, W, and Mugny, G (1984), *The Social Development of the Intellect*, Oxford: Pergamon.

Donaldson, M (1978), *Children's Minds*, Glasgow: Fontana/Collins.

Ennals, J R (1984), *Beginning micro-PROLOG* (2nd Edition), Chichester: Ellis Horwood.

Evans, J St B T (1982), *The Psychology of Deductive Reasoning*, London: Routledge & Kegan Paul.

Fletcher, B (1985), 'Group and individual learning of junior school children on a microcomputer-based task: Social or cognitive facilitation?', *Educational Review*, **37**, 251-261.

Freeman, D, and Tagg W (1985), 'Databases in the classroom', *Journal of Computer Assisted Learning*, **1**, 2-11.

Glachan, M, and Light, P H (1982), 'Peer interaction and learning: Can two wrongs make a right?', in G E Butterworth and P H Light (eds), *Social Cognition: Studies in the Development of Understanding*, Brighton: Harvester Press.

Green, T R G (1980), 'Programming as a cognitive activity', in H T Smith and T R G Green (eds), *Human Interaction with Computers*, London: Academic Press.

Hasemer, T (1984), 'A very friendly software environment for SOLO', in M Yazdani (ed), *New Horizons in Educational Computing*, Cnichester: Ellis Horwood.

Hawkins, J (1983), *Learning LOGO Together: The Social Context*, Technical Report No 13, Bank St, College of Education, New York.

Hawkins, J (1984), *Computers and Girls: Re-thinking the Issues*, Technical Report No 24, Bank St College of Education, New York.

Hinde, R, Perret-Clermont, A-N, and Stevenson-Hinde, J (1985), *Social Relationships and Cognitive Development*, Oxford: Clarendon Press.

Hoyles, C, Sutherland, R, and Evans, J (1986), 'Using LOGO in the mathematics classroom', *Computing and Education*, **10**, 61-72.

Hutchins, E L, Hollan, J D, and Norman, D A (1986), 'Direct manipulation interfaces', in D A Norman and S W Draper (eds), *User Centred System Design: New Perspectives on Human-Computer Interaction*, Hillsdale, N J: Lawrence Erlbaum.

Jackson, A, Fletcher, B, and Messer, D (1986), 'A survey of microcomputer use and provision in primary schools', *Journal of Computer Assisted Learning*, **2**, 45-55.

Johnson-Laird, P N (1983), *Mental Models: Towards a Cognitive Science of Language, Inference, and Consciousness*, Cambridge University Press.

Kahney, H (1983), 'Problem solving by novice programmers', in T R G Green, S J Payne and G C van der Veer (eds), *The Psychology of Computer Use*, London: Academic Press.

Kareev, Y, and Avrahami, J (1985), 'Teaching children AI,' *Proceedings of the 2nd International Conference on Artificial Intelligence and Education*, University of Exeter, 2-3 September 1985.

Kowalski, R (1984), 'Logic as a computer language for children', In M Yazdani (ed), *New Horizons in Educational Computing*, Chichester: Ellis Horwood.

Light, P H, Colbourn, C J and Smith, D J, (1986), 'Peer interaction and logic programming: A study of the acquisition of micro-PROLOG', *Pegboard*, **1/1** (Spring), 100-105.

Light, P H, Colbourn, C J, and Smith, D J (1987), 'Peer interaction and logic programming: A study of the acquisition of micro-PROLOG', *Economic and Social Research Council, Information Technology and Education Programme, Occasional Paper*, ITE/17/87.

Light, P H, Foot T, Colbourn, C J, and McClelland, I (1987), 'Collaborative interactions at the microcomputer keyboard', *Educational Psychology*, **7**, 13-21.

Light, P H, and Glachan, M (1985), 'Facilitation of individual problem-solving through peer interaction', *Educational Psychology*, **5**, 217-255.

Nichol, J, and Dean, J (1984), 'Pupils, computers and history teaching', in M Yazdani (ed), *New Horizons in Educational Computing*, Chichester: Ellis Horwood.

O'Shea, T, and Self, J (1983), *Learning and Teaching with Computing: Artificial Intelligence in Education*, Brighton: Harvester Press.

Papert, S (1980), *Mindstorms: Children, Computers, and Powerful Ideas*, Brighton: Harvester Press.

Pea, R D, and Kurland, D M (1984), 'On the cognitive effects of learning computer programming', *New Ideas Psychology*, **2**, 137-68.

Perret-Clermont, A-N (1980), *Social Interaction and Cognitive Development in Children*, London: Academic Press.

Pollard, P (1982), 'Human reasoning: Some possible effects of availability', *Cognition*, **12**, 65-96.

Richards, M P M, and Light, P H (Eds) (1986), *Children of Social Worlds*, Cambridge: Polity Press.

Sage, M, and Smith, D J (1983), *Microcomputers in Education: A Framework for Research*, London: Social Science Research Council.

Simon, H A (1975), 'The functional equivalence of problem-solving skills', *Cognitive Psychology*, **7**, 268-288.

Vygotsky, L S (1978), *Mind in Society*, Cambridge, M A. Harvard University Press.

Wason, P C (1983), 'Realism and rationality in the selection task,' in J St. B.T Evans (ed), *Thinking and Reasoning: Psychological Approaches*, London: Routledge & Kegan Paul.

Wason, P C, and Green, D W (1984), 'Reasoning and mental representation', *Quarterly Journal of Experimental Psychology*, **23**, 63-71.

16. Making front-ends friendly: designing PROLOG to fit children's minds

Geoff Cumming and Elizabeth Abbott
Department of Psychology
La Trobe University
Bundoora
Victoria, Australia 3083

INTRODUCTION

In educational computing, we can think of the computer as the medium we use to support learning activities. We want children to be able to give maximum attention to the curriculum materials and educational activities, with minimum distraction by the system. So the computer system must be user-friendly, consistent, predictable, easy-to-use. A promising way to approach these design goals is to think in terms of the user's mental model of that system.

In this chapter we consider mental models and how they may contribute to system design, then give an account of our search for a front-end for micro-PROLOG that makes it as easy as possible for children to use.

MENTAL MODELS

Psychologists are beginning to study the mental models people have of devices or processes they use. Norman (1982) is an excellent and simple introduction; see also Gentner and Stevens (1983). Results to date suggest several conclusions:

1. Learners can differ greatly in their mental models of some device or system, despite all having had similar experience and all being basically competent users.
2. Learners often develop impoverished or incorrect models, especially if learning has been unstructured or haphazard.
3. An incorrect model may serve a learner reasonably at first with troubles only emerging later when more complex aspects of the system are encountered. So reasonable performance now may disguise inappropriate conceptualization, and problems emerging later may have their roots in a poor mental model acquired early on.
4. Learners can be encouraged to form and use a good mental model from the start. The design of both the system and the learning activities can contribute to this.

With a good mental model the user's guesses about system behaviour should be more often correct, memory for commands and formats should be better, learning should be faster, errors fewer and understanding of what is going on should be better. In general the user should have more capacity to devote to the task of real interest, since less is required to cope with the medium or tool being used to carry out that task.

This last point is likely to be especially important for less able children: with a less than excellent system they are likely to have a larger proportion of their attention and capacity diverted by foibles of the system than are more capable children. So a concern for effective educational computing across the full ability range makes good system design even more vital.

Edinburgh LOGO

The development of Edinburgh LOGO is an example of the use of mental model ideas. The designers of this LOGO were very concerned that the children using the language should be encouraged to form a clear conceptualization of how the whole system — machine, language, and user interfaces — works (du Boulay and O'Shea, 1978). All aspects of the system should fit the child's model as consistently as possible: the hardware, the instruction manual, the teaching materials, the very words chosen as primitives in the language.

Following this philosophy the Edinburgh workers carefully chose the names to use in the language, aiming to make the everyday meaning of the words as consistent as possible with what they referred to in the model. So they chose *change* rather than *edit*, and *multiply* rather than *product*, in each case preferring a familiar term that described closely the operation to be carried out. They give examples of confusions produced by some of their early, less than ideal, choices of names: children often used *remember* in the sense of 'bring to mind' rather than 'memorize' as intended. And *show* was often used by children as if it might display what a procedure draws when executed, when in fact it caused the listing of the procedure definition.

PROLOG FOR CHILDREN

Turning to our main interest here, the development of a good front-end for children using PROLOG, we start with core micro-PROLOG, then consider front-ends intended to make logic programming more accessible, especially for children.

Micro-PROLOG

Micro-PROLOG, from Logic Programming Associates, has a LISP-style syntax relying on multiple parentheses. Programs consist of data statements such as:

((likes Jose eating))

and rules such as:

((makes X cakes)(has X recipe)(likes X eating))

An example query is:

?((makes Jose cakes))

which will result in the prompt **&** for success and **?** for failure

SIMPLE

The designers of micro-PROLOG developed SIMPLE as a friendly front-end to micro-PROLOG. The SIMPLE syntax is used by Ennals (1983) and in several other books, and by most applications in schools so far. SIMPLE offers a much more friendly syntax while still supporting virtually all the facilities of micro-PROLOG.

Rules now look much more like English, the example above becoming:

**add (X makes cakes if X has recipe and
X likes eating)**

Data is held in the more natural infix form:

Jose likes eating

or in the equivalent prefix form:

likes (Jose eating)

or, more generally:

student (Susan 23 psychology hang-gliding).

Queries are of the form:

is (Jose makes cakes)

giving a reply of **yes** or **no** as appropriate, or:

which(x: x makes cakes)

or equivalently:

which(x: makes (x cakes))

possibly giving the reply **Jose** in either case.

SIMPLE uses **X,Y,Z,x,y,z,X1,Y1,** etc, as variable names. New sentences can be added to the program:

add (Angela likes drinking)

Using SIMPLE with children

In our first pilot tests we used SIMPLE with three classes of grade 6 children (11- and 12-year-olds). Accounts of this work are given by Cumming and Richardson (1984) and Cumming (1985). The work was generally successful, but there were very large individual differences among the children. It took only a few isolated instances of noticing a child confuse whether, for example, 'add' or 'which' was needed, for us to realise that at least some children had very poorly-formed, or inappropriate mental models. Our teaching strategies and materials needed improvement, but part of our difficulty seemed to be caused by some of the characteristics of SIMPLE syntax. We now report some observations arising from our experience with this syntax.

The fairly close match to English seemed to be of benefit; children appreciated this while also coping with the need to keep relation and object names precisely consistent, even in violation of English syntax.

The use of **X, Y, Z**, and so on for variables was generally well-accepted. In fact it was surprising that the children, who had had no exposure to algebra, took so easily to the idea that a letter symbol meant 'something' and that the same symbol appearing again on the same line meant the same something. Our observation may be contrasted with Ennals's report that 'for many [of his middle school pupils beginning to learn PROLOG] the concept of variables was difficult, but the variable convention was the same as the one to which they were being introduced in their mathematics classes' (Ennals, 1984. p3). Neither his nor our impression is supported by data, but the relation between understanding of variables in computing and in mathematics may warrant study. We found that re-use of the same variable symbol on a different line for a different purpose was not a problem, but it was a problem that when a program — or a single line — is listed, the variable symbols shown in rule definitions are not in general the same as those used when the rule was typed in.

A second difficulty arose from the non-specificity of the available symbols. For example, in our library program, **X overdue Y** gives no immediate clue that **X** is a borrower's name and **Y** a book title. It is true that merely having helpful variable names would not prevent PROLOG from instantiating **X** with any object name giving a match — no type-checking is being proposed — but mnemonic variable names would be a help.

The SIMILE syntax for queries allows the use of an answer template. So asking:

which (X is a terrific person: X likes PROLOG)

might give as output:

Mary is a terrific person.

This is a powerful facility, allowing the design of interactions having something of a conversational feel, but the potential for confusion between the first part of the query, which is text, and the second part, which is PROLOG, led us not to use it with the children. So queries became:

which (X : X likes PROLOG)

and the first variable symbol (the vestigial answer template) seemed arbitrary and unnecessary and did cause confusion.

The format for adding to the program requires an extra set of parentheses, and we would like to economize on keystrokes — especially those requiring use of the shift key — where doing so would simplify the child's task. Many children persisted in expecting sentences to be added to the program if they were simply typed on a new line, so lines frequently had to be retyped in order to insert **add** and brackets.

SIMPLE supports the **accept** command to save typing time when many statements about the one relation are to be added to the program. But the statements appear on the screen in what was for us the non-standard prefix format, which was found highly confusing. We used this command, but should have avoided it.

The version 3.1 update of SIMPLE, while having some good points, allowed prefix and infix confusion to flourish. It attempted to give the user maximum choice and then itself to use whichever format the user seemed to prefer. In practice it often gave oddly confused mixtures of infix and prefix. Even if a user adopted one format consistently, the fact that another format was acceptable meant that error messages could not be as tight and helpful as would be ideal. While freedom of choice might be appreciated by experienced adults, for children — and perhaps for any learners — it is preferable to have a single, well-chosen, consistent way of doing things, with immediate helpful prompting the moment the user strays from this correct and narrow path. More generally, error messages need to be fuller and more specific than those provided by SIMPLE.

We considered the line editor too awkward for use with the children. So in the case of error the child had to delete the full, unwanted statement and then add the correct version. The children were concurrently learning to use a simple text processing program, and when working at PROLOG they sorely missed the basic cursor movement and screen editing facilities they were becoming familiar with as part of their creative writing work.

We considered the trace facility also to be too awkward for child use; the screen layout of the output seemed especially confusing.

The section above should not be construed as any sort of attack, but rather as a report of our experience and some suggestions about the needs of child learners. Micro-PROLOG and SIMPLE represent, in fact, an early and generally very successful attempt to squeeze a great deal into a 64K 8-bit machine.

MITSI

Given our worries about SIMPLE, we were delighted when MITSI appeared (Briggs, 1984). MITSI was designed as a simpler-than-SIMPLE beginner's front-end. It answers many of the concerns we had with SIMPLE, but is quite limited by comparison with SIMPLE since it was conceived as an easy way into SIMPLE rather than as a replacement for it.

MITSI uses only infix format and all relations are binary, ie, take two objects. Few parentheses are needed. A statement is added to the database by simply typing it, followed by a full stop. Commands are followed by !. A query is posed by typing the sentence, followed by ?. For variables, MITSI uses any name starting with **some** or **any**, so **somebody**, **anyx**, and **somebook** are all acceptable variable names. MITSI retains the exact variable name originally typed in and so this name is shown when a rule, or the whole program, is listed.

The limitation to binary relations only is not a serious restriction: if in SIMPLE we had **male(Carl)**, in MITSI we can easily write **Carl is-a male**, thus replacing a unary relation with a binary one.

MITSI does not give us an improved editor, but it does give an excellent if limited explanation facility: type **why?** after a query has been answered and see an explanation of the final step of inference before the answer was found. For example, we could add to our MITSI program the same information given earlier:

Jose has recipe
Jose likes eating.
someone makes cakes if someone has recipe and
someone likes eating.

If we then asked:

someperson makes cakes?

the reply would be:

YES Jose makes cakes

and if we followed up with **why**? we would get:

Jose makes cakes because
**   Jose has recipe and**
**   Jose likes eating.**

We could press the explanation further back up the inference chain, but to do so we have to type again the sentence of interest. For example we could ask:

Why Jose has recipe?

and get earlier sentences if this sentence was deduced using a rule. In the present case we would get the bland statement:

Jose has recipe is stated

because this fact appears itself in the program.

Using MITSI with children
In 1985 we used MITSI with grade 5 and grade 6 children (10- 11- and 12-year-olds). It was very well accepted by both children and teachers and was considered a marked improvement over SIMPLE by those who had also participated in the first pilot tests. We interpreted the advantages of MITSI in terms of a simpler, more consistent user model. We felt so positive about MITSI that we did not want to use it merely as a stepping stone to SIMPLE. Instead, when we wanted to use features of SIMPLE not supported by MITSI, we started making extensions to MITSI. Our fuller front-end, EMITSI, now offers nearly all the facilities of SIMPLE and two additional very valuable features.

Enhanced MITSI
The first reason to enhance MITSI was to promote better child understanding of what was going on by improving the error messages. Our detailed observation identified errors for which the messages were not helpful. For example, if a child made a query without having loaded the program the error message stated only that there are no sentences about the relation being queried. Our revised message adds the hint to check that the correct program has been loaded. Several of the messages have been made more detailed in this way, suggesting extra things the child should check as possible causes of the problem.

In some cases we have trapped error conditions at an earlier stage and so have been able to make the error messages more specific to the particular error occurring, and thus more helpful to the child. For example, in original MITSI a variety of errors received this one error message:

error ... not a MITSI question

despite having quite different causes. We could isolate three such errors and give more specific messages:

1. incorrect punctuation: **list is-in?**
   error message: **error ... use ! not ? for commands**
2. incorrect understanding of the role of rules in querying:
   something is-in brass-band if something made-of brass?
   error message: error ... you cant have ... if ... in a question
3. incorrect format: **something is in brass-band?**
   error-message: **error... not an EMITSI question — check for object relation object patterns**

Our experience is that introduction of improved error messages can have an immediate and marked effect on the children's ability to recover from problems by themselves.

The second reason for enhancing MITSI was simply to add extra features. Some were equivalents of useful features supported by SIMPLE, for example the ability within a program to add or delete sentences, to kill a relation, and to read from the keyboard and print to the screen. The valuable **is-told** feature of SIMPLE was also taken over to EMITSI ('enhanced' MITSI). These facilities allow the development of programs that can engage the user in dialogue, and then modify the database to incorporate information given by the user in response to questions posed by the program.

'Exploring' a program is often advocated as a useful PROLOG activity. The practical problem of how to start is too often solved by listing the program, or parts of it, to find out something about object and relation names appearing in the program. Having to scan a listing suggests a computer may hardly be required at all, and is in any case impractical if the program is large. Our solution to this problem is to implement a command we call **seek**. When **seek** is used with a name, EMITSI states whether the name is of an object or a relation. If the former, it gives all the relations that appear in statements with that object; if the name is of a relation it gives an example statement from the program that includes the relation. Knowing only a single name appearing in the program it is possible in most cases to use a combination of **seek**ing and querying to explore a program fully.

The other major extension we have implemented is to make **why?** able to track back up through a tree of inferences an arbitrary number of levels. The first response to **why?** is as illustrated above for standard MITSI. If **why?** is asked again the user is invited to nominate one of the sentences appearing after **because** for further explanation. If the user does so, the inference is tracked back one more step and again the user can choose any sentence that has been given in an explanation — at any level — and not so far followed up, and nominate it for further analysis.

As an example, suppose we were using a modified and extended version of the program about Jose. We first ask:

someone makes cakes?

and receive the answer:

YES Jose makes cakes

If we then keep asking **why?** and entering selected numbers when requested, the interaction might start as follows:

> **why?**
> **Jose makes cakes because**
> **   Jose has necessaries and**
> **   Jose likes eating**
> **why?**
> **I can explain why**
> **1. Jose likes eating**
> **2. Jose has necessaries**
> ** type the number you want explained**
> **2**
> **Jose has necessaries because**
> **   cupboard contains supplies and**
> **   Jose has recipe**
> **why?**
> **I can explain why**
> **1. Jose has recipe**
> **2. cupboard contains supplies**
> **3. Jose likes eating**
> ** type the number you want explained**

Further questioning would reveal any rules used to arrive at the numbered statements, and eventually lead back to facts stated in the program. These facts may be described as **is stated**, as in the earlier example, if they were added in the normal way when the program was written. If, however, a fact was acquired by the program as the answer given by the user to a question asked by the program its status is indicated by **was told by user**.

Our work so far with these facilities, with our primary children and with undergraduates, suggests that EMITSI is both very powerful and easy to use. Some of our programs can be regarded as toy expert systems (Cumming and Abbott, 1986).

Space is of course a problem. If we include all the facilities mentioned there is only a little of 64K remaining for program and workspace. With EMITSI, as with SIMPLE, the best strategy is to leave out facilities not needed for some specific activity, meanwhile itching for the not-too-far-away demise of the 64K barrier.

The problem of editing remains. We would like a full screen editor similar to that familiar to the children through their use of word-processing programs, but this seems impossible to achieve within 64K.

MacPROLOG

The excellent interface offered by the Macintosh should be an ideal environment for development of a PROLOG system supporting a good user mental model. Our brief experience with MacPROLOG suggests that, while the basic facilities of mouse and windows are as attractive as ever, further work is required to exploit Macintosh features in the service of PROLOG. A trace and explain facility making good use of graphics — perhaps showing tree-like diagrams — would be valuable.

CONCLUSION

All of us cope — more or less — despite working with systems that have certain irrational, inconsistent and ambiguous features. Why should learners be cocooned? Why should we agonise about the odd bracket or naming detail? Is the design of the front-end really so important? We contend that it is, and especially so for children of lower ability.

It is true that whatever front-end we use the big problems of curriculum design remain: how best should knowledge be organised for expression in a PROLOG program? How should querying be conducted to tap this information? Nonetheless, our general conclusion is that we should have sufficient respect for the children who will use our systems and materials to take the trouble to get the small things right; they will then have as good a chance as possible to grapple successfully with the big things.

[*This work was made possible by the generous co-operation of the Principal, staff and children of St Clare's Primary School, Thomastown West, Victoria. The work was supported under the Australian Research Grants Scheme. An earlier version of this chapter appeared in* Australian Educational Computing.]

REFERENCES AND FURTHER READING

Briggs, J (1984), *micro-PROLOG Rules!* London: Logic Programming Associates.
Cumming, G (1985), *Logic programming and education: Designing PROLOG to fit children's minds*, Paper presented at the First Pan-Pacific Computer Conference, Melbourne, September 1985.
Cumming, G, and Abbott, E (1986) 'Exploiting expert systems in education,' in Salvas, A D, and Dowling, C (eds) *Computers in Education: On the Crest of a Wave?*, Melbourne, Computer Education Group of Victoria. (Proceedings of the Fourth Australian Computer Education Conference) pp129-134.
Cumming, G, and Richardson, J (1984), 'LOGIC PROGRAMMING: PROLOG and education,' in Salvas, A D (ed) *Computing and education — 1984 and beyond* Melbourne: Computer Education Group of Victoria (Proceedings of the Sixth Annual Conference of the CEGV, La Trobe University, May 1984) pp113-125.
du Boulay, B, and O'Shea, T (1978), *Seeing the works: A strategy for teaching interactive programming*, Working paper No. 28, Department of Artificial Intelligence, University of Edinburgh.
Ennals, J R (4983), *Beginning micro-PROLOG*, Chichester: Ellis Horwood.
Ennals, J R (1984), *Context and Customs: The Beginnings of PROLOG Cultures*, Paper presented to the Conference of the British Psychological Society.
Gentner, D, and Stevens, A L (1983), *Mental Models*, Hillsdale, N J: Erlbaum.
Norman, D A (1982), *Learning and Memory*, San Francisco: Freeman.

17. Models, micro-worlds and minds

Jon Nichol
PROLOG Education Group
School of Education
University of Exeter
Exeter EX1 2LU
UK

In the Humanities ideas of using models in education have been in circulation for well over twenty years (McLeish, 1970). They played an influential role in the development of 'New Geography' teaching in the late 1960s, and specifically underpinned the gaming and simulation movement (Chorley and Haggett 1967; Walford, 1969). Ideas of modelling were also seminal to developments within History teaching in the early 1970s, generically called the 'New History'. The 'New History' took the view that History was a problem-solving discipline based upon the processing of historical evidence, as opposed to seeing historical learning as the assimilation of a body of predetermined facts and ideas (Schools Council, 1976).

Modelling in this context tended to be disguised, in deference to the anti-positivistic stance of the majority of non-Marxist historians, by the use of words such as 'frameworks' and 'situations' (Barker, 1977; Birt and Nichol, 1975). In a more academic milieu than that of History education, modelling ideas thrived in the world of Social and Economic History (Desai, 1968; Chaudhuri, 1978). For a while they threatened to carry all before them, consigning traditional approaches to the study of Economic History to the junk heap, although now it is the econometricians who have the appearance of academic rag and bone men (Fogel and Elton, 1983). Outside the study of the Arts, the concept of modelling is of seminal significance in the scientific (Gentner and Stevens, 1983) and mathematical (Bundy, 1983) domains and underlies the varied uses of LOGO (Papert, 1981; Squires and McDougall, 1986).

What do we mean by modelling in the Humanities? The key elements are the identification and abstraction of determining elements and the relationships between them in analogous situations and their representation in a generalisable form. A Humanities model will normally contain:

place
a time
objects — things
animals/creatures
people/sentient beings

relationships
forces

At its most abstract an Arts model need only contain people, or some other sentient, thinking beings. The building of models becomes more complex when we introduce three axes: simplicity/complexity, abstraction/reality, and time. This allows us to build a model of models. There is a fourth element already mentioned, the *relationships* between the different elements in the model; indeed, these are the factors which give the model its identity. Take them away, and all you have are bits of discrete information.

What, if anything, has this to do with the computer? Models have been a convenient teaching device for a long time. When given a dynamic, decision-making dimension they can take the form of simulations. A model in this sense means the mental representation inside the computer of a world **external** to the user, with which the user can interact. Already there is a plethora of computer simulations which represent within the micro a world with which the pupil can interact — a micro-world. Here the micro-world is external to the pupil, in the same way as any other form of modelled reality — be it a simulation, physical model, picture, or a verbal or written representation. Why bother to use the computer? The research of Cass and Bennett into pupil-use of CAL suggests why indeed (Cass and Bennett; 1987).

A fundamental difference comes when the pupil can produce his *own* model within the computer. Such models can be a mechanical micro-world: for example, last year one of our 14-year-old specific learning difficulty (dyslexic) pupils wrote a program to analyse the building of a light circuit using a battery, bulb and assorted pieces of wire and clips. When the model has an animate dimension the pupil can create a living micro-world, be it the ecological environment which Jens Rasmussen has been developing (Rasmussen, 1987), the fishing world of one of Jennifer Raffan's 9-year-old dyslexics (Nichol and Raffan, 1987), or the horror world of Crediton in 1743 when the town burned to the ground. Last year a group of 11-12-year-old pupils wrote such a micro-world using the adventure game shell, THE PLAN.

It is here also that we begin to tread gingerly into the worlds of cognitive science, with ideas of schema, frames and scripts to lull our senses, or perhaps our common senses. Minsky's theory of frames, adumbrated in 1975, is very seductive. If we argue that a model is analogous to a frame, we can accept the idea that a model can be made up of fixed slots, and an array of empty slots of infinite number. These slots can be filled up or emptied in relation to the changing circumstances which the model mirrors. (Minsky, 1975). The dynamic of the model comes from the relationships which exist between the different and variable elements in the slots. Another dimension to the idea is added if we can think of the model frame as linking in to the slots of other frames — in other words a three-dimensional structure of potentially bewildering complexity. Here there can be interdependency between the frames, which will alter in relation to one another. The model can be represented as a semantic network, which describes the relationships between the different elements and the way in which they interact (Shastri and Feldman, 1986). When the model becomes a computerized environment which pupils can both create and explore, it takes the form of a micro-world.

For the creation of a micro-world we need open-ended software which provides the slots within which the world can be created, and the computation of the relationships between the elements which fill the slots. The relationships can take the form of logical links — the micro-world's *procedures*, which provide the model's structure. The model's semantics depend upon the nature of the information to be entered into the slots, and whether we can provide an additional semantic framework for such data. The existing shell DETECT already provides such a structure, and the new shell SLOTS, for building up the meaning of words and sentences, is an even richer semantic environment.

The creation of such software — an environment — passes through a number of stages. These mirror much of the work in the 1970s in the development of educational gaming and simulation. The stages are:

1. The abstracting from particular situations of the general analogous elements which make up the model.
2. The framing of *rules* (not laws) which determine the possible outcomes of a situation as identified within the model. At its simplest this takes the form of *x* occurs if *y*, but we are soon into a world of possibilities and probabilities through the description of the conditions under which a rule applies. Choices in simulations, like those for the choice of a Saxon village site and the building up of the Saxon village or the possibilites facing a diplomat, take this form.
3. The identification of features common to similar models, for example in settlement, negotiation, discussion or debate simulations. The structure can then be repeated, be it in modelling the Congress of Vienna or the Treaty of Versailles, the enclosure of a Tudor or 18th century village or a Viking or Elizabethan voyage.
4. The stripping down of these super models and saying what, if any, are their common identifiable features, and how we can get the computer to replicate them.

If we can achieve 4., we can perhaps provide pupils with the tools to create their own micro-worlds. At present we are experimenting with four such micro-world shells, DETECT, LINX, SLOTS and THE PLAN (see above) in three primary schools, a Specific Learning Difficulties (dyslexic) unit attached to another primary school, and an 11-18 comprehensive school. Within these environments the shells are in use five days a week in a multiplicity of ways. The common factor is pupil use of them to write their own programs. Such programs are a representation of the pupil structuring of ideas and information about a problem or topic. The learning occurs from the researching, thinking about, planning and expressing understanding in the form of the program. Below we will discuss the use of one of the shells, LINX, in a variety of contexts.

What are the main features of the LINX shell which pupils can use to write their own simulations? LINX can:

- allow choices at any specific point or node
- allow links between the outcomes of a choice
- carry consequences forward from one choice to any subsequent choice
- remember what has happened at each node, and why
- forget what has happened
- add text at any node
- add or subtract

In other words, it enables the creation of a changing micro-world, as do THE PLAN and SLOTS. LINX is a very powerful tool with which pupils can write the whole range of pencil-and-paper simulations of the early and mid 1970s, with the exception of those requiring arithmetical computation. In addition, the computer can explain the outcomes of decisions, deal with a multiplicity of different potential results of developing situations, review the progress of a player through a simulation, and link current outcomes to different previous choices.

The micro-world need only contain a single category delineated on pp.185-6. For example, during the 1985/86 academic year our 11-12-year-old pupils created micro-worlds of the Greek gods as an element in their Classical Studies course. They built their micro-worlds from a description of the gods and the links between them. To write their micro-worlds we asked each member of our form of thirty pupils to write a computer program which modelled the world of the Greek gods. To write the program each pupil had to research the information and identify the relationships between the gods.

Figure 17.1 is one pupil's structure diagram. The diagram shows the links between the different elements within her pantheon. Each entry is a node in a declarative database, from which hangs the relevant text. Information in the program deals with individuals, their characteristics, thoughts and actions. The arrows show the relationship between the different blocks of information. The program was entered into the computer using our shell DETECT (see above). This particular micro-world is a static one, in that there are no dynamic relationships between different elements in the program.

An example of a simple abstract, yet dynamic, micro-world occurred in 1986/87 in the Religious Studies element of our current first-year Humanities form's programme. We wanted to see if the pupils could collectively write a program to help see what form the gods might take in an imaginary island they were settling as a primitive tribe in a conventional pencil-and-paper simulation. The program is called 'IDENTI-GOD'. It contains under separate headings the different features a god might have. Singly or in pairs the pupils worked out god characteristics for a particular feature, such as clothes. When they had done this we had fifteen forms to type into the computer:

colour, height, dress, eyes, legs, shape, sex, mortality, weapons, where lives, good/evil, married, what it created, strong/weak, magic powers

The following is one pair's entry for clothes:

FEATURES — SUBJECT *clothes*
   1. Robes
      REMEMBER The god wears lots of clothes
   2. Daily robe
      REMEMBER Daily robe for daily use
   3. Royal robe
      REMEMBER The god wears a blue robe
   4. Jungle robe
      REMEMBER The god wears a robe that is camouflaged
   5. Armour
      REMEMBER The god wears a big shiny armour with a shield

The pupils typed the program into the computer using the simulation shell LINX (see above). The pupils were then able to ask the program about a particular god — for example, the god of water. The program gives a list of choices for each feature of the god, for example for clothes it would ask the user:

what clothes will your god wear?
a) armour
b) (jungle robe)
c) (royal robe)
d) (daily robe)
d) robes

The pupil types one of a, b, c, d, or e, and the program stores the reply and details linked to it, ie the **REMEMBER** element linked to the choice, as already entered. When the pupil has worked through the fourteen features, making a choice for each, the program then describes what the god is like when the pupil types in **review**.

A more complicated process is the creation of a micro-world combining several determining elements (see list on pp.185-6). For two years we have had pupils creating a whole range of micro-worlds from the trivial to the complex. An example of a complex program is one called DOCTOR which three 12-year-old boys wrote during their course on medieval medicine. Their form was one we had taught Humanities to for the previous year. The boys were one of three groups extracted from their normal lessons to work on the micro for 14 half-hour sessions spread over eight weeks.

The DOCTOR program simulates the work of a medieval doctor. To write it, the pupils used a range of History books and sources to research the information contained in the program. Figure 17.2 is the diagram they drew to plan the simulation. It shows the structure of the program, which contains 37 choices, 14 links and 16 remembered pieces of information. From each node hangs a piece of text. The program was developed in a top-down manner, with each layer being developed in sequence and linked to the previous one. One pupil worked out the basic structure, which he discussed fully with the other two, who researched the information for entering into the program.

How does the program work? The node **do.** has the text:

You are a medieval doctor
Patients come to you with all sorts of complaints
The complaints are sorted into five categories

The node **do.** has five choices leading from it:

Which will you choose?
a) headache
b) sickness
c) smallpox
d) toothache
e) constipation

The player, taking the role of the doctor, then has to treat one of the patients. He is faced with a choice of possible cures. For example, headache can be cured by cutting the head or cutting the throat. The program then links back to the start or carries on, depending on whether the cure has been effective. The program continues with a second set of patients — although the outcome of the decision to cure them might be different. For example, the doctor who chooses to cure smallpox will contract the disease and die, while the doctor who treats and cures other complaints lives on to deal with other patients. At any point the player can review what has happened during the simulation, ie what effect his treatment of the patients has had. For example, if for treating the Black Death he had decided on a traditional remedy — take a dried toad and place on the swelling — when he asked to review the program the computer would tell him:

Black Death — toad
The toad did nothing to cure the Black Death

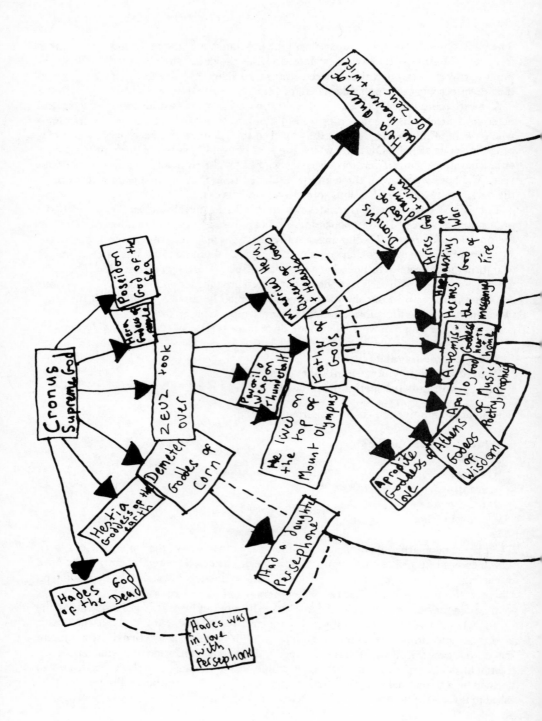

Cronus Supreme god

Zeus took over

Poseidon God of the sea

Hera Goddess of marriage

Hestia Goddess of the earth

Demeter Goddess of Corn

Hades God of the Dead

Favourite weapon thunderbolt

He lived on the top of Mount Olympus

Father of gods

Married Hera Queen of Heaven +

Hera Queen of Heaven + wife of Zeus

Dionysus God of wine + a man of

Ares god of war

Hermes the messenger

Hephaestus God of fire

Artemis Goddess hearth home

Apollo god of Music Poetry, Prophecy

Athens Goddess of wisdom

Aphrodite Goddess of love

Had a daughter Persephone

Hades was in love with Persephone

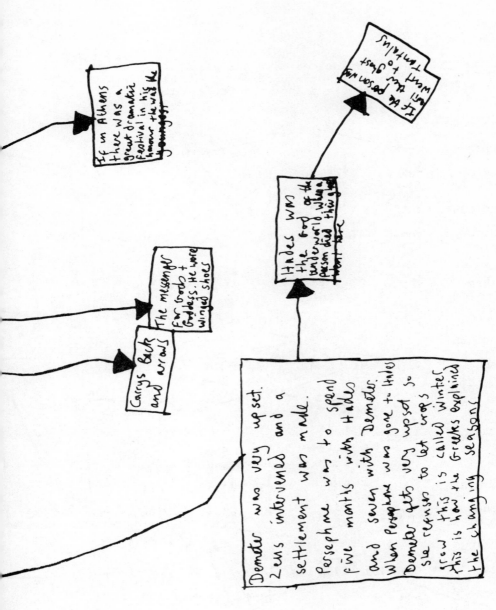

Figure 17.1

If in Athens there was a great dramatic festival in his honour the winner the youngest

If the person died their ghost went to Tantalus

The messenger for Gods + Goddess. He wore winged shoes

Carrys back and arrows

Hades was the God of the underworld where a person died they went there

Demeter was very upset. Zeus intervened and a settlement was made.
Persephone was to spend five months with Hades and seven with Demeter.
When Persephone was gone to Hades Demeter gets very upset so she refuses to let crops grow this is called winter this is how the Greeks explained the changing seasons

DOCTOR STRUCTURE   37 choices 14 links 29 blocks of text
                    entries in brackets ( ) indicate
                    previous choice affects outcome

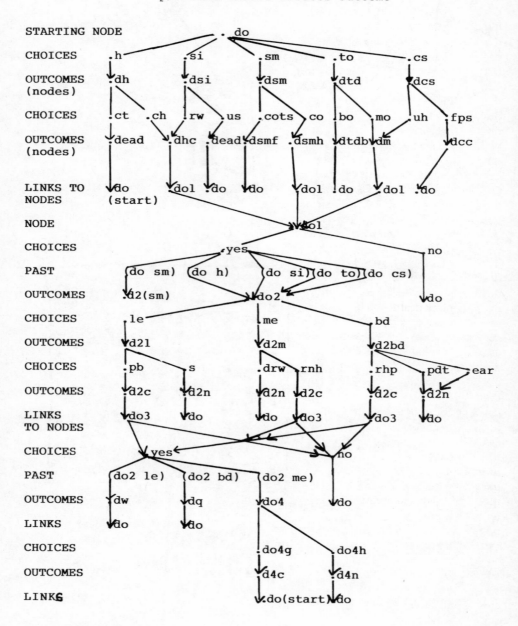

KEY TO NODES

bd	Black Death
cots	cut off the spots — mixed herbs on the wounds
cos	cut off the spots — feed to patient

cs	constipation
ct	cut throat
ch	cut head
d2	doctor dead from smallpox
d2bd	the patient has black death
d2c	the disease is cured
dcc	constipation not cured
d2l	leprosy — choice of cures
d2m	measles — choice of cures
d2n	disease not cured, the patient dies
dead	dead
dh	headache — choice of cures
dhc	headache, cut head, cured
dm	constipation, cured
do	doctor, first set of patients
dol	doctor, second set of patients
do2	doctor 2, third set of patients
do3	doctor 3, fourth set of patients
do4	doctor 4, fifth set of patients
do4c	queen is cured
do4n	queen is not cured — you are beheaded
do4g	feed the queen ground up grasshoppers
do4h	feed the queen honey and lemon juice
dg	black death, you die
drw	measles, cured
dsi	sickness — choice of cures
dsm	smallpox — choice of cures
dsmf	smallpox — dies
dtd	toothache — choice of cures
dtdb	toothache, not cured
dcs	constipation — choice of cures
dw	leprosy, your head drops off
ear	eat a rat
h	headache
le	leprosy
me	measles
mo	myrrh and opium
no	no
pdt	place a dried toad on the swelling
rhp	take a red hot poker and burn the swellings
rnh	measles, not cured
rw	river water
s	swim
si	sickness
sm	smallpox
to	toothache
us	use salt
yes	yes

Figure 17.2

The building of the DOCTOR micro-world involved the pupils in carefully planning out the structure of each layer of the program before entering it into the computer. The information inside the program required careful researching, collating, organizing and structuring before it was entered.

In creating a dynamic environment like that of the medieval doctor, the pupils develop an awareness of the nature of their own micro-worlds. The following is part of a structured interview with the pupil who planned the DOCTOR program:

> **Q.** Do you think you built up an imaginary world inside the computer? ... Would you like to say any ideas about what this micro-world was like, and so on?
> **A.** Well, I suppose it was just like you were a doctor who had patients coming to you, you just have patients, not actual names and characters.
> **Q.** Where was this micro-world?
> **A.** Somewhere in England in medieval times.
> **Q.** What sort or objects and things did your micro-world contain?
> **A.** Basically just the things for a cure, like splatterated cats.
> **Q.** What kinds of people and animals were inside this world?
> **A.** There's the patients but they didn't really have individual identity. Then there was the doctor, who was the person playing the game.

The three boys have been able to build a computerized environment which reflects elements in their understanding of a particular problem. To do this they had to carefully plan out the logical structure of the program before it was entered into the computer.

The creation of such micro-worlds can involve a high degree of:

1. Peer interaction and co-operative learning (where pairs or groups produce their micro-worlds).
2. Mental modelling and representation of knowledge in the computer.

The precise nature of that peer interaction and knowledge representation, and the question of whether the pupils are developing logical thinking and transferable skills through writing programs, are subjects for subsequent research. Whether PROLOG, either directly through logic programming or indirectly through the use of shells, can foster the kind of thinking and transferable skills which have been claimed for LOGO (Harvey, 1984; Papert, 1981), is for research to decide.

REFERENCES AND FURTHER READING

Barker, B (1977), 'History Situations', *Teaching History*, **17**, pp 19-23.
Birt, D, and Nichol, J (1975), *Games and Simulations in History*, Longmans.
Bundy, A (1983), *The Computer Modelling of Mathematical Reasoning*, Academic Press.
Cass, A, and Bennett, N (1987), Research in progress on the impact of CAL on pupils. Address: School of Education, University of Exeter, EX1 2LU
Chaudhuri, K N (1978), *The Trading World of Asia and The English East India Company, 1660-1760*, Cambridge University Press.
Chorley, J, and Haggett, P (1967), *Models in Geography*, Methuen.
Desai, M (1968), 'Some Issues in Econometric History', *The Economic History Review*, Second Series, XXI.
Fogel, W, and Elton, G R (1983), *Which Road to the Past?* Yale University Press.
Gentner D, and Stevens, A L (1983), *Mental Models*, Lawrence Erlbaum, New Jersey.

Harvey, B (1984), 'Why LOGO?', in M Yazdani, (ed) *New Horizons in Educational Computing*, Ellis Horwood.

McLeish, J (1970), 'Systems, models, simulations and games in education: A description and bibliography', in R H R Armstrong and J L Taylor, (eds), *Instructional Simulation Systems in Higher Education*, Cambridge Institute of Education.

Minsky, M (1975) 'A framework for representing knowledge', in P H Winston, (ed) *The Psychology of Computer Vision*, McGraw Hill, New York.

Nichol, R, and Raffan, J (1987), see Chapter 7: 'Using PROLOG Tools for Teaching Children with Specific Literacy Difficulties'.

Papert, S (1981), *Mindstorms*, Harvester.

Rasmussen, J (1987), see Chapter 4:, 'Using PROLOG In The Teaching of Ecology'.

Schools Council (1976) *A New Look at History*, Holmes McDougall.

Shastri, L, and Feldman, J A (1986), 'Neural Nets, Routines and Semantic Networks', in Sharkey, N E, (ed) *Advances in Cognitive Science I*, Ellis Horwood.

Squires, D, and McDougall, A (1986), *Computer Education*, **10**, Nov 3, pp375-86.

Walford, R (1969), *Games in Geography*, Longman.

Part V: Fifth generation computing and curriculum development

Preface

Jon Nichol

The problem of introducing PROLOG into the educational system arises from its transfer from the milieu in which it evolved to an alien environment. As with the analogous area of organ transplant, there have been major difficulties with rejection of the transplanted organ. Chapter 18 addresses a range of issues raised by the attempt to introduce PROLOG into the school curriculum.

The decision to adopt the 8-bit BBC machine as the educational standard in Britain — the equivalent of making Spinning Jennies the standard spinning machine during the Industrial Revolution — has raised some serious issues. The 8-bit micro has proved to be a Procrustean bed. It fails to fit the needs of the educational software and learning environments which are now being developed. All the major British educational computing development teams have adopted 16-bit machines for implementing their ideas. In Chapter 18 the Danes describe how they have overcome this major problem by using IBM PCs. The Danish developments are rooted within an intensive, bottom-up classroom-based pattern which draws upon a range of expertise.

Chapter 19 looks towards the future. Tom Conlon raises some exciting possibilities for the use of the next series of languages. His account of PARLOG reminds us vividly that we are all functioning within a rapidly developing milieu which continually opens up exciting new vistas and possibilities.

18. Logic programming in a computerized learning environment

Jorge Aage Jensen and Bent B Andresen
Institute of Informatics
Royal Danish School of Educational Studies,
115B Emdrupvej
DK-2400
Copenhagen NV
Denmark

INTRODUCTION

In this chapter, within the framework of a Project on Informatics in a Computerized Learning Environment (PILE), use of PROLOG as a knowledge structuring tool is discussed. An illustration of the interplay between conceptual analysis and formalization of a domain of knowledge using PROLOG is presented, and lines of further work are indicated.

PROJECT: INFORMATICS IN A COMPUTERIZED LEARNING ENVIRONMENT (PILE)

The aim of the project (PILE) is to establish and maintain a framework for exploring the pedagogical potential of a computerized learning environment. By this we mean an environment with abundant access to micro-computers, to be used when pedagogical intentions and plans so advise. The intention is to accustom the teacher groups and the students to having computers around, and using them every day.

One argument for establishing a computerized learning environment is that we want to secure the co-operation of the teachers and the students in these sub-projects without having (as significant issues) the news value of the computer, or its ascribed 'motivational power'. This expresses the belief that it is of pedagogical interest to investigate the use of computers in education, when these are available, to an extent that makes them unsensational, to be used when the 'tools' and 'media' that they offer seem to facilitate the attainment of pedagogical and developmental goals. We believe, as an overall hypothesis, that those tools and media will challenge both the content and the ways of learning and teaching in the school system.

This goes for all the software that we are using, but an obvious example will be word-processing. The reason for using it is not that traditional essay-writing be performed more efficiently. The editing and layout facilities may result in a mutually *beneficial* different interchange between teacher and student, and among students. Both teachers and students will be able to occupy themselves with precision of expression, agreement of text with intentions, cross-curricular use of texts produced in different subjects, and the relation between text and other forms of expression.

Three types of software will be used in PILE:

1. Programming languages: PROLOG with various front-ends and tools on top of it; LOGO, and possibly COMAL.
2. General applications software: the Assistant series of IBM + IBM's Display Write.
3. Dedicated tools for use in particular subject areas, such as Mathematics and Geography.

Our intention is that the software be used as a tool or vehicle for learning about the subject-matter, which may be a subject, or may be an inter-disciplinary 'project' over a long period.

The organizational framework of the project: two schools in the Copenhagen area act as project schools. Two sets of IBM PCs, each consisting of eight machines, were placed in two seventh grade classes (age 13-14, about 20 students in each class) in November 1985, and they will remain there through the eighth and ninth grades. The group of teachers teaching the two classes will also substantially remain intact. The period of time for the project is thus (at least) three years. During this time the research team from the institute will observe, analyse, and teach the teacher group and the students the use of computers in education.

The observations that are of interest will emerge from two sources. Firstly, the teachers and the students, by regular reports of a general character, will furnish us with information (amount of time spent, the kind of programs used, etc). Secondly, various sub-projects will aim at systematic theory-based observations concerning cognitive processes in educational contexts.

One sub-project is concerned with PROLOG across the curriculum. It will be pursued in accordance with the following research agenda (Hillel, undated):

1. Construction of a PROLOG environment appropriate to the grade of the students involved. The term 'environment' includes:
   - A set of commands which is given to the students as part of the program language vocabulary or as part of PROLOG toolkits, either created by the teacher or developed or supplied by the researcher.
   - A set of programming techniques and system operations which are made available to the students.
   - The instructions, including the tasks which are given or suggested as part of the curriculum.
   - The strategies of intervention of the teacher and the researchers.
   - The physical set-up: the number of students involved, the student: computer ratio, the length and number of sessions, etc.
2. Analysis of the concepts implicit in the PROLOG environment, which might be accessible to the students via their activities, including:
   - The disciplinary concepts.
   - The programming concepts.
3. Improvement of the environment according to the results of stage 2.
4. Investigations of the students' behaviour in the PROLOG environment, including:
   - Their projects: initiation, implementation and application in further studies.
   - Their level of planning.

- Their problem-solving procedures.
- Their ways of coping with errors (errors within PROLOG, and discrepancies concerning the relation between the knowledge-base and observations from other sources).

5. The analysis of the data obtained in stage 4 as evidence for the emergence and acquisition of:
   - Different forms of representation of the problem solved.
   - Disciplinary, or subject-matter, concepts.
   - Programming concepts.

ON THE USE OF PROGRAMMING LANGUAGES IN EDUCATION

Computer applications to educational processes are often roughly categorized as follows (UNESCO, 1986):

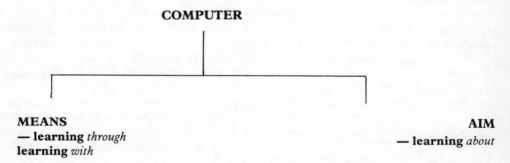

COMPUTER

MEANS
— **learning** *through*
learning *with*

AIM
— **learning** *about*

Computers can be either tools of education or the actual subject-matter of computer science.

As a tool the computer can be used in two different ways:

1. Learning *through* computers, eg the use of the computer as a vehicle through which the teacher gives instructions and asks questions (CAL, CAI, drill-and-practice, etc).
2. Learning with *computers*, eg the use of the computer as a tool towards the acquisition of knowledge, on the assumption that more powerful ways of representation in the minds of students can thereby be achieved.

In order to learn with a computer, it is necessary to introduce some knowledge about computers, eg programming languages, applications software, etc. Using computers, then, is not only a means of education, but becomes an educational aim in itself, so that learning with computers is also, somehow, learning *about* computers in the fullest meaning of the phrase.

Educational research may be concerned with PROLOG in at least two ways:

1. The pupils' writing of PROLOG programs to organize their knowledge and understanding concerning a particular topic. These programs are 'traces', so to speak, to be studied as expressions of cognitive processes. Their style, their sequence, their changes are also functions of the teacher-pupil-subject interaction. In this case the user interface is a feature of particular concern.
2. The researcher using student interaction with a PROLOG program as a description

of the student's structure of knowledge about a particular topic at a particular point of time (Law, Ogborn and Whitelock, 1986). Again, a series of such descriptions will be the material for analysis of cognitive processes and cognitive development. In this case, front-ends will not be a particular issue, only how powerful a version of the language is available in order to capture as many details and nuances as possible. Our research materials will be interviews with the pupils, solving of particular problems assumed to indicate different forms of understanding within the particular topic: and work with various sets of teaching materials.

ON FRONT-ENDS

As indicated above, the students' use of PROLOG to structure knowledge raises the question of special adaptations of both the syntax and the semantics of the language. In working on this problem, we will build on the rich British experiences of logic programming in educational contexts. The aim is to implement the essential ideas of logic programming without having the notational intricacies of PROLOG standing in the way. The openness, the general accessibility of micro-PROLOG has inspired a number of attempts at constructing user-friendly interfaces as well as a number of 'dedicated' programs, using a subset of micro-PROLOG, for studying particular topics. The Exeter software is an example (Briggs, Dean and Nichol, 1986).

One important feature of front-ends like Jonathan Briggs' MITSI (1985), is a change of the prefix notation of PROLOG into an infix notation, ie from the *objects* as arguments to the *predicate*, to the *relation* standing between the *objects*. The aim is to approach natural language, on the assumption that the closer one comes to expressing oneself in natural language, the easier it will be to learn and to use the programming language. While the assumption may have a considerable face validity, it is nevertheless important to keep in mind the fact that whatever is done to approach natural language, it is still a formalism that one imposes, with rules and regulations set up exactly in order to achieve the structuring capability. (Incidentally, note as an example the often induced incorrect use of the present tense, third person marker, in English, imposed by the rules of PROLOG.)

A second point is that when one chooses to use a front-end to facilitate the novice's use of PROLOG, it is important to retain the possibility of progressing into the language itself, without having to abandon the work done via the front-end. This demand is met, fortunately, by the version mentioned above — MITSI. Both these points are important when the use of PROLOG progresses from simple family trees or bicycle repair programs to more complex tasks, set by educational goals and curricula.

A third point concerns the *model* one chooses for teaching about the language. In our analysis of an example, to be presented below, we use the object/attribute/value triplet, instead of object/relation/object. We do not think one is good and the other bad. We mainly argue for our choice because of the nature of the subject domain being programmed. A number of the facts and rules seem to be conceived more naturally by formulating them as objects-attributes-values than by a relation between objects.

Finally, a fourth point in this discussion concerns how the system prompts the user. In our adapted version of MITSI, we operate a screen with two horizontal windows, a *writing* window and an *answer* window, or an input and output window.

There are four main types of user input:
1. The user's description of a given problem field.
2. The user's questions to the system.
3. The user's answers to questions from the system.
4. The user's commands to the system.

For each of these a particular prompt is given. First, the prompt that tells that the system is ready. We use the standard sign > for this. What the user writes depends, of course, on his intentions and judgements of the system's output from a preceding step of the program execution. But it also depends on the prompts of the system. The reaction of the system depends on the type of input.

For the first type, the user's description of a given problem field, the system will provide an evaluation, so that the knowledge base is updated if the input accords with structural and syntactical criteria. The user can inspect this updating, as it is presented in the output window. If the entry is incorrect, no change in the knowledge base is made, and the system's prompt will comprise a message about the error.

The second type of input, the user's questions, activates the inference engine. In fact, it is through asking questions that the user executes the program. Again, depending on the syntactical correctness, the user may be given either messages of error ending in a particular prompt, or messages about the result of the execution.

The third type of input concerns answers from the user to questions from the system. Again, the system provides prompts to be answered by yes or no.

The fourth type of input, the commands to the system, comprises listing, editing, saving, loading, and so on. In each case, the system provides prompts, informing the user about four kinds of states:

● Error messages.
● Questions requiring additional information, or questions to ensure that the user really intends his command to be executed.
● Messages that the command is executed, in particular for cases when this state is not shown otherwise.
● Display of contents of knowledge base.

This analysis has guided our adaptation of MITSI to produce a consistent interface for experimental use.

FORMALISATION OF KNOWLEDGE: AN EXAMPLE

Three ways of using PROLOG may be distinguished:

1. A finished PROLOG program is made available, and the students apply the search mechanism to obtain answers to their questions.
2. The students themselves construct the program by formulating the rules and selecting the information.
3. A mixture of the preceding two, in which the structure of the knowledge base is presented by the teacher/researcher, together with templates of how to represent information and rules, and then the students build the knowledge base.

In the first case, the program is a sort of 'black box', while in the second and third cases, it may be a 'glass box'. In any case the use of PROLOG must be preceded by a conceptual analysis.

As an example of such a conceptual analysis we shall comment on one aspect of a larger project, which used PROLOG as a knowledge structuring tool. The study was carried out in the spring of 1986 with an eighth grade class in a suburban school in Odense, Denmark. It was run by one of us (BBA), together with Mr Jens Rasmussen and the teacher of the class, Mr Hans Jantzen. The subject area was cross-curricular, dealing with ecological matters such as food chains, cyclical transformation of matter, respiration, nutritive salts and metabolism, and is more fully reported in this volume in Chapter 4. A model of the ecological system studied is shown in Fig. 18.1. The work comprised such features as identification and classification of flora and fauna, and discussion of themes like respiration, photosynthesis and food chains. Experiments in Biology and Physics/Chemistry were done, and a one-day excursion to a brook near the school was made.

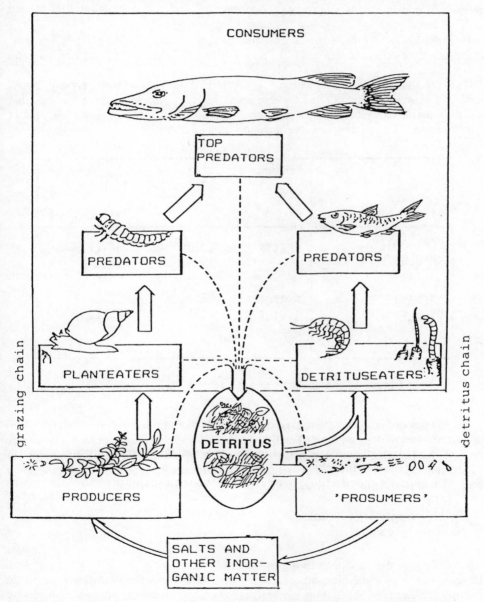

Figure 18.1 *Model of a Freshwater System. From Abrahamsen, S. E. Forurening i Ferskvand — MAKRO-INDEX metoden. (Pollution in freshwater — The Macro-Index method) Copenhagen, Forum, 1981.*

In this study we chose the third way of using PROLOG. The groups of students were set to work on an analysis that distinguished two epistemological dimensions — 'episodic' and 'semantic' knowledge. Episodic knowledge is based on concrete experiences, comprising modes of appearance of phenomena. Roughly speaking, the knowledge is 'situation-bound', immediately related to experiences. Semantic knowledge forms a network of meaning. It is knowledge about 'essence', and is conceptual and formalised (more or less).

Episodic knowledge concerns *entities*, like plants, animals, bacteria, while semantic knowledge concerns processes like photosynthesis, metabolism, respiration and putrefaction.

The processes of the ecosystem were categorised into three main types. Firstly, processes that *supply* matter to the ecosystem (production): secondly, processes that *consume* matter (consumption); and thirdly, processes that *supply and consume* matter (prosumption). These categories are shown in Fig. 18.2.

	PRODUC-TION	CONSUMP-TION	PROSUMP-TION
"EPISODIC" KNOWLEDGE	PLANTS	CARNIVORE HERBIVORE	BACTERIA FUNGI
"SEMANTIC" KNOWLEDGE	PHOTO SYNTHESIS	METABO-LISM	PUTRE-FACTION

Figure 18.2 *Model of metabolism in an ecological system*

On the basis of this analysis it is relatively simple to formulate rules in PROLOG for the metabolism of the ecosystem. For example, a rule about photosynthesis can be seen to rest on the fact that it takes place in plants. The plants exploit the light energy for production of organic matter. The 'semantic' content of the rule is that a species supplies organic matter, if it grows in light. In PROLOG it may look like this:

**species supply organic-matter
if species grow-in light;**

The binding of the variable will depend on the facts that the students have supplied. Imagine that they have been on a field trip to a brook nearby, and they have found examples of surface vegetation, bottom vegetation, and vine plants, or examples of particular plants such as water-thyme. These facts are put into the system like this:

surface-vegetation grow-in light;
bottom-vegetation grow-in light;
vine-plants grow-in light;

or alternatively:

water-thyme grow-in light;

Immediate observations of the students' use of the analysis seem fairly encouraging. The observations concerning the provision of facts to the system showed variations as to what aspects of the ecosystem were dealt with. One group was much preoccupied with the most common sources of water pollution. They supplied their knowledge base with facts like:

liquid-manure is-common source-of-pollution;
sewage is-common source-of-pollution;
ensilage is-common source-of-pollution;
sulpho-detergent is-common source-of-pollution;

Another group dealt with facts about systems of respiration. The intention was to represent Darwin's view about 'survival of the fittest' in the database. Roughly stated, in the case of a diminishing supply of oxygen (which is the most frequent cause of extinction in waters), one species will survive another species if the first species has a less sensitive respiration system with respect to oxygen than that of the other species. And the rule must of course be applied to facts about respiration systems, such as:

butterfly-gnat breathe-through snorkel;

rat-tailed-larva breathe-through snorkel;
aquatic-beetle breathe-through bladder;

gnatl breathe-through skin;
gnat2 breathe-through skin;

worm1 breathe-through skin;
coelenterata breathe-through skin;
mayfly-larva breathe-through tracheal gills;

fish breathe-through gills;
mussels breathe-through gills;
snails breathe-through gills;

While the facts may be considered as the *atoms* of the knowledge base, its *molecules* are the rules. Not surprisingly, the variations among the student groups as to formulation of rules were fewer than for the facts. The rules were seen as a kind of 'bridge' between conceptual subject-matter knowledge and the 'episodic' experiences. The students were encouraged to formulate rules on a template presented to them at the beginning of the study, an issue elaborated in Chapter 4.

REFLECTIONS ON THE USE OF PROLOG IN EDUCATION
(LOGIC PROGRAMMING)

In planning an educational course in natural science we consider it important, as noted above, that a conceptual analysis precede the students' activity. We regard logic programming as an essential tool in attempts to escape a barren dilemma between the 'science-organized' and 'experience-organized' curriculum. One can neither build solely on the subject-matter as organized in today's science, nor can the immediate experience of the students be the only basis for choice of content.

PROLOG, as a tool for bridging the gap between often intuitively organized knowledge about phenomena and the formalized knowledge of science, seems to us to have exciting potential. It offers, firstly, a means of externalizing knowledge by building a knowledge base; secondly, a vehicle for establishing a kind of Socratic dialogue to expose one's own thinking and to reveal incompleteness and inconsistencies in knowledge; and thirdly, it offers students the chance to work with models, including the assumption that one always looks at the world from a particular perspective, and that different perspectives of a given 'slice of reality' may exist. (Incidentally, it may be noted that when we talk in Danish about PROLOG programs, we use the word 'information' rather than 'facts', as the latter term has connotations which may mislead in not suggesting a particular perspective.)

The perspective used in the example, and with which we shall continue in our own project, is that insight into the functioning of a domain is achieved through the view that the phenomena may be seen as three-part-atoms, consisting of: an object, eg a plant: an attribute, eg that the plant grows in something; and a value, eg that the plant grows in light. As mentioned earlier we do not consider that this choice is right, and the choice of object-relation-object wrong, but we have found the object-attribute-value triplet expedient.

When the students work with the knowledge base, a continual evaluation of it is possible. Questions, the answers to which are known in advance, may be put to the system for checking that particular facts and rules have been established. In case the expected answer does not turn up, corrections can be made.

Further, this learning process may in principle be interrupted and resumed many times. After having established the basic rules for the ecosystem, the PROLOG work may be interrupted for a while, and themes like pollution (why do the fish die in polluted water?), evolution (what was, more precisely, meant by 'survival of the fittest'?), etc, may be explored by more conventional means, then the PROLOG may be resumed. The knowledge base may be enlarged, eg with rules about an ecosystem as a system in which various species compete with each other, from a Darwinistic or a Marxist point of view (Capra, 1981). Both Darwin and Marx, inspired by Malthus, stressed conflict relative to harmony. A single rule suffices to represent this point of view. Since the rule must deal with competition in the system, the students may attempt formulations such as:

> __species compete with __anotherspecies
>   if __species consume oxygen
>   and __anotherspecies consume oxygen;

Contrary to this will be a rule that describes co-operation in the system. Such a rule must express the knowledge that a species exists due to the existence of another species, because the latter supplies something to the system that the former consumes. For example, plants supply oxygen which the animals need:

__species help __anotherspecies
if __species supply oxygen
and __anotherspecies consume oxygen.

We see great potential in PROLOG for increasing the complexity of such micro-worlds. When a knowledge base contains few facts and rules, one is not surprised by the answers provided: one gets answers already known. But when the knowledge base becomes more complex, ie when answers appear by the combination of several rules, representing 'new knowledge', then it is of prime importance that the students have the chance to wonder, and reflect upon it, and to request an account of the reasoning that led to the answer, ie an exposition of the way the inference engine has combined rules and facts (the 'why-function' of MITSI).

PILE'S NEXT STEP

According to our research agenda our next task will be within item 1: 'Construction of a PROLOG environment...', defining the set of commands given to students. As indicated we will explore further an adaptation of MITSI (Briggs, 1986). Introduction of MITSI to the students will begin in October. Two lessons per week will be devoted specifically to teaching and using MITSI.

The teacher groups will be introduced to PROLOG, starting in September, with the intention that they come to appreciate the potential of PROLOG as a means of structuring knowledge of subject-matter. For the year 86/87, we have established a frame of three lessons per week for the teacher groups, as part of the in-service teacher training scheme in Denmark.

In parallel with this introduction we will analyse, in co-operation with the teachers, some of the subject-matter topics planned for spring '87, in order to see how PROLOG can be put to use in the teaching and learning process. What we have in mind is the kind of conceptual analysis indicated in connection with the pilot study of an ecological system.

Further, we intend to use Jonathan Briggs' PLAN (Briggs, 1986) in the teaching of English as a foreign language. The first task will be an adventure game created by the English teacher for learning vocabulary.

Finally, subject to the experiences gained with MITSI during Spring 87, we plan to prepare for using APES (Hammond and Sergot, 1985) in the third and final year of the project.

REFERENCES AND FURTHER READING

Briggs, J H (1985), *MicroPROLOG Rules!*, Logic Programming Associates Ltd, London.
Briggs, J H (1986), *THE PLAN Adventure System*, London.
Briggs, J H, Dean J, and Nichol, J (1986), *LINX, PLACES, DETECT*, from PEG-Exeter, School of Education, University of Exeter, EX1 2LU.
Capra, F (1981), *The Turning Point*, Berkeley.
Hammond, P, and Sergot, M (1985), *APES User Manual*, Logic Based Systems Ltd, Richmond, Surrey.
Hillel, J, Concordia University, Canada, personal communication.

Law, N, Ogborn, J, and Whitelock, D (1986), 'Knowing what the student knows: A use of APES in science education,' *Pegboard*, Vol **1**/1, Exeter.

UNESCO (1986) International Centre for Chemical Studies; *Final Report, Microcomputers in Science*, Ljubljana.

19. Who's afraid of parallel logic?

Tom Conlon,
Moray House College of Education,
Holyrood Road,
Edinburgh
EH8 8AQ
UK

INTRODUCTION

PARLOG provides concrete proof that logic programming is not synonymous with PROLOG. Furthermore, it seals the place of logic programming as the main software paradigm for fifth generation computing.

The use of PARLOG should not affect our basic logic programming perspective, in which program development proceeds from logic to control. However, the PARLOG control view is very different from that with PROLOG. The basis of the language is and-parallelism, in which several processes are active on sub-problems together. Mode constraints synchronise the processes in a natural way, by specifying which arguments of a process are inputs and which are outputs; a process suspends until its input arguments are made available by other processes. Processes communicate by passing messages through variables which provide communication channels. The search strategy commits choice to one clause instead of attempting an exhaustive search through all possible clauses.

This Chapter is an introduction to PARLOG, which indicates some possible pedagogical devices. It assumes a knowledge of PROLOG.

FROM PROLOG TO PARLOG

The two most important things about PARLOG are: first, PARLOG is a logic programming language; second, it is designed for efficient implementation on parallel hardware. The first point reveals the common ground between PARLOG and PROLOG, whilst the second distinguishes the two languages from one another.

Most readers of this chapter, who are looking at PARLOG from an experience of PROLOG, will probably be asking the obvious question: what does this mean in practice, when we try to solve a problem by computer using PARLOG in place of PROLOG? The answer to the question partly depends on our approach to programming. If we adopt a good logic programming approach, as proposed for example by Kowalski (1985), we will follow a two-stage approach to computational problem-solving which proceeds from logic to control, as follows:

1. In the first stage we specify the problem to be solved together with the information which is required for its solution; these specifications may be informal initially, but eventually formal logic specifications should be derived.
2. In the second stage we transform the logic into a form which is efficiently executable by the target logic interpreter.

The use of this methodology is what gives logic programming its problem-oriented quality, in which programming begins at the stage of specifications rather than algorithms. Of course it is possible to bypass it, and to use logic programming languages whilst maintaining an essentially algorithmic approach to computing, but this is perverse. Let us assume that we are logic programmers: we base our programming perspective on 'logic first, control second'. This perspective, then, should not change when we move from one logic programming language to another.

In the first stage of problem-solving, when logic considerations dominate, it makes no difference whether we are using PROLOG or PARLOG. The declarative interpretations of programs written in the two languages are the same. PARLOG syntax too will be highly familiar to PROLOG users, so that a PARLOG program will not only be entirely understandable (in its declarative reading) to a PROLOG programmer, it will actually be necessary to look quite closely to avoid mistaking the PARLOG program for one written in PROLOG.

It is in the second stage of program development that the difference matters. When control considerations come to the fore we focus on the imperative interpretation of the program. PROLOG programs are evaluated sequentially, whereas PARLOG uses a parallel evaluation. As we will show, the two behaviours are usually very different.

AND-PARALLELISM

Consider the following problem specification:

> **John is invited to join a September fishing holiday in Shetland. He hates travelling by sea, but it may be possible to fly. On balance, he decides that if Shetland has an airport and the weather forecast for that month in Edinburgh is poor, then he will go.**

A PROLOG programmer might represent the problem as a query:

> **?-has-airport(Shetland) & forecast(Edinburgh, September, poor)**

The corresponding query in PARLOG is:

> **:has-airport(Shetland), forecast(Edinburgh, September, poor)**

The two sub-problems are connected in the PROLOG query by the **&** operator, denoting 'sequential and'. The comma in the PARLOG query denotes 'parallel and'. Where PROLOG solves the two sub-problems one at a time in left-to-right order, PARLOG solves the two together. There are obvious human analogies for the two behaviours. For the case of PROLOG, John works alone. He first rings the travel agent and then he checks with the meteorological office. In the case of PARLOG, John has help from a friend and they each make a phone call. By doubling the resources given to solving the problem, the work can be completed in half the time.

The counterpart computing behaviour should be clear. When there are two processors available then the query

:has-airport(Shetland), forecast(Edinburgh, September, poor)

can be answered by giving one sub-problem to each processor. If the predicates are defined by a database of facts such as, say,

> **has-airport(Edinburgh)**
> **has-airport(Dundee)**
> **has-airport(Inverness)**
> **has-airport(Aberdeen)**
> . . . .
> **forecast(Wick, August, fine)**
> **forecast(Aberdeen, August, fair)**
> **forecast(Shetland, August, fair)**
> **forecast(Dundee, September, poor)**

then the processors are each working on a different part of the database. It is as if John and his co-worker were together tracing with their fingers down through the facts, taking one set each. The two processes are completely independent: they need not communicate with one another. It does not matter whether they start together or at different times. There is no data in common between the two processes. This kind of parallelism is highly natural and unproblematic.

Even where two sub-problems share data in common, if the shared data is only input data then the sub-problems can be regarded as independent. Separate processes can be set up to solve each one. An example is the problem of finding the minimum and the maximum elements of a given list. The PROLOG programmer represents this problem as a goal statement:

> **? -min-of(__list, __min) & max-of(__list, __max)**

The PARLOG query is:

> **: min-of(__list, __min), max-of(__list, __max)**

PARLOG sets up two processes which run together, each having its own copy of the given list to which to refer. Again, the processes need not synchronize nor communicate. PROLOG can manage only one process at a time, and each sub-problem must wait for the completion of earlier sub-problems before receiving attention. In the human analogy, the question is whether the problem is to be solved by two persons or one. The fact that there are two copies of the input list makes no difference.

It is easy to point to another efficiency gain which arises from this 'and-parallel' problem-solving behaviour. When several processes are active on sub-problems together, if one process fails (because its problem is unsolvable) then all the other processes can be terminated at once. A single processor might be unlucky, doing a lot of wasted work before discovering the unsolvable problem in the conjunction. By analogy, when John is alone it is possible that he might spend a very long time confirming the existence of the airport with the travel agent, only then to be told that the weather condition is not met. When operating with a friend we would expect the two to cease working as soon as the weather information was revealed to one of them.

Notice that we are now referring to *processes* rather than processors. There is not likely to be a one-to-one relationship between the two. PARLOG has been designed for efficient implementation on any granularity of hardware architecture, including fine-grain dataflow machines, coarse-grain graph reduction machines, and even the extreme coarse-grained case of a monoprocessor (sequential) machine. It is too early to be sure about future parallel architectures but it seems certain that the job of mapping processes (ie behaviours initiated by relation calls) to physical processors will be that of the system software and not of the PARLOG programmer. For the same reason, it would be more accurate to refer to concurrent rather than parallel evaluation of programs.

MODE CONSTRAINTS FOR SYNCHRONIZING PROCESSES

Consider the problem of finding the total of four numbers. One approach is exemplified by:

$$1 + 2 + 3 + 4$$
$$= (1 + 2) + (3 + 4)$$
$$= 3 + 7 = 10$$

in which we 'balance' the addition into a set of similar sub-additions. A group of four numbers requires three such additions. With realistic data sets, balanced addition has a real value in reducing rounding errors, but it will serve our purposes to stick to sets of four numbers here.

A PROLOG programmer might express the general problem with a triplet of calls:

> SUM(__n1, __n2, __totA) & SUM(__n3, __n4, totB) &
> SUM(__totA, __totB, __total)

whilst the PARLOG equivalent may be:

> sum(__n1, __n2, __totA), sum(__n3, __n4, __totB),
> sum (__totA, __totB, __total)

Proceeding as before, we anticipate that PARLOG will not spawn three processes, one to handle each sum process. However, if the third process tries to proceed it will surely enter an error state since its inputs will not yet be ready. In the PROLOG evaluation, this problem does not arise because the left-to-right sequencing ensures that the answers to the first two additions are available before the third is attempted.

How can the difficulty with the parallel evaluation be resolved? Summoning the human analogy, we imagine three people working together on the balanced addition problem and taking one addition each. The third person will know not to start adding until being told what to add by the two who are working on the preliminary additions. That is, the third person is synchronized by his inputs: when his inputs are both available, he can become active; until that point he is in a state of suspension. In fact, this suggests the actual means by which PARLOG solves the synchronization problem. Each relation is given a mode declaration which specifies which arguments are inputs and which are outputs. The mode declaration for the sum relation is:

MODE sum (?, ?,ˆ)

which specifies that the first two arguments are inputs and the third is an output. A process becomes suspended if its inputs are not ready. So, if sum is defined by a large database of facts, such as:

sum(0, 0, 0)
sum(0, 1, 1)
sum(1, 0, 1)
sum(1, 1, 2)
sum(0, 2, 2)
sum(1, 2, 3)

then a call such as:

sum(__totA, __totB, __total)

in which **__totA** and **__totB** have not been given values, will be suspended. As soon as they both have values the process will proceed. Of course, if they are given values (such as non-integers) which cannot be matched with the arguments in any sum clause, the call will fail. We might now like to define a relation **add-four**, say, which expresses the balanced addition of four integers. A suitable PARLOG program for the relation might be:

MODE add-four(?, ?, ?, ?,ˆ)
add-four(__n1, __n2, __n3, __n4, __total)
    <— sum (__n1, __n2, __totA),
        sum (__n3, __n4, __totB)
        sum (__totA, __totB, __total)

The mode declaration specifies that an **add-four** process expects inputs on its first four arguments and delivers output on its fifth. In the parallel terminology, it is a *consumer* of four items of data and a *producer* of one.

Many PARLOG evaluations have a clear graphical interpretation. We illustrate a relation call as a process which consumes and produces data items according to the mode declaration. See, for example, the diagram in Fig. 19.1.

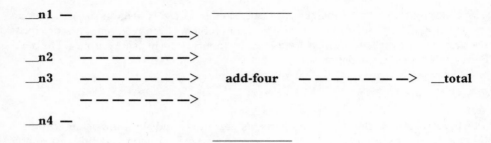

Figure 19.1

The system of sub-processes which is spawned by a call to a relation can be shown in a similar way. For example, a call to **add-four** spawns three sum processes, as in Fig. 19.2.

Such diagrams give a good idea of the dataflow generated by a process and between sub-processes. Conceptually, as soon as some data has arrived on all the input channels of a particular process, the process 'fires'. In the diagram above, the third sum process is in suspension until the values for **totA** and **totB** are placed on its input channels. At that point it fires — it becomes an active process. An active process consumes its input data and may spawn further sub-processes. Eventually it either succeeds, often producing data which is then placed on its output channels, or fails. In either case it terminates.

PARLOG's use of mode declarations to synchronize communication between processes means that, in contrast to PROLOG, the order of calls in a conjunction is immaterial. The PROLOG query given earlier will fail if the programmer changes the position of the third call. On the other hand, PARLOG programs in general can only have a single mode of use. There is no way in PARLOG to define a single relation **append** and then use it both to join and to split lists, for example. The PARLOG programmer must write a different version for each pattern of use, and supply a mode declaration for it accordingly.

PROCESS COMMUNICATION

The reality of parallelism forces us to change the way we think about the communication of data between processes. In sequential languages such as Pascal, 'parameter passing' is an ephemeral event which accompanies a procedure call. Actual parameters are completely formed by the calling procedure and transmitted on a once-for-all basis to the called procedure. Execution of the first procedure stops and the second one starts. PROLOG generalizes parameter passing into unification, thus giving it a basis in logic, but the behaviour is still that of instantaneous message passing accompanying the transfer of control. For example, in the PROLOG calls:

producer(__data) & consumer(__data)

the first procedure binds **__data** and immediately terminates, at which point the second procedure begins.

The human analogy for communication in the style of Pascal and PROLOG is obvious. A company of people in an office (say) are all asleep, save for one active soul who for some reason is doing some work. When eventually the worker decides that he needs to

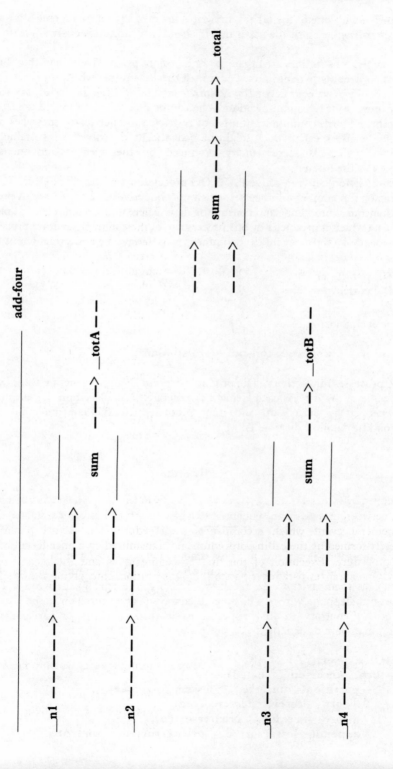

Figure 19.2

communicate with one of the others, he writes his message on to a memo slip, wakes up the chosen colleague, stuffs the paper into his hands and simultaneously falls into oblivion himself.

Fortunately, most offices are organized rather more productively than this. First, they usually keep sleeping to a minimum; or at least there is no rule which says that everybody but one should be asleep. Secondly, a worker (assuming he is not asleep) is capable of simultaneous two-way communication — he can be receiving one memo whilst handing over another. Third, communication is not restricted to once-for-all messages on memo pads; there is also speech, which might be pedantically described as a sustained flow of information which is incrementally produced by the speaker and incrementally interpreted by the listener.

Communication between active PARLOG processes is comparable to this. There is no restriction on the number of processes which may be active at any one time. A process can be simultaneously producing and consuming data. There is also stream communication — a list of data which is produced by one process can be consumed by another process *as it is being produced*. To illustrate this last point, suppose that we have two relations as follows:

MODE producer (^)
MODE consumer (?)

Then the evaluation of:

producer(__listofdata), consumer(__listofdata)

sets two processes into activity. The producer process begins to generate values which are the elements of the list. As each element is generated it is placed on the output channel from where it is picked up and duly processed by the consumer process. The corresponding dataflow diagram is:

```
_____                          __listofdata                    _____

producer..................................................consumer

_____              — — —>    — — —>                        _____
```

The communication is continuous. This is not the memo-writing of parameter passing; it is more like speaking down a telephone, in which the listener comprehends the words and even acts on them as they are received. Actually, the analogy between a PARLOG variable and telephone wire as a channel of communication turns out to be a rather good one, because contrary to first appearances it turns out that a variable can carry information in both directions.

```
MODE q-sort(?,^)
q-sort(__unsorted, __sorted)
   <— partition(__unsorted, __lesser, __greater),
       q-sort(__lesser, __lessersorted),
       q-sort(__greater, __greatersorted),
       append(__lessersorted, __greatersorted, __sorted)
```

We will now give the definitions of **partition** and **append.** Their mode declarations are:

MODE partition (?,⁻,⁻,)
MODE append(?,?,⁻)

A **q-sort** process immediately forks into a system of four sub-processes. At first all but **partition** suspends, since the others have no inputs. However, as soon as **partition** generates any elements of the lists **lesser** and **greater,** these elements are placed on the output channels and consumed by the **q-sort** processes. Similarly, the **append** process is fired by the incrementally produced outputs of **q-sort.** The result is a highly parallel dataflow behaviour. A dataflow diagram for **q-sort** is shown in Fig. 19.3.

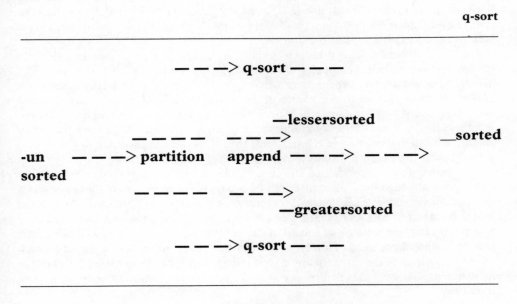

Figure 19.3

COMMITTED CHOICE SEARCH STRATEGY

Let us suppose that our problem is to find out how much insurance premium an individual is due to pay for some policy. The problem can be represented in logic by the goal:

premium(__person, __policy, __amount)

There may be several ways to solve the problem, each corresponding to one rule for the relation:

```
premium(__person, __policy, 10) if .....
premium(__person, __policy, 15) if .....
premium(__person, __policy, 20) if .....
premium(__person, __policy, 25) if .....
```

PROLOG's strategy in this situation is to attempt an exhaustive search. It tries the first rule, then the second rule, and so on. Moreover, PROLOG tries to find all the ways to solve the problem with each rule by tracking backwards and forwards through the conditions of the rule. This is the backtracking depth-first search strategy with which we are familiar.

PARLOG's search strategy is very different. Initially PARLOG regards all the clauses for the relation as candidate clauses, any one of which could be selected to solve the call. But then the candidates are all inspected in parallel, and one is selected as the clause to use. The evaluation becomes committed to this selected clause: the discarded alternatives will not be re-tried. There is no backtracking.

PARLOG's search strategy has the important advantage that it can be efficiently implemented on parallel computers. It is also very easy for humans to understand. The disadvantage is that only one answer can be produced by any evaluation. Since the evaluation commits itself to one branch of the search tree at each choice point, without ever backtracking, any solutions which lie on the unexplored branches will not be found. It follows that to make a false commitment is a disaster. If PARLOG chooses the wrong clause (one which cannot solve the problem) then the evaluation will fail — there is no going back, as there is with PROLOG, to explore the others.

The consequences of committed choice search are not as severe as they appear on first sight. First, although only one answer can be produced by an evaluation, it is permitted that the answer can be a set. Second, the 'inspection' which was described above as the means by which PARLOG selects a clause from among the candidate clauses is very flexible. It can mean testing any sub-set of the conditions in the clause as well as just test matching with clause head. Thirdly, it is a fact that many of the logic programs which have been written to date are virtually deterministic — they can be executed with little or no searching. This suggests that the committed-choice strategy may not be too restrictive in practice.

CONCLUSION

This paper has barely scratched the surface of PARLOG. More information about the language, and about related developments such as other parallel logic languages and advances in parallel hardware, is available from research sources and especially in the various papers published by the Logic Programming Research Group at Imperial College.

An important event in PARLOG history is expected shortly with the publication of Steve Gregory's book, which is based on his pioneering PhD thesis (1986). However, this book, as with the rest of the existing PARLOG literature, is academic in its approach. This is understandable, but there is also a need for material which is addressed beyond the community of computing science academics, just as there was with PROLOG in the 1970s. Let us hope that with PARLOG we do not repeat all the old mistakes.

The use of PARLOG should not affect our basic logic programming perspective, in which program development proceeds from logic to control. However, the PARLOG control view is very different from that with PROLOG. The basis of the language is and-parallelism, in which several processes are active on sub-problems together. Mode constraints synchronize the processes in a natural way, by specifying which arguments of a process are inputs and which are outputs; a process suspends until its input arguments are made available by other processes. Processes communicate by passing messages through variables which provide communication channels. The search strategy commits choice to one clause instead of attempting an exhaustive search through all possible clauses.

PARLOG provides concrete proof that logic programming is not synonymous with PROLOG. Furthermore, it seals the place of logic programming as the main paradigm for fifth generation computing. PROLOG supports a declarative view of computing but its execution is essentially a conventional sequential one, geared for efficiency on Von Neumann computers. PARLOG combines the declarative view with an execution mechanism which can exploit the highly parallel hardware architectures which are now being developed. It is too early to make many predictions about the language, but it is impossible not to be excited by its potential and invigorated by its ideas.

ACKNOWLEDGEMENTS

I would like to thank the members of the PARLOG Group at Imperial College, and especially Steve Gregory, for the discussions, help and encouragement which they have given me in developing my knowledge of and interest in PARLOG.

REFERENCES AND FURTHER READING

Gregory, S (1986), *Design, Application and Implementation of a Parallel Logic Programming Language*, PhD Thesis, Dept Computing, Imperial College, University of London, (In Press) Addison-Wesley.
Kowalski, R (1985), 'Logic programming and specification', in: Hoare, C A R, Shepherdson, J C (Eds) *Mathematical Logic and Programming Languages*, Prentice-Hall.